In the Bubble

In the Bubble

Designing in a Complex World

John Thackara

The MIT Press
Cambridge, Massachusetts
London, England

First MIT Press paperback edition, 2006
© 2005 Massachusetts Institute of Technology

MIT Press books may be purchased at special quantity discounts for business or sales promotional use. For information, please e-mail special_sales@mitpress.mit.edu or write to Special Sales Department, The MIT Press, 55 Hayward Street, Cambridge, MA 02142.

This book was set in Stone Sans and Stone Serif on 3B2 by Asco Typesetters, Hong Kong.
Printed and bound in the United States of America.

Library of Congress Cataloging-in-Publication Data

Thackara, John.
In the bubble : designing in a complex world / John Thackara.
    p. cm.
Includes bibliographical references and index.
ISBN 0-262-20157-7 (alk. paper), 0-262-70115-4 (pb)
1. Engineering design. 2. Design, Industrial. I. Title.
TA174.T52   2005
620'.0042—dc22   2004062531

10 9 8 7 6 5 4 3

Contents

Acknowledgments

They say that it takes a village to raise a child. The same goes for this book; it's the result of encounters and shared experiences over several years that gave rise to the questions, first raised at Doors of Perception conferences, that are now addressed here. The most insightful of these questions are not mine: They come from the late Peter Dormer, John Chris Jones, Derrick de Kerckhove, Jouke Kleerebezem, Ezio Manzini, Caroline Nevejan, Jogi Panghaal, Chee Pearlman, Aditya Dev Sood, and Marco Susani. A number of the examples in the book are based on encounters in Japan and East Asia enabled by Tadanori Nagasawa and Kayoko Ota. Kayoko also introduced me to my first Amsterdammer, Willem Velthoven, who, in turn, helped organize the first Doors of Perception conferences. I owe a lot to Harry Swaak, who hired me to run the Netherlands Design Institute in 1993; it was there that many of the perplexities in this book crystallized, and where Doors of Perception was born. Our journey since then has been much enlivened by the presence of fellow explorers: Janet Abrams, Conny Bakker, Ole Bouman, Rob van Kranenburg, Bert Mulder, Michiel Schwarz, and Gert Staal. Doors speakers, who inspired us with their insight, have also been unfailingly generous in spirit. The warmth and insistent collaboration of the Doors tribe—the compost that has nurtured this book—are due to the stewardship of our producer, Janneke Berkelbach, and her live-wire colleagues. My optimism about the future of design comes from working with some fabulous practitioners in recent times: Michael Samyn and Remon Tijssen on the Doors and Netherlands Design Institute websites; Wouter van Eyck and Ton Homburg on publications; Edith Gruson and Lynne Leegte on venues; and Abhishek Hazra on Doors East. Debra Solomon has artfully connected Doors with food and design. Aya van Caspel and Jane Szita have been wordsmiths to die for, and Livia Ponzio helped many journalists keep us on our toes. Together with our software and engineering maestros Jan Jaap Spreij and Paul Jongsma, I've been truly privileged to learn about design, on the job, with such an amazing group of people. Ivo Janssen, who animated the whole enterprise with his piano performances at Doors, also introduced me to the music of Simeon ten Holt, which has provided me with the metaphor that concludes the book. Doors has flourished as a fledgling enterprise thanks to the stewardship of our Board: Dingeman Kuilman, Christian Oberman, Ben Pluijmers, Walter Amerika, and Krijn van Beek.

A central theme of this book is the design of projects and institutions. The subject has been brought to life for me by working with some highly enlightened commissioners. Jakub Wejchert, at the European Commission, enabled many of us in Europe to put social issues at the center of technology innovation projects for the first time. Paola Antonelli, at MoMA, gave me the opportunity, as one of her helpers on Workspheres, to explore the future design of work. Roger Coleman and Jeremy Myerson at the Royal College of Art, Elena Pacenti at Domus Academy, and Tim Brown at Ideo were inspiring partners on the Presence project about elders online. Franco Debenedetti, Barbara Ghella, and Gillian Crampton Smith invited me along on a fabulous adventure: to get Interaction Design Institute Ivrea up and running. Most of what I know about interaction design (and Canavese food) I've learned from them and the Institute's gifted faculty: Walter Aprile, Michael Kieslinger, Simona Maschi, Stefano Mirti, Casey Reas, Dag Svaenes, and Jan-Christoph Zoels. Sean Blair and Kevin Gavaghan in London and Claire Byers at One North East in Newcastle involved me in the design of a region-specific institution—and in my hometown, to boot. Victor Lo and John Frazer, on the Hong Kong Design Task Force, introduced me to the complexity of developments in China. Without Yrjo Sotamaa, Eija Salmi, and Jan Verwijnen in Helsinki, Peter Gall Krogh in Aarhus, Alessandro Biamonti in Milan, and Arvo Parenson in Tallinn, I would not have been able to visit the farthest and most fascinating corners of Europe for the Spark! project. Cathy Brickwood and Martine Posthuma de Boer, and my colleagues in Virtual Platform, introduced me to Europe's best media art when we did E-Culture Fair together. Luuk Boelens, of Urban Unlimited, opened my eyes to the need for services connecting high-speed trains to the places where they stop; he also alerted me to the emerging phenomenon of design-free zones.

James Bradburne, Malcolm McCullough, and Ben Reason and Chris Downs plowed through early drafts of this book; they were kind enough to say that there were bits worth saving. At The MIT Press my manuscript has been made presentable by kind and expert editors: Doug Sery, Michael Sims, Kathleen Caruso, and, especially, Michael Harrup.

At the heart of the village that raised this book are friends and family who have had to tolerate a preoccupied author for too long. Tony Graham told me most of what I've written, in the pages that follow, about theater. Hilary Arnold and Colin Robinson gave me both professional and moral support when it was most needed. My daughter Kate has been my inspiration. Kristi van Riet is the fire in the village square. I don't know where it will lead, but I do know where it came from: This book is dedicated to my parents, Lex and Eleanor Thackara.

Introduction

"In the bubble" is a phrase used by air traffic controllers to describe their state of mind, among their glowing screens and flows of information, when they are in the flow and in control. Lucky them. Most of us feel far from in control. We're filling up the world with amazing devices and systems—on top of the natural and human ones that were already here—only to discover that these complex systems seem to be out of control: too complex to understand, let alone to shape, or redirect.

Things may seem out of control—but they are not out of our hands. Many of the troubling situations in our world are the result of design decisions. Too many of them were bad design decisions, it is true—but we are not the victims of blind chance. The parlous condition of the planet, our only home, is a good example. Eighty percent of the environmental impact of the products, services, and infrastructures around us is determined at the design stage.[1] Design decisions shape the processes behind the products we use, the materials and energy required to make them, the ways we operate them on a daily basis, and what happens to them when we no longer need them. We may not have meant to do so, and we may regret the way things have turned out, but we designed our way into the situations that face us today.

The premise of this book is simply stated: If we can design our way into difficulty, we can design our way out. "Everyone designs," wrote scientist Herb Simon, "who devises courses of action aimed at changing existing situations, into preferred ones."[2] For Victor Papanek, too, "design is basic to all human activities—the placing and patterning of any act towards a desired goal constitutes a design process."[3] Designing is what human beings do.

Two questions follow this understanding of design. First, where do we want to be? What exactly are the "preferred situations" or "desired goals" that Simon and Papanek talk about? Second, how do we get there? What courses of action will take us from here to there?

Although this book addresses those two questions, it is not about the future, and it is not really about the new. I have organized the chapters that follow around ten themes that deal with daily life as it is lived now—not around fantastical science fiction futures. And I will tell you about aspects of daily life in which radical innovation is already emerging: Nothing you read here is a promise or a fantasy that may, one day, come true.

One of the things that drove me to write this book was boredom with the schlock of the new. Many of the "preferred situations" that Simon talked about already exist—but in a different and often unexpected context. One of the things you can do next Monday morning, after reading this book, is walk out of your door and take a look around. I am confident you will be surprised by the variety of social innovation taking place in your environment. I have been.

That said, addressing the question "Where do we want to be?" brings us up against an innovation dilemma. We've built a technology-focused society that is remarkable on means, but hazy about ends. It's no longer clear to which question all this stuff—tech—is an answer, or what value it adds to our lives. Too many people I meet assume that being innovative means "adding technology to it." Technology has become a powerful, self-replicating system that is accustomed to respect and receives the lion's share of research funding. In NASDAQ, tech even has its own stock exchange.

During the first part of the industrial age (and we are still in the industrial age, by the way), progress and development meant the continuous production of technology and more products, period. The spirit of that age is captured in an old Matsushita song:

Let's put our strengths and minds together
Doing our best to promote production
Sending out goods to the peoples of the world
Endlessly, and continuously.[4]

On the basis of this mindset, technology has evolved from a collection of tools used for doing things into a self-perpetuating system.[5] At the time, the benefits of technology seemed to be self-evident: better, faster, smarter—and usually cheaper—products. But as the extent of technology's penetration into daily life has grown, the differences between gadgets have decreased; technology has become at best a commodity, at worst an infringement on personal space—a form of trespass even, or pollution. One reason the dot-coms failed is that they offered little value other than "tech" at a time when the culture had changed and tech was no longer an end in itself in our daily lives.

I do not suggest that we have fallen out of love with technology, more that we are regaining appreciation and respect for what people can do that tech can't. Throughout the modern age we have subordinated the interests of people to those of technology, an approach that has led to the unthinking destruction of traditional cultures and the undermining of forms of life that we judged, once, to be backward. The victims of this approach to modernization have not just been hapless people in rain forests. "Getting people to adapt" to new technology has affected us all. We believed that the assembly line and standardization would make the world a better place, yet along with efficiency came a dehumanization of work. We act no less as slaves to the machine today when we lambaste teachers as "obstacles to progress" when they do not embrace the latest technological fix for education.[6]

The introduction of a new mass technology—telegraph, railway, electrification, radio, telephone, television, automobiles, air travel—has always been accompanied by a spectacular package of promises. A certain naïveté is excusable for the inventors of those early technologies: They had no way of knowing about the unforeseen consequences of their innovations. Today, we don't have that alibi. We *know* that new technologies have unexpected consequences.[7]

The worst kind of tech push combines irresponsibility with wishful thinking. One of the worst current offenders is biotech. When Eugene Thacker (no relation) studied the biotech industry for a book he was writing, he encountered "blatant disparity between hyper-optimism and an overall lack of concrete results."[8] The future promises of biotech are many and far reaching, but Thacker could not help noticing the comparative absence of any concrete, widespread, sustainable results of the application of biotech in medicine and health care. We are victims, says Thacker, of "biotech imagineering" by vested interests that participate in the assemblage of enticing future visions.[9]

Being skeptical about technology does not mean rejecting it. There's a lot of technology in this book. For one thing, we don't have an either/or choice: Terra firma, and terabits, are both here to stay. Broadband, smart materials, wearables, pervasive computing, connected appliances, and other stuff we don't know about yet will continue to transform the ways we live. The question is, how?

Means and ends have lived apart too long in discussions of innovation. Understanding *why* things change—and reflecting on how they *should* change—are not separate issues. In the pages that follow, I try to reframe issues of technology and innovation in ways that make it easier for non-specialists to engage in meaningful dialogue—as things happen. Theodor Zeldin calls this the transition from an age of specifications to one of deliberation.[10]

We cannot stop tech, and there's no reason why we should. It's useful. But we need to change the innovation agenda in such a way that people come before tech. It will be an ongoing struggle, of course. From nineteenth-century mill owners to twentieth-century dot-commers, businesspeople have looked for ways to remove people from production, using technology and automation to do so. A lot of organizations will continue on this path, but they're behind the times.

This book is about a world in which well-being is based on less stuff and more people. It describes an approach to innovation in which people are designed back into situations. In these situations, we will no longer be persuaded that to be better off, we must consume more trashy products and devices.

The following pages describe the transition, which is already under way, from innovation driven by science fiction to innovation inspired by social fiction. I've collected the best examples I could find of designed services and situations in which people carry out familiar, daily-life activities in new ways: moving around, learning, caring for each other, playing, working. Some of these services involve the use of products, or equipment, to carry them out. This equipment ranges from body implants to wide-bodied jets. But objects, as a rule, play a supporting role. New principles—above all, lightness—inform the ways they are designed, made, used, and looked after. The design focus is overwhelmingly on services and systems, not on things.

As well as designing people back into the picture, we need to design ourselves more time to paint it. Many of the so-called rebound effects of innovation—results that are the direct opposite of what we intended—occur because we have inadequate time to try things out small, observe what happens, and reflect on how the bigger picture is changing. As I argue in chapter 2, velocity may be an imperative in the computer industry, but speed can be damaging in social situations.

One issue we need time to reflect on concerns the sheer number of people we have in the world. The planet's population has doubled in my generation's lifetime—something that never happened to a generation before. You and I are the first human beings who have had to adjust to such an explosion of numbers. And yet we persist in the pursuit of "labor-saving" devices and services—using tech as the means.

It's not that we're dumb. On the contrary, many millions of people have exerted great intelligence and creativity in building the modern world. It's more that we're being swept into unknown and dangerous waters by accelerating economic growth. On just one single day of the days I have spent writing this book, as much world trade was carried out as in the whole of 1949; as much scientific research was published as in the whole of 1960; as many telephone calls were made as in all of 1983; as many e-mails were sent as in 1990.[11] Our natural, human, and industrial systems, which evolve slowly, are struggling to adapt. Laws and institutions that we might expect to regulate these flows have not been able to keep up.

A good example is what is inaccurately described as mindless sprawl in our physical environment. We deplore the relentless spread of low-density suburbs over millions of acres of formerly virgin land. We worry about its environmental impact, about the obesity in people that it fosters, and about the other social problems that come in its wake. But nobody seems to have designed urban sprawl, it just happens—or so it appears. On closer inspection, however, urban sprawl is not mindless at all. There is nothing inevitable about its development. Sprawl is the result of zoning laws designed by legislators, low-density buildings designed by developers, marketing strategies designed by ad agencies, tax breaks designed by economists, credit lines designed by banks, geomatics designed by retailers, data-mining software designed by hamburger chains, and automobiles designed by car designers. The interactions between all these systems and human behavior are complicated and hard to understand—but the policies themselves are not the result of chance. "Out of control" is an ideology, not a fact.

To do things differently, we need to perceive things differently. In discussing where we want to be, breakthrough ideas often come when people look at the world through a fresh lens. One of the most important design challenges I pose in this book is to make the processes and systems that surround us intelligible and knowable. We need to design macroscopes, as well as microscopes, to help us understand where things come from and why: the life story of a hamburger, or time pressure, or urban sprawl. Equipped with a fresh understanding of why our present situations are as they are, we can better describe where we want to be. With alternative situations evocatively in mind, we can design our way from here to there.

Macroscopes can help us understand complex systems, but our own eyes, unaided, are just as important. All over the world, alternative models of organizing daily life are being tried and tested right now. We just need to look for them. When Ezio Manzini ran design workshops in Brazil, China, and India to develop new design ideas for an exhibition about daily life, he encountered dozens of examples of new services for daily life he had never thought of before—and also new attitudes. In many different cultures, he discovered, "an obsession with things is being replaced by a fascination with events." Both young and old people are designing activities and environments in which energy and material consumption is modest and more people are used, not fewer, in the ways we take care of people, work, study, move around, find food, eat, and share equipment.[12]

In a less-stuff-more-people world, we still need systems, platforms, and services that enable people to interact more effectively and enjoyably.[13] These platforms and infrastructures will require some technology and a lot of design. Some services will help us share the load of everyday activities: washing clothes on the roof of apartment blocks, looking after children, communal kitchens and gardens, communal workshops for maintenance activities, tool and equipment sharing, networks and clubs for health care and prevention. The most important potential impact of wireless communications, for example, will be on the resource ecologies of cities. Connecting people, resources, and places to each other in new combinations, on a real-time basis, delivers *demand-responsive services* that, when combined with location awareness and dynamic resource allocation, have the potential to reduce drastically the amount of hardware—from gadgets to buildings—that we need to function effectively. Most of us are potentially both users and suppliers of resources. The principle of *use, not own* can apply to all kinds of hardware: buildings, roads, vehicles, offices—and above all, people. For more or less anything heavy and fixed, we don't have to own them—just know how and where to find them.

There are many things wrong with design in our world, but designers, as a group of people, are not the problem. Thirty years ago, in *Design for the Real World*, Victor Papanek observed that "there are professions more harmful than industrial design—but only a few."[14] This kind of blaming and shaming is counterproductive and unjustified. The world contains its share of selfish and incurious designers, of course. But no designer that I ever met set out to wreck the planet, force us to eat fast food, or make life miserable. Our dilemma is that small design actions can have big effects—often unexpectedly—and designers have only recently been told, with the rest of us, how incredibly sensitive we need to be to the possible consequences of any design steps we take.

Another reason not to blame designers for our ills is that many of them are working hard, right now, to fix them. They are designing new services and systems that are radically less environmentally damaging, and more socially responsible, than the ones we have now. This book contains many examples of their often-inspiring work. But the challenges and opportunities that face us will not be solved by designers acting on our behalf. On the contrary: As we suffuse the world with complex technical systems—on top of the natural and social systems already here—old-style top-down, outside-in design simply won't work. The days of the celebrity solo designer are over. Complex systems are shaped by all the people who use them, and in this new era of collaborative innovation, designers are having to evolve from being the individual authors of objects, or buildings, to being the facilitators of change among large groups of people.

Sensitivity to context, to relationships, and to consequences are key aspects of the transition from mindless development to *design mindfulness*.[15] At the heart of *In the Bubble* is a belief that ethics and responsibility can inform design decisions without constraining the social and technical innovation we all need to do. Design mindfulness involves a determination to

• think about the consequences of design actions before we take them and pay close attention to the natural, industrial, and cultural systems that are the context of our design actions;

• consider material and energy flows in all the systems we design;

• give priority to human agency and not treat humans as a "factor" in some bigger picture;

• deliver value to people—not deliver people to systems;

• treat "content" as something we do, not something we are sold;

• treat place, time, and cultural difference as positive values, not as obstacles;

• focus on services, not on things, and refrain from flooding the world with pointless devices.

Values and manifestos are an important guide to design decisions. But design defined only by limits and prohibitions will not flourish. Telling people to be good seldom works. As the underground classic *BoloBolo* puts it, "too many visions of the future stink of renunciation, moralism, new labors, toilsome rethinking, modesty and self-limitation. Of course there are limits, but why should they be limits on pleasure and adventure? Why do most alternativists only talk about new responsibilities and almost never about new possibilities? Why be modest in the face of impending catastrophe?"[16] The creation of interesting social alternatives has to be as exciting and engaging as the buzz of new technology used to be. A culture of community and connectivity has to be fun and challenging, as well as responsible. An aesthetics of service and flow should inspire us, not just satisfy us.

In the Bubble is about sustainable and engaging futures and the design steps we need to take to realize them. Our journey is not an easy one. We need to think, connect, act, and start processes with sensitivity. We need to foster new relationships outside our usual stomping grounds. We have to learn new ways to collaborate and do projects. We have to enhance the ability of all citizens to engage in meaningful dialogue about their environment and context, and foster new relationships between the people who make things and the people who use them. The "we" here is important. In a world of complex systems and constant change, we are all, unavoidably, "in the bubble." The challenge is to be both in the bubble and above it, at the same time—to be as sensitive to the big picture, and the destination we are headed for, as we are to the smallest details of the here and now.

1 | Lightness

I am driving along the Languedocienne motorway from Barcelona to Marseille, in the middle lane of three. The traffic is a solid line of sixteen-wheeled trucks, nose to tail, a couple of meters apart. In front of me is a Croatian truck: "Engine parts from Zagreb." Behind me is a Spanish truck full of tomatoes. The lines of trucks stretch as far ahead, and as far behind, as the eye can see. From the crest of a hill, I can see hundreds of trucks flowing in each direction. A big Opel whooshes up from behind, in the fast lane. The driver, who is doing 200 kilometers (120 miles) an hour, is talking on a mobile phone. Suddenly, the Croatian truck veers left to avoid something. The Opel, startled, first bangs into the crash barrier and then, braking hard, swerves in front of the Croatian truck. Horns blare, brakes slam, wheels lock, tires smoke. We all stop. By a miracle there is no squashed car, and nobody is dead. The Opel has come to a halt between fifty thousand pounds of engine parts in front and fifty thousand pounds of tomatoes behind. I notice a slogan on the tomato truck: "Trans-Inter: Your Partner in Closed Loop Logistics." The Opel driver has stopped talking on his phone—thinking, perhaps, how close he came to closing his loop with all those tomatoes.

The shock of that near miss in France made me think that this was not the "weightless" new economy we were told the Internet would bring. Rather than the displacement of matter by mind, life seems to have become heavier—physically and psychologically—than ever. That torrent of trucks was a reminder that thanks to all the design we do, man-made flows of matter and energy all around us are growing in volume. We buy more hardware than ever. We print more paper. We package more goods. We move more stuff, and ourselves, around at ever-increasing rates. In my lifetime, global population has doubled, energy production has more than tripled, economic output has risen by a factor of five, and computer processing speeds and storage have both increased over a millionfold. It took from the beginning of human history to the year 1900 to grow a world economy that produced six hundred billion dollars in output; today, the world economy grows by that amount every two years. This acceleration is like a cultural centrifuge. The faster the economy grows, the heavier we feel.

A few years ago we hoped that digital communication networks would lead to a lighter economy and a cleaner environment. But that has not happened. Global temperatures are rising faster than ever before recorded, bringing increased instability to weather systems across the world.[1] With heat comes dust. More than one hundred million European and North American citizens live in cities in which the air is unsafe to breathe. When I visited Hong Kong during research for this book, the news broke that a ten-million-square-mile, two-mile-thick "Asian brown cloud" of man-made pollutants had been discovered. It contained a dynamic soup of vehicle and industrial pollutants, carbon monoxide, and minute soot particles or fly ash from the regular burning of forests and wood used for cooking in millions of rural homes. The cloud was spreading across the whole Asian continent and blocking out up to 15 percent of the available sunlight.[2]

At ground level, too, the information age is heavier than we anticipated. I realized after my near miss on the Languedocienne that we made a fundamental error with the theory of dematerialization. We supposed that an information society would *replace* industrial society, whereas the information society has in fact been *added* to the industrial one and increased its intensity.

Apart from its impact on the wider economy, information technology is heavy in itself. It's a heavy user of matter in all the hardware needed to run it. One of the hidden costs of the misnamed silicon age is the material and energy flows involved in the manufacture and use of microchips. It takes 1.7 kilograms of materials to make a microchip with 32 megabytes of random-access memory—a total 630 times the mass of the final product.[3] The "fab" of a basic memory chip, and running it for the typical life span of a computer, eats up eight hundred times the chip's weight in fossil fuel. Thousands of potentially toxic chemicals are used in the manufacturing process.[4] A single microchip is, it is true, a small thing—on its own. But there are a lot of them about—and many more to come. Promoters of ubiquitous computing promise us that *trillions* of smart or embedded devices are on the way.[5]

The ecological footprint of computing is not limited to the chips. The manufacture of electronic devices also involves highly intensive material processes. A great deal of nature has to be moved during the production of communications equipment. Many components require the use of high-grade minerals that can be obtained only through major mining operations and energy-intensive transformation processes. One of the most startling pieces of information brought to light in Paul Hawken, Amory Lovins, and Hunter Lovins's *Natural Capitalism* is that the amount of waste matter generated in the manufacture of a single laptop computer is close to four thousand times its weight on your lap.[6] Fifteen to nineteen tons of energy and materials are consumed in the fabrication of one desktop computer.[7] To compound matters: As well as being resource-greedy to make, information technology devices also have notoriously short lives. The average compact disc is used precisely once in its life,[8] and every gram of material that goes into the production and consumption of a computer ends up rather quickly as either an emission or as solid waste. In theory, electronic products have technical service lives on the magnitude of thirty years, but thanks to ever-shorter innovation cycles, many devices are disposed of after a few years or months.[9]

Information networks also stimulate the use of old-media matter, such as paper. Ethernets, which enabled computers and printers to talk to one another, were one reason the use of paper in offices rose eightfold *after* the paperless office was predicted. Every single employee of the European Commission, which is a digital-savvy organization, prints out 247 pages of hard copy a day.[10]

Information networks don't just use a lot of stuff. They also guzzle energy. George Gilder predicts in his book *Telecosm* that Internet computing will soon consume as much power as the entire U.S. economy did in 2001—some three trillion kilowatt hours.[11] The PC on your desk, whirring away in standby mode, uses its own share of that; but the real energy gluttons are server farms—entire floors, or whole buildings, filled with powerful computer servers. A single server farm consumes the same amount of energy as a city the size of Honolulu.[12] Information technology has been added to the world; it has not made it lighter.

If highways like the Languedocienne carry the lifeblood of our economy, they are like the arteries of a fat-addicted man on the brink of a massive coronary. Most of the flows they carry are wasteful. Only 1 percent of material flows in the U.S. economy ends up in, and is still being used within, products six months after their sale. Hawken and his colleagues reckon that so-called developed economies are less than 10 percent as efficient as the laws of physics allow.[13] Every product that enters our lives has what they call a "hidden history"—an undocumented inventory of wasted or lost materials used in its production, transport, use, and disposal. Industry, say the writers, "moves, mines, extracts, shovels, burns, wastes, pumps and disposes of billions of pounds of material in order to deliver the products we take for granted, but which are needed for roads and buildings and infrastructures." They go on to list waste in the form of tailings, gangue, fly ash, slurry, sludge, slag, flue gases, construction debris, methane—and other wastes of the extractive and manufacturing processes, overuse of resources, pollution, and destruction of natural areas—that continue to threaten life on the planet."[14] The pièce de résistance in the extraordinary analysis of *Natural Capitalism* is that the amount of matter and energy wasted, or caused to be wasted, by the average North American consumer is roughly one million pounds a year: a "million-pound backpack."[15]

These numbers may sound implausible, but they are based on serious long-term research. The material flows of industrial society, its "metabolism," have been measured with increasing precision since the 1960s.[16] Materials flow analyses (in Germany called *Stoffflussanalyse*) register, describe, and interpret these otherwise unseen metabolic processes. In Germany they call all this waste the "ecological rucksack" of a product or lifestyle. A million pounds of weight is an awfully big rucksack to carry around. It's the same as ten thousand one-hundred-pound bags of cement. I once had the idea, before a lecture, of piling this many cement bags on the stage, as a stunt, to illustrate this point. But when the venue management worked out that this would result in a pile of cement the area of a tennis court, sixty feet high, they called it off, saying the stage would collapse. All the world's a stage, I told them.

Individual companies are not uniquely responsible for environmental impact. Communities add their own weight, which has been measured in the form of *ecological footprints*. Researchers at the University of British Columbia have translated various categories of human consumption into areas of productive land needed to support them. They discovered that the ecological footprint of one Canadian is 4.8 hectares (an area 220 meters long by 220 meters wide—roughly comparable to three city blocks). This statistic means that if everyone on Earth lived like the average Canadian, we would need at least three Earths to provide all the material and energy essentials we currently use.[17] The World Wildlife Fund calculates that mankind's ecological footprint is already 1.2 Earths.

Another way to describe environmental impact is called "weighting." In weighting, different impacts—or "endpoints," as they are described in the dry terminology of international standards—are assessed in tandem: damage to human health, damage to ecosystem quality, and damage to resources. Damages to human health are expressed in disability-adjusted life years (DALYs), a system used by the World Health Organisation and the World Bank.[18]

Collecting all these data is one thing; making sense of them holistically is another. Other researchers are working on that. A British project, Environmental Life Cycle Information Management and Acquisition (ELIMA), integrates data on human, ecological, and industrial processes. The assessment of environmental impacts on human health (from carcinogens, respiratory organics and inorganics, climate change, radiation and ozone layer depletion, and so on) is linked to data about ecosystem quality (from ecotoxicity, acidification/eutrophication and land use, and so on). These data, in turn, are connected to data about industrial processes such as raw-materials use, especially minerals and fossil fuels.[19]

Environmental impact researchers are also bringing us harder and better information about individual products. A Dutch group called PRé has developed software for product and packaging designers that enables them to model a complex product and its life cycle. Built into the software package are more than two hundred eco-indicators for commonly used materials such as metals, plastics, paper, board, and glass, as well as production, transport, energy, and waste treatment processes. The software calculates the environmental load and shows which parts of the product "weigh" the most. These can then be rethought.[20]

Environmentally sound product life cycle design takes into account all processes that occur in relation to the product during its life cycle, from cradle to grave—or even better, from cradle to cradle. One of the methods used to document findings is the so-called MET matrix—a scorecard for the materials, energy, and toxicity impacts of a product during its production, use, and disposal. One counterintuitive outcome of this method's application is the finding that although natural materials are commonly believed to be more environmentally friendly than artificial or man-made ones, the picture is more complicated than that. Yes, a product incorporating one kilogram of wood causes fewer emissions than the same product made with a kilogram of plastics. But once the paint needed to preserve the wood, or sawing losses, are factored in, it can turn out it takes about ten times as much wood as plastic to make some products. And while plastics can often be recycled, wood cannot.

As we saw with information technology, energy consumption has often been underestimated in measuring a product's environmental impact: A coffee machine, for example, uses three hundred kilowatt-hours of electricity during its lifetime; this is equivalent to the amount of energy generated from sixty kilograms of oil. It sometimes turns out to be better to use materials that have a high environmental load per kilogram to manufacture, if it means energy use can be reduced during their life of operation. This is particularly true in transport equipment, in which less weight means less fuel consumption. The designers and researchers at PRé insist that environmentally sound materials do not exist; environmentally friendly design approaches do.

A designer can influence a product's lifetime by making it more durable from a technical point of view or by making it upgradeable in a functional sense—for example, by enabling the latest chip to be installed in an existing computer or washing machine. Most products could be recycled, but only a few will be, because only products that are easy to disassemble and yield a decent return when one does so will be chosen for recycling. Designers increase the chance that a product is recycled by optimizing its assembly to that end. Increased product lifetimes also make a difference—but not automatically a good one. When a group of Dutch designers called Eternally Yours investigated the issue, it discovered that designing a product to last a long time does more harm than good if the product is energy-inefficient.[21]

Small Actions, Big Effects

For product designers, the lesson is that small actions can have big effects. In many industries, measures to integrate environmental considerations into product development have resulted in substantial positive achievements. Europe leads the way internationally: Countries such as Denmark, Germany, the Netherlands, Austria, and Sweden are front-runners in impact assessment, design method development, and eco-design education. Their efforts contributed to an overall reduction of carbon dioxide emissions from EU manufacturing of over 11 percent between 1985 and 2000.[22] Internationally, some large multinationals now address the issue of environmental product design in a comprehensive way, particularly in the fields of electrical and electronic goods, motor vehicles, and packaging. These firms have responded to a variety of drivers and now pay as much attention to environmental and social aspects related to their products, from a life cycle perspective, as they once did to economic and market aspects only.

Weighty Factors

Three factors throw a shadow over this otherwise positive picture. The first is that industry is changing, but too slowly relative to overall economic growth. During that same period in which carbon dioxide emissions were reduced, manufacturing production as a whole rose by 31 percent—with the result that industrial production still accounts for a considerable share of pollution. Much-maligned global corporations are less of a problem than small and medium-sized enterprises (SMEs), for whom eco-design continues to play a very small role.

A second brake on progress is inadequate information diffusion. A lot of potentially weight-reducing research goes unreported. Environmental design information tends to be scattered and fragmented, and many eco-design tools and data that could help us remain hidden from view and underused. Kathalys, a research group in Holland, turns ecological footprints into design action points by measuring pressure on the environment in terms of everyday activities in the home—such as taking a shower. Taking just one shower in a top-of-the-range cubicle, Kathalys has discovered, consumes as much as thirty-five kilojoule-pounds in energy and two hundred liters of water. Kathalys is testing a mist shower that, combined with water and heat recycling, reduces those numbers tenfold, to five megajoule-pounds of heat and twenty liters of water per person. These numbers are impressive, but too few people know about them. I live less than an hour away from the Kathalys offices, for example; I have met the gifted and dedicated people there on numerous occasions, and I am known to have an interest in their work. But I did not hear about, still less see their book, *Vision on Sustainable Product Innovation*, until eighteen months after its publication—some three years after they started to produce the shower.[23]

The third factor holding back eco-design is our slow transition to whole-systems thinking. Switching to misty showers will not of itself resolve our underlying problems, which are systemic. As the authors of *Natural Capitalism* explain, living systems have been in existence for three and a half billion years; human systems, such as agriculture, began more recently, about thirty thousand years ago; but industrial systems are new—two hundred years old or less—and have affected human and natural systems in dramatic and unforeseen ways. "What is happening is not by intention," Hawken, Lovins, and Lovins explain, "so we can put aside the theory that there are 'bad' people that we can get rid of to make everything OK. The fact is that the rate of loss [to the environment's capacity to sustain the economy] is a systemic problem inherent in assumptions that have only recently begun to be questioned."[24]

The good news is that enlightening system models and frameworks are being developed and disseminated around the world. They have names such as Triple Bottom Line, Five Capitals Model, and Twelve Features of a Sustainable Society. One of the whole-systems frameworks introduced to give us a better grasp of the bigger picture is called The Natural Step (TNS) Framework. TNS is based on an all-embracing definition of the conditions that must apply in any sustainable society. These conditions, known as system conditions, and delineated by an international network of scientists, describe a sustainable society in which nature is not subject to systematically increasing concentrations of substances extracted from the Earth's crust, concentrations of substances produced by society, or degradation by physical means. In this society, human needs are met worldwide. TNS is one among several all-encompassing frameworks within which several principles of sustainability and lightness are pretty much agreed upon:

- Minimize the waste of matter and energy.
- Reduce the movement and distribution of goods.
- Use more people and less matter.

These principles are easy enough to state, but their implementation requires us to redesign industrial and societal systems that deliver material necessities—food, clothing, shelter, mobility—to us, not to mention the cultural systems that shape our attitudes and expectations.[25]

So systems are important. The trouble is that because it's seldom obvious who should look after them, nobody does. One way to persuade society to value, and therefore look after, its systems is to reframe them as forms of capital. Jonathon Porritt, director of Britain's Forum for the Future, tells policymakers, industrialists, and educators that five types of capital enable us to deliver goods and services we need to sustain and improve the quality of our lives: natural, human, social, manufactured, and financial capital.[26]

Big capitalist companies already follow a whole-systems approach. They tend naturally to think in terms of product life cycles, not of discrete objects, and some are enthusiastic users of resource efficiency measurement tools and techniques. They routinely measure costs of products from the extraction of the materials used to produce the products through to their ultimate disposal. Most large organizations are well aware that in a whole-systems context, design is important because it can change the processes behind products and services, as well as the resources used to make them, use them, and dispose of them. Resource efficiency brings not only ecological, but also economic, benefit to an enterprise,[27] and many companies have been won over to the proposition that because avoidable waste is avoidable cost, improved resource productivity increases profit.[28] It's because a product or service redesigned to use less matter or energy costs less to deliver that "market-based environmentalism" has caught the business imagination.[29] John Elkington, a British advisor to many international companies, says the evolution of sustainable corporations is "not further along than aviation was when Wilbur and Orville were still running their cycle shop"—but he nonetheless anticipates "explosive" growth in sustainability experimentation in the coming years.[30]

Big Picture, Small Steps

The sustainability challenge is a design issue. Eighty percent of a product, service, or system's environmental impact is determined at the design stage.[31] If it is true that we are using the Earth's resources faster than we replace them, then design can help reverse this trend by changing the processes behind products, as well as the resources used to make them and use them. This is how a commitment to sustainability drives innovation. When organizations put design at the heart of product and service development, they are triggered to ask fundamental questions about what they make, how they make it, and who for.[32] End-to-end system integration closes energy and matter loops. Design thinking, in combination with Internet-enabled networks and wireless communications, can reshape whole production processes, even the entire logic and structure of an industry.

Design has achieved critical mass in many industries—if not cultural visibility—because it looks at ways to make products less wasteful of materials, less polluting, and easier to recycle. If the so-called green design approach (better known in the United States as "design for the environment") has a limitation, it is that it intervenes at the "end of the pipe." It modifies individual products or services but does not transform the industrial process as a whole.

Use, Not Own

Structural changes to whole systems, in the way markets are organized, in the way our transport infrastructures are organized and used, and in the way we work and live, are the hardest changes to effect. But just such changes in these areas are already under way. The shift to a service-based economy is one of the most important features of this transition. Think of your mobile phone. You may have paid fifty dollars for the handset—or maybe you got it free. Either way, you probably pay hundreds of dollars for calls and services *each year*—and those, to all intents and purposes, are immaterial in the sense that you do not need to purchase or use a new device each time you make a call. Many of us already lease, rather than purchase, a device as part of a service contract—a car, a refrigerator, an answering machine, a photocopier. In so doing, we purchase performance—moving, cooling, message taking, or copying—rather than the product itself. Companies are finding, today, that by switching from simply selling a product to selling the optimal performance of a product, they obtain significant financial rewards through, among other things, increasing resource productivity.[33] The trend is to supply enabling platforms rather than stand-alone devices.

Power tools are another example. The average consumer power tool is used for ten minutes in its entire life—but it takes hundreds of times its own weight to manufacture such an object. Why own one, if I can get ahold of one when I need it? A *product-service system* provides me with access to the products, tools, opportunities, and capabilities I need to get the job done—namely, power tools for me to use, but not own.

Service design is about arranging things so that people who need things done are connected to other people and equipment that get things done— on an as- and when-needed basis. The technical term, which comes from the logistics industry, is "dynamic resource allocation in real time." Agricultural cooperatives that purchase tractors and sell their use-time to associates are well-known examples, but once one starts looking, examples spring up everywhere: a home delivery service for detergents in Italy, a mobile laboratory for industrial users of lubricants in Germany, dozens of car-sharing schemes, an organic vegetable subscription system in Holland.[34] Industrial ecologists François Jégou and Ezio Manzini found enough examples to fill a book, *Sustainable Everyday: A Catalogue of Promising Solutions*,[35] which is filled with novel daily life services that they discovered around the world. These are "planning activities whose objective is a system," Manzini told me. Hundreds of services suitable for a resource-limited, complex, and fluid world are being developed by grassroots innovators: those that enable people to take care of other people, work, study, move around, find food, eat, and share equipment.

Examples of extended homes and cohousing are emerging in many countries, for example. The integration of private and common space is enabling the creation of communities of people who choose to live together on the basis of shared facilities such as kitchens, laundries, do-it-yourself workrooms, children's play areas, guest rooms, gardens, and garden tools. In Hong Kong, the majority of recent buildings have been constructed to incorporate this kind of sharing. A wide range of neighborhood multi-service centers has been opened in various cities: a bookshop that houses a bar and cultural center (Tikkun, Milan), a bakery that offers space for the preparation and refrigeration of food (Cottage Baker, Rugby, England), a grocery shop that offers meetings and study courses (Nature Ride, Milan).[36]

My favorite example of a light product-service system is telephone voice mail services. When my wife and I first moved in together, we discovered that we owned, between us, *seven* stand-alone telephone answering machines. Only one of these actually worked; the rest were awaiting repair in a tangled heap of boxes and wires. One of them had been inoperative for seven years.[37] Flemming Heden, a researcher with Telia, a telecommunications company in Sweden, has compared the impact of owning such machines—that is, the effects produced by their manufacture, distribution, ownership, power consumption, maintenance, and disposal—to that of using an online answering service. Examining such factors as power consumption and contribution to the greenhouse effect, Heden calculated that using the online service has between one hundred and eight hundred times less impact on the environment than employing an answering machine for the same purpose. The savings in power consumption alone achieved annually by the seven hundred thousand or so customers in Sweden who subscribe to just one such service are equivalent to that required to heat two thousand houses with electricity for a year. If the five hundred thousand remaining Swedes who still have an old-style answering machine were to subscribe to an online service, it would reduce carbon dioxide emissions by ten thousand tonnes a year.[38]

Or take digital photography. The various branches of analog photography—the businesses that develop and print photographic film and paper, and radiography in the spheres of medical and dental care—are responsible, between them, for thirty million square meters of "developed surface" each year—an area the size of Belgium. Printing hard copies in Belgium involves chemical industries whose collective environmental impact is immense. Problems include the leakage into the atmosphere of gases that affect the climate and toxic waste that includes harmful mercury, silver compounds, and chromium. The industries concerned have invested heavily n recycling, waste processing, and the development of closed systems. But digitization is far more effective as an antidote to all this waste. For the local government of Stockholm alone, digitization of radiography means producing 230,000 square meters less of X-ray film, 100,000 liters less of developer, and 120,000 liters less of fixer.[39]

Now if you're in some kind of "thing" business, such as vacuum cleaners, or chairs, or buildings—don't panic. The knowledge and expertise you have now is still needed. We still need products in product-service systems. But the designers of those products will have to learn new tricks, so that the products they design can be deployed differently than we have been accustomed to.

Chris Pacione has already done so. He did not set out to be the designer of a wireless product-service system. On the contrary: This cofounder of

BodyMedia took a communication design course at an engineering school—Carnegie Mellon University—and fully expected to become a product designer. "But as soon as we started BodyMedia," says Pacione, "it became clear that our object was only one part of a bigger picture. We had to become service designers—and after that, business model designers—in order to survive."[40]

BodyMedia's product is a hybrid of hard and soft features. What you see on Pacione's arm is a wearable computer, with wireless capability. But that object is just one part of the story. The company develops and sells wearable body monitors and software that collect, store, analyze, and display continuous and accurate physiological and lifestyle data, such as energy expenditure (calories burned), level of activity, sleep states, and other important physiological data—anytime, anywhere. A website shows wearers charts that compare their body's performance to average or ideal charts, thus enabling them to see at a glance if they are getting enough exercise, sleeping too much, or consuming too many calories. As well as object design—the industrial design of the object on your arm, its shape, weight, materials, engineering, and so on—Pacione and his colleagues had to design the appearance and organization of information on the website. They also had to design the ways people would buy the product and pay for it; they have had to adjust the company's business model continuously. At first they thought consumers might obtain the product free of charge and pay for a "wellness monitoring service," in much the same way as we sometimes get a satellite dish, or television set-top box, free and pay for programs through a monthly subscription. But the marketing costs of that business model were too high, so BodyMedia switched to selling the product to sportsmen and -women as a high-tech training aid. This did not work—the unit price was too high—so now, BodyMedia sells its hybrid product-service to insurance companies and health care providers in a business-to-business model. Says Pacione, "we never stop designing the object, the way it's used, the way the information is presented, and the way people pay for it."[41] BodyMedia's story is paradigmatic of the way traditional "thing" design is evolving.

Liftoff

Global companies are integrated enough, today, to move steadily toward lighter modes of production. Most of them dislike being ahead of the market—namely, us—so if we change, they'll change. The reason is that we do not yearn for lighter ways of living most of our collectively wasteful behaviors are hidden from view. So we persist in our wasteful ways. Many heavy actions that I take, for example, seem trivial in themselves: leaving the light on, printing out an e-mail, eating a plate of Kenyan beans. It's the accumulation of such tiny acts that weighs heavily on the planet. A relationship, or flow, or accumulation, or change, is by its nature invisible. An important new task of design is to make these behaviors and changes within systems intelligible. We need new ways to understand the morphology of systems—their dynamics, their "intelligence": how they work, what stimulates them, how and why they change.

I was outraged to be told recently that in Amsterdam I put 563 kilograms of trash onto the street for collection each year. This was clearly a slander: All I do is put a couple of black bags on the street once or twice a week. They weigh only 5 kilos (I put paper and bottles in their own banks for recycling), and they don't pile up in a huge heap; they disappear. And that's part of the problem. My bags disappear from view, but not from the big picture.

So how might we make aggregate heaviness visible? The science fiction writer Bruce Sterling once challenged the Doors of Perception conference (a biannual event for designers that I run) to imagine what it would be like if carbon dioxide were red, and our wasteful emissions turned the sky to the color of blood, or if we had the eco-equivalent of a Geiger counter and sensors that would click, eerily, whenever we left the tap on. The conference's audience visibly squirmed as the idea sank in. We ignore environmental phenomena, or take them for granted, in much the same way that we take our bodies for granted. We don't think about them until they go wrong—and then we demand instant action from the person in charge. As we saw just now with BodyMedia, devices strapped to the body will constantly monitor its vital signs: What would it mean to monitor our planet's virtual signs in such a way?

Many affective representations of complex phenomena have been developed in recent times. Physicists have illustrated quarks. Biologists have mapped the genome. Doctors have described immune systems in the body and among communities. Network designers have mapped communication flows in buildings. Managers have charted the locations of expertise in their organizations. But these representations have been made and used mainly by and among specialists as objects of research—not as the basis for feedback and sense-and-respond behavior by wider groups of people. We need to foster ecological and systems literacies.

Changing attitudes is not just about enhancing perceptions. There are also psychological factors to contend with. One reason we don't see the bigger picture is that we don't want to: It's so grim. On the wall behind me, as I write, is a newspaper cutting with the headline "Life on the Planet under Threat." The story begins, "The human race has only one or perhaps two generations to rescue itself." Now you'd think this would be a front-page story, but the editor of the *Guardian* chose to run it on page 13 under "International News."[42] And I can't say I blame him. We have been bombarded for years by a stream of ghastly forecasts and warnings about the environment. Eco-trends always seem to be getting worse; our prospects on the planet always seem to be dire. And it's all our fault. But eco-guilt doesn't sell newspapers, and being told that a planet-wide calamity is one's fault is a splendid reason for turning straight to the sports pages.

It's also demotivating to be confronted by a task that seems too hard. I well remember the first time a scientist told me about "factor 20." Factor 20 refers to the idea that in order to achieve a balance of energy and matter consumption, with rising living standards and growing population calculated in, we need to improve the efficiency with which we use matter and energy by a factor of *twenty times* within one or two generations. Now the number twenty is not scientifically provable; the correct number may turn out to be four, or eight, or eighty. The actual factor numbers are best treated as parables. What they signify is that we need to effect a radical change in the way we live on the planet. When I heard that we have to change things by a factor of twenty, I thought: "Well that's it. The game's up. We're finished."[43]

In fact, radical change is already under way. It's just not visible. We've embarked on an operation compared by Ezio Manzini to "changing the engines of an aircraft while in flight." "It may appear a difficult task," understates Manzini, "but consider this: during two centuries of innovation, until now, we have reduced the role of labour in production by even larger proportions. We have done it before."[44] Hawkens and his coauthors, in *Natural Capitalism*, are resolutely confident, too. They state that "90 to 95 percent reductions in material and energy flows are possible in developed nations without diminishing the quality of the services people want."[45]

Attitudes are changing: People do think it's doable. The Australian economist Clive Hamilton, who writes powerfully about the emptiness of affluence in his book *Growth Fetish*, has uncovered research that shows that despite high and sustained levels of economic growth in the West over a period of fifty years, "four fifths of Americans believe they consume far more than they need to."[46] The richest people in the world say they are miserable, that it's not worth it, and that they'd like to change.

From End of Pipe to Whole of Life

Among the multiple interacting cycles of change now under way are incremental improvements to present products; this is the so-called end-of-pipe approach to eco-design. A second cycle involves the radical redesign of products and services in which an element is transformed, even though the model stays the same: Putting hydrogen power plants into private cars is an example of this. A third cycle involves the development of product-service systems that replace those in old models: Car-sharing schemes enabled by the Global Positioning System (GPS) are a good example of this. A fourth cycle involves the redesign of entire spatial, agricultural, and industrial systems to meet the goal of a fully sustainable society. The radical decentralization of production—in food, goods, and care—that has already begun is an example of such a systemic change.

These four change cycles operate at different timescales, but they influence each other. Much of our physical infrastructure needs to be replaced, for example, and a missed opportunity now can delay important change for decades. The average life span of what economists call "climate-relevant capital stock"—such as heating and ventilating systems—runs into many years: Electrical appliances such as office equipment and consumer and household goods should last five to twenty years (although, as we have seen, actual life cycles are often shorter). Residential heating and cooling systems last ten to twenty years. Cars, too, ten to twenty; trucks and buses, ten to twenty-five; commercial heating and cooling systems, ten to thirty; industrial production facilities, ten to forty; power plant electricity transmission, thirty to fifty; and transport and urban infrastructure, forty to two hundred.

Losing Weight, Gaining Lightness

"If you want to build a ship, don't divide the work and give orders; teach them to yearn for the vast and endless sea."[47] The French aviator and writer Antoine de Saint-Exupéry got it right. More than rational argument, and more than persuasive or scary representations, are required for the idea of lightness to "take" in our collective imagination. Although we have been culturally and economically entrenched in a particular way of doing things, the "jump" to renewables, and to a light, sustainable economy, is the result of a cultural, not a technological, transformation. One indication of cultural change is the success of books like *Natural Capitalism* and the speed with which industry, government, and education are embracing whole-system models such as The Natural Step. These seismic changes in mindset are making the jump from the ecological fringe into mainstream thinking.

One of the best codifications of a lightness-based industrial culture was made by the architect William McDonough following a commission by the organizers of the 2000 World's Fair in Hannover, Germany. At one of the epicenters of global capitalism, what have come to be known as the Hannover Principles were adopted without major controversy:

1. Insist on rights of humanity and nature to coexist in a healthy, supportive, diverse, and sustainable condition.

2. Recognize interdependence The elements of human design interact with and depend upon the natural world, with broad and diverse implications at every scale. Expand design considerations to recognizing even distant effects.

3. Respect relationships between spirit and matter Consider all aspects of human settlement including community, dwelling, industry and trade in terms of existing and evolving connections between spiritual and material consciousness.

4. Accept responsibility for the consequences of design decisions upon human well-being, the viability of natural systems, and their right to coexist.

5. Create safe objects of long-term value Do not burden future generations with requirements for maintenance of vigilant administration of potential danger due to the careless creation of products, processes, or standards.

6. Eliminate the concept of waste Evaluate and optimize the full life cycle of products and processes, to approach the state of natural systems, in which there is no waste.

7. Rely on natural energy flows Human designs should, like the living world, derive their creative forces from perpetual solar income. Incorporate the energy efficiently and safely for responsible use.

8. Understand the limitations of design No human creation lasts forever, and design does not solve all problems. Those who create and plan should practice humility in the face of nature. Treat nature as a model and mentor, not an inconvenience to be evaded or controlled.

9. Seek constant improvement by sharing knowledge Encourage direct and open communication between colleagues, patrons, manufacturers and users to link long-term sustainable considerations with ethical responsibility, and reestablish the integral relationship between natural processes and human activity.[48]

The critical issue—for people, organizations, and governments alike—is *knowing where we want to be*. The imaginary, an alternative cultural vision, is vital in shaping expectations and driving transformational change. Shared visions act as forces for innovation, and what designers can do— what we can all do—is imagine some situation or condition that does not yet exist but describe it in sufficient detail that it appears to be a desirable new version of the real world.

We've done it before and can do it again. The last quarter of the nineteenth century was seething with enticing possibilities. The social historian William Uricchio has investigated the ways that nineteenth-century technology "simultaneously gave form to, and was shaped by, conceptions of space, time and event which defined the culture of modernity."[49] Early variations of the telegraph and telephone reinforced an intense cultural interest in speed and simultaneity. Film, together with the telephone and phonograph, extended our perception of events and locations beyond their physical and temporal bounds. "Global simultaneity, or something close to it, was finally achieved," says Uricchio. "Popular and scientific culture embraced the notion of speed and celebrated the ever diminishing interval between transmission and reception."[50] For Uricchio, this cultural shift, at the dawn of modernity, explains the ignorance of the past, and disinterest in the present, that we suffer from today.

"The filters of the future will be in our heads, not at the end of pipes," agree Bill McDonough, author of "The Hannover Principles."[51] Frames of meaning cannot be changed at will or by passing laws. Shaking off our culture's mechanical conception of the world, the idea of controllability, and our all-round anthropocentrism will be especially difficult. Writes Theodore Roszak: "Ecology, as the study of interconnectedness, has a psychological dimension—the transition from egocentrism, to ecocentrism. Copernicus took us out of the centre of the solar system; we now need to take ourselves out of the centre of the biosphere."[52]

Lightness is not a new idea. I've been inspired to stick with lightness, as a peg upon which to hang my other themes, by a book two decades old: Italo Calvino's *Six Memos for a New Millennium*. One of Calvino's essays therein,

"Lightness," reminds us that the word does not need to refer to perfection and utopia. "Whenever humanity seems condemned to heaviness," writes Calvino, "I think I should fly like Perseus into a different space. I don't mean escaping into dreams, or into the irrational. I mean I have to change my approach, look at the world from a different perspective, with a different logic, and with fresh methods of cognition and verification."[53]

2 | Speed

The English travel writer Bruce Chatwin wrote about a group of white explorers who were trying to force the pace of their African porters. The porters, within sight of their destination for the day, sat down and refused to move. As they explained to their frustrated employers, "we are waiting for our spirits to catch up with our bodies."[1]

Have we reached a similar juncture, when it comes to speed? For generations, speed and constant acceleration have defined the way we communicate, eat, travel around, and innovate products. Our designed world reinforces the value we place on speed. We produce and consume at an ever-increasing pace, and speed is worshipped uncritically as an engine of investment and innovation. Michael Dell's proclamation is typical: "Velocity, the compression of time and distance backward into the supply chain, and forward to the customer, is the ultimate source of competitive advantage," he said in 1999.[2] Or as Hitachi more punchily put it in the 1990s, "Speed is God, Time is the Devil."[3] (Hitachi's current slogan is "Inspire the Next.")

But the signs are that speed is a cultural paradigm whose time is up. Economic growth, and a constant acceleration in production, have run up against the limited carrying capacity of the planet. The carrying capacity of business is also under pressure. When continuous acceleration is the default tempo of innovation, it leads to "feature bloat" in products and the phenomenon, which we are seeing now, of customers who resist the pressure to upgrade devices or software continually. Absolute speed—in computers, as much as in cars—remains powerfully attractive for many of us, but *acceleration* seems to have lost its allure. Many of us want faster computers, but we also want to live more balanced lives—lives lived at speeds we determine, not at speeds dictated by the logic of systems beyond our control.

Questioning speed and acceleration raises interesting design and innovation questions. Should we continue to design only to make things faster? Is selective slowness consistent with growth and innovation? How might faster information help us live more lightly on the planet?

A-Forces

Many of the problems that unnerve us have less to do with speed than with acceleration. Graphs everywhere seem to be heading off the chart. In the economy, for example, it took from the beginning of human history to the year 1900 to develop a world economy that produced six hundred billion dollars in output. Today, the world economy grows by that amount every two years.[4] In my lifetime, energy production has more than tripled, and economic output has risen by a factor of five.

Cultural evolution has also accelerated. In his book *Consilience*, the biologist Edward O. Wilson plots the evolution of artifacts since the controlled use of fire 450,000 years ago. According to Wilson, the brain of modern *Homo sapiens* was anatomically fully formed by no later than 100,000 years before the present. From that time forward, material culture at first evolved slowly, later expanded, and then exploded. It passed from a handful of stone and bone tools at the beginning of the interval, to agricultural fields and villages at the 90 percent mark, and then—in a virtual eye blink—to prodigiously elaborate technologies. Marvels Wilson: "Cultural evolution has followed an exponential trajectory."[5]

It took centuries for information about the smelting of ore to cross a single continent—and bring about the Iron Age. During the time of sailing ships, it took years for knowledge and technologies to spread around the world. Subsequently, as Dee W. Hoch, founder of Visa, points out, with the telegraph and telephone it became possible to deliver information point to point, simultaneously.[6] Radio, television, and satellite increased the informational footprint—so that by the time man landed on the moon, half the world's population could witness the fact a second later. The push toward simultaneity continues in today's artifacts: Computer processing speeds and storage have both increased over a millionfold in a couple of decades, and the Internet has transformed the dynamics of information distribution within a few years.

Travel speeds have plummeted at similar rates. It took the Pilgrim fathers sixty-six days to sail from England to America in 1660, bringing news from the old country with them. The Concorde could do the same journey in four hours: two hundred times faster. In France, the division of the country into departments was based on how far a man could travel on a horse in a single day. Back in 1867, the journey from Paris to Marseille took sixteen hours; today, I do the journey in three hours and a bit by the Train Grande Vitesse (TGV). Netscape founder Jim Clark proclaimed these trends as the "law of continuous acceleration."[7] But acceleration is a trend, not a law. The pace of life has indeed quickened remorselessly all our lives—but that need not continue.

One reason to change gear is that speed is not free. As the environmentalist Wolfgang Sachs points out, the victory against distance and duration carries a heavy cost. The conquest of space and time requires what he calls "the mobilisation of nature."[8] Fuels and vehicles, roads and runways, electricity and electronic equipment, satellites and relay stations call for a gigantic flow of energy and materials. As we go faster, we use a disproportionately growing amount of energy to beat friction and air resistance. An average car consumes five liters of gasoline at eighty kilometers per hour but needs four times the energy—and hence four times the fuel—to go twice as fast. An increase in speed from two hundred to three hundred kilometers per hour caused the French TGV trains that I take to Marseille to consume not just 50 percent more energy, but 100 percent more. "In general," says Sachs, "the more speed outdoes natural time-scales, the more environmental resources have to be expended. Incremental gains in eco-efficiency will never cancel out the basic law which governs the physics of speed."[9]

Ecologies of Speed and Time

"Thank heaven, literally, for the moon," says the economist Susan George. "If it weren't there, supplying the gravity to slow down the earth's rotation, our days would last only about four hours, with constant gale-force winds. Nature doesn't work on the principle that faster is better."[10] Industrial society, unfortunately, does work on that principle. As a consequence, it weighs heavily upon nature. As we saw in chapter 1, its metabolism has reached a velocity and intensity at which the ecosystems it depends upon are thrown into disorder.

The time scales of modernity have collided with the time scales that governed life on Earth in premodern times. Every year, our industrial systems burn as much fossil fuel as the Earth has stored up in a period of nearly a million years. At this rate, we'll use up all of the planet's fossil fuel reserves within the equivalent of a second in geological time. The acceleration of the speed of human population growth means that in a single human lifetime, the Earth may lose half of its living species, species that it took tens of millions of years for evolution to create through the process of speciation.[11]

The collision between industrial and biological time is most evident in agriculture. "It is the same story over and over again," says Sachs; "natural rhythms of growth and maturation are considered much too slow by the industrial and post-industrial mind, and an enormous amount of resources and ingenuity are deployed to squeeze out more output in shorter periods of time."[12] Cows, chickens, rice, or wheat are selected, bred, chemically treated, and increasingly genetically modified, in order to accelerate their yield. But the imposition of industrial time on natural rhythms is achieved at a heavy price. Animals are kept in appalling conditions, disease spreads, pollution advances, soils degenerate, species diversity is narrowed, and evolution is not given enough time to adapt. A host of ecological problems in the area of agriculture derive from the fact that the rhythms of nature are displaced by the demands of a higher-speed economy.

Another break with natural speed came with the invention of powered vehicles—and in particular, the railroad. From the time of Caesar to that of Napoleon, there had not been much progress in speed. It was only when fossil energy reserves deep under the surface of the Earth were tapped, in order to obtain fuel for the propulsion of vehicles, that the gates to the new age were thrown open. The combustion engine made possible a transformation of the Earth's treasures into vehicle speed. The mission of successive armies of transport technologies was nothing else than the reduction and gradual abolition of duration and distance. With the arrival of the railroad, the speed of engines supplanted the speed of bodies, and vehicular space gradually settled upon natural space. This radical break inaugurated *the age of acceleration.*

From Event Time to Clock Time

Lewis Mumford declared in 1934 that "the clock, not the steam engine, is the key machine of the industrial age."[13] Before the clock was invented we lived time, but we were not regulated by it. We were regulated by nature when deciding when to begin and end activities. We would work until a task was finished, or until the sun went down. This was the era of event time: We started and ended events when the time was right for them. Time did not run in a straight line from now into the future; different kinds of time came and went with the seasons.

The transition to a clock-based system began, in Europe at least, at the end of the Middle Ages, when monks invented clocks in order to structure prayer times.[14] Tradesman and mechanics adopted these clocks and took them into the cities. In the beginning each city ran on an independent clock and hence had its "own time." Mechanical timepieces have always been used not only to mark the passage of time, but also to dictate the scheduling of activities; they regulate the speed of action and therefore the pace of society. "Contemporary ideas about promptness would have been incomprehensible to the vast majority of our predecessors," concludes Robert Levine in his book *A Geography of Time*.[15]

The Greeks, Levine explains, had two words for time: *chronos* and *kairos*. *Chronos* means absolute time: linear, chronological, and quantifiable. *Kairos*, however, means qualitative time—the time of opportunity, chance, and mischance. If you go to bed because the clock says 10:30, you are adhering to a chronological time system. If you go to sleep because you're tired, you are following kairological or event time. We are all born with a sense of event time. Before they shifted to a more clock-based way of doing things, people listened to their bodies to tell them when to do things. Babies, so much in touch with their internal needs, are perfect examples of humans tuned to kairological time. The clash between personal time flow (getting food, going home) and the public time flow (standing in a queue) is experienced as disturbing. People have to continuously adjust their personal time (*kairos*, event time) to the public time (*chronos*, clock time). Public time flows are based on other people, services, or processes that have their own timing.[16] Excessive social speed degrades social quality. The religious calendar, interestingly, incorporated long periods of slowness, of waiting, such as Advent and Lent.

The costs of speed are not just environmental. We also pay a social and personal price. Remember Henry David Thoreau's famous dictum, "we don't ride on the railroad, it rides on us"?[17] For one thing, we work longer hours in a speed society. The more the speed, the less the time. The U.S.

standard of living of 1948 could be reproduced in four hours of today's earning capacity.[18] Life in Stone Age times was even easier. Then, we survived on three or four hours of work a day. According to "P.M.," the anonymous author of *BoloBolo*, hunter-gatherers usually had to work only a few hours a day to meet their subsistence needs. Most of their time was used for socializing, ritual, artwork, or just relaxing. "We stuck it out that way for several hundred thousand years," writes P.M.; "this was a long and happy period compared to the two hundred years of our present industrial nightmare of accelerated industrial 'progress.' Utopia is behind us!"[19]

In *BoloBolo* we are all viewed as cogs in a continuously accelerating Planetary Work Machine. The Machine's activities are governed by the needs of an economy, which P.M. defines as "a system for the impersonal, indirect exchange of crystallized life-time. You spend your time to produce some part; this is used by somebody you don't know, to assemble some device, that is in turn bought by somebody else you don't know, for goals unknown to you. The circuit of these scraps of life is regulated according to the working time that has been invested in raw materials, its production, and in you."[20] In Europe through the Middle Ages the average number of holidays per year was 115.[21] Robert Levine recalls that farm wives in the 1920s, who were without electricity, spent less time at housework than do suburban women today.[22]

An accelerating pace of life scrambles our sense of time. Many of our daily activities are now governed by the so-called objective time of clocks in factories, schools, offices, and transport systems. As we pass through and interact with these systems, we are exposed to a huge amount of sensory stimulation, but we lose contact with the lived time, the natural time, of our ancestors, whose genetic makeup persists in our bodies. Most of us have experienced some of the ways time affects how we feel. Jet lag, for example, is what we feel as our regular sleep cycle struggles to keep pace with adjusted bedtimes. Levine says two hundred physiological changes take place on a daily basis and have an impact on our health. Researchers and pharmaceutical companies discovered in the 1980s that by dosing medications in synchrony with rhythms in these processes, they could optimize the therapeutic benefit of medications. This time-based approach to disease treatment is known as *chronotherapy*, in which medications are prescribed to be taken at specific times in synchrony with the body's circadian rhythms.[23]

According to the psychologist David Winnicott, the loss of temporality engendered by modern life is also a feature of psychotic and deprived individuals who have lost the ability to connect the past with the present. The bridging of the present into the past, and into the future, says Winnicott, is a crucial dimension of psychic integration and health. By scrambling our mind-and-body clocks, speed society creates the preconditions for psychosis.[24]

Sociability, too, suffers at speed. "A rapid pace of life virtually requires a disregard of strangers," laments Levine.[25] Some cultures are less well placed to resist than others. The English language, for example, has no word with a positive connotation to describe lingering on the street; we have at our disposal only negative words like "loitering." Italians, on the other hand, speak of *dolce farniente*, which, loosely translated, means "sweet doing nothing"—a nonactivity that is highly treasured in some cultures as a productive and creative force. The Kabyle people in Algeria, the sociologist Pierre Bourdieu discovered, despise any semblance of haste in their social affairs and refer to the clock as "the devil's mill."[26] For the Kelantese people of the Malay Peninsula, an emphasis on slowness is deeply embedded in their beliefs about right and wrong, and haste is considered a breach of ethics. "At the core of this ethical code," writes Levine, "is a willingness to take the time for social obligations, for visiting and paying respects to friends, relatives and neighbours."[27]

Critiques of speed by writers like Robert Levine and Jeremy Rifkin follow a long tradition. Complaints about speed occur throughout the modern age. In a book about the first industrial age cities in England, *Building Jerusalem*, the historian Tristram Hunt gives dozens of examples of writers complaining about speed. "How men are hurried here," wrote Thomas Carlyle of London in 1843; "how they are hunted and terrifically chased into double-quick speed, so that in self-defence they must not stop to look at one another." Alexis de Tocqueville described "crowds hurrying this way and that, their looks preoccupied and their appearance sombre and harsh."[28] In 1881, George Beard published *American Nervousness*, in which he introduced the term "neurasthenia" to describe a new mental illness caused by the increased tempo of life made possible by the telegraph, railroads, and steam power.[29] Beard deplored the fact that a businessmen could conduct one hundred times more transactions in a given period than could his eighteenth-century predecessor. Other nineteenth-century medical experts also warned that the acceleration of life, the use of the telephone, and the "annihilation of space and time" experienced by early train travelers would cause "serious mental degeneration."[30] In the 1930s, according to Hunt, Byron referred to London as a "Babylon," a chaotic labyrinth of the jabbering and the jostling.

All this sounds quaint today. But the fact remains that we have been talking about the negative impacts of speed for nearly two hundred years—but have not taken effective remedial action.

From Clock Time to Real Time

Time scarcity has always been a feature of industrial life, but the Internet has ratcheted up the pressure. Clock time is being supplanted by Internet-enabled "real time." The probable author of this term, at least in a business context, is Don Tapscott. Tapscott began discussing the real-time enterprise in his 1992 book *Paradigm Shift* and fully developed the idea in *The Digital Economy*. He wrote in 1995 that "the new economy is a *real time economy*. Commerce becomes electronic as business transactions and communications occur at the speed of light rather than the post office. The new enterprise is a *real time enterprise*—continuously and immediately adjusting to changing business conditions."[31] The growth of networked communications has accelerated the emergence of an always-on, 24/7 society whose premise is that if anything *can* happen anytime, it *should* happen now.

The drive toward real time has its origins in attempts by large companies to integrate their global systems in space and time. They are wiring up digital nervous systems that connect everything involved in their operations: information technology (IT) systems, factories, and employees, as well as suppliers, customers, and products. These processes of interconnection have names like customer relationship management (CRM), enterprise resource management (ERM), and supply chain integration (SCI). As Ludwig Siegele wrote in *The Economist* in 2002, these companies are collecting data from any point in space or time where a customer "touches" a company— such as a store, a call center, or a website; their aim is to develop "dashboards" that will use these disparate data feeds to measure key indicators, compare their performance against goals, and alert managers if a deviation becomes large enough to warrant action. "Some of the world's biggest companies want to convert their worldwide information flows into a vast spread-sheet—creating, not a new economy, but a 'now economy,'" reported Siegele.[32] When Siegele talked to Gary Reiner, chief information officer of General Electric, he was told that the company's most important initiative was to digitize and integrate as much of its business information as possible.

I remain intrigued, but also troubled, by the idea of GE's prototype global dashboards. The idea is troubling because it exemplifies the kind of high-altitude thinking that is divorced from the reality on the ground and therefore blind to social and environmental consequences. Vivek Ranadive, author of *The Power of Now*,[33] says that to become real time, not only must companies have an overarching spreadsheet that connects everything they do; they also need tools that can help them easily change "macros." Managers confronted by rows and rows of columns need an intuitive overview of the information they really care about. Ranadive dreams of what he calls the "event-driven firm." Running such a company, he says, "will be rather like running an IT system today: Machines monitor the business, solve problems by themselves, as far as possible, and alert managers when something is amiss." Ranadive calls this "management by exception."[34]

Real time will not necessarily be quality time. There are serious downsides to the real-time economy aspired to by firms like GE. Those of us charged with tending to the system will experience increased pressure and time compression. Real time also means low control—and is seldom free. A FedEx delivery carries with it the implied command: Act now! We lose autonomy as technology strives to render us, through its devices, *always-on*. Nokia reckons (and will presumably make it happen) that 70 percent of all teenagers will be in always-on mode by 2010. As I write, 60 percent of mobile workers already carry technologies that offer instant response by voice and hourly response by e-mail (mobile phones, personal digital assistants [PDAs], wearables, etc.). According to writer Danielle Gobert, an electronic performance support system (EPSS) is "an electronic environment available to and easily accessible by employees that is structured to provide on-line access to all information to permit them to do their jobs with minimal intervention by others."[35] It started with emergency workers and doctors, spread to FedEx and pizza delivery boys—but why should it stop there? The always-on schoolchild is only a matter of time.

Real time also threatens to erode insight and understanding in research and innovation. Always on means no time to reflect critically on the bigger picture. Speed, in this context, undermines the foundations of professional knowledge. The inclination, capacity, and time to reflect on longer-term issues and consequences is what used to set the professional apart from the mere technician.[36]

"Without consciousness there is never succession, never a before and after—just a lonely cloud of discrete and discontinuous points," wrote the philosopher Henri Bergson. Bergson called this kind of time *lived time*, experienced time, or *durée* (duration).[37] Narrative time is created when human beings, inveterate interpreters and storytellers that we are, "join up the dots" between the discrete space-time we would otherwise experience as lived time. This is surely true of research and innovation. A success factor in research is time—time to understand a user community, time to get to know individuals within it, time to conduct research at a speed that does not threaten people, and time to reflect on results.

From Real Time to Quality Time

Perhaps it's a bit of a jump, but I have the feeling that Bergson's concept of *durée* is the acorn from which we can grow a new approach to time, speed, and distance. By separating time from space, we can reprioritize the information and experiences available to us here and now—and not spend our lives searching for the there and next.

As I explained earlier, the demand for change is strong. Time values seem to be changing. Fewer people seem to wear watches nowadays. Fountain pens are back in fashion. In a celebrated time values study in 1991, Hilton Hotels found that two-thirds of respondents would take salary cuts in exchange for getting time off from work.[38]

In science, too, as our understanding of complex systems grows, the virtues of slow growth are becoming apparent. According to Ilya Prigogine, the father of complexity theory, "if changes in one small area are too quickly communicated across a system as a whole, they would tend to be dampened out. New and dissenting ideas need time to accumulate evidence and argument."[39]

Slow travel is also growing in popularity. It used to be just the poor who took the slowest means of travel, but the richest people are now substituting connectivity for velocity. Jim Clark, the founder of Netscape, who, as we saw earlier, proclaimed the "law of continuous acceleration," is also famous for his obsession with (admittedly high-tech) sailing boats. Destinations too will now sell you the opportunity to be quiet and reflective; the market for spas and retreats is booming.[40] Agri-tourism is growing fast in popularity, and one-fifth of all travelers say they prefer to travel in an ecologically sound way (i.e., to practice eco-tourism).[41]

Some transport designers are exploring forms of motion that are not tied into perpetual acceleration. Michael Douglas, an Australian designer, believes tramways are a great way to move slowly in a rich context. "Tramways curiously run against the grain of industrial logic," he says. "Travelling back and forth, day in and day out, tramways help us encounter and learn about small things of value whilst participating in the larger choreography of a city's metabolism." Many tram systems were eliminated from cities during years of car-oriented urban planning since the 1950s, but they are now coming back. Douglas, in a project called Tramjatra, based in Melbourne and Kolkota, celebrates their cultural, as well as functional, value. "In our enthusiasm for electronic technologies, it's too easy to neglect the value of networks like tramways which already exist," he says. "Tramways facilitate a way of knowing that is embedded in the dynamic time and place of its situation. We need to pursue design practices which weave themselves through the social fabric without damaging it."[42]

Some transport planners regard Kolkota as a paragon among cities because such a high proportion of its citizens walk to and from work. It's a great test bed for the study of pedestrian flow and human behavioral factors. For transport ecologist John Whitelegg, "Kolkota is still very much the weather vane or 'canary in the cage' of world transport. It is one of the finest examples in the world of an accessible city. All of the recent rhetoric about creating livable cities or sustainable cities in Europe and North America is nothing compared to the reality of Calcutta which can provide thousands of everyday destinations for its 14 million citizens within walking and rickshaw distances that can be covered in less than half an hour."[43]

Compared to Kolkota's trams and pedestrians, today's high-speed train (HST) is a marvel of speedy travel—but also of profligate resource consumption. Fast trains are transforming the experience of space and time of thirteen million travelers who already use them each year—and of citizens who live in places where the trains deign to stop. Enormous infrastructure projects are under way, but we are only now beginning to reflect on the cultural and social consequences of it all and whether they are desirable.

To fill this gap, however belatedly, the High Speed Network Platform, an association of fifteen European regions, and Urban Unlimited, a planning firm, asked me in 2004 to organize a cultural-expert workshop on the theme "quality time." I gathered together a dozen international cultural experts to help answer the question, What does it mean to design for fast and slow speeds in a city or town about to be transformed by the arrival of the high-speed train?

Fast Trains, Slow Food

The aim was to develop project ideas for services and situations that connect people, cultural resources, and places in new combinations. Food, for some reason, dominated our discussions of quality time. Slow Food has grown into a large-scale international movement, with over sixty thousand members in all five continents.[44] Debra Solomon, an artist-chef based in Amsterdam, persuaded our group that slow food and quality time are linked in cities everywhere. Solomon herself had just returned from working with dumpling vendors in Nanjing, China, and street food sellers in Bangalore, India. Systems for the distribution of organic and seasonal slow food are emerging everywhere, it turned out—even in the speediest cities. Organic produce, products of certified origin, and fresh, natural, seasonal produce are becoming easier to find throughout all metropolitan areas. Often these are accompanied by attempts—parallel to the ones seen in logistics—to make the whole line of production and distribution more visible. Some organic fruit and vegetable home delivery organizations (e.g., Odin in Holland, Aarstiderne in Denmark, and Le Campanier in Paris; a similar service is provided by Handan Organic Vegetables in China) connect the producer directly to the end user, providing a delivery service for seasonal fruit and vegetables. Subscribers receive a weekly crate of fruit and vegetables, the contents of which vary according to the season and what has actually been harvested.

A particularly interesting collaboration network enables Bombay Lunch Delivery in Bombay. This initiative organizes the daily distribution of thousands of home-cooked meals produced by the wives of employees in offices throughout the city. The success of the service is due to the organization of its underlying structure. A network of "meal porters" (the *dabbawallah*) acts as a link between the wives who cook the meals and their husbands working in the offices; each pays a monthly subscription for the service provided. Today, people who do not have a family but wish to receive a home-cooked meal can also subscribe to the system, which has been so successful that since late 2003, it has also been possible to order meals online.[45]

Another way to close farm-to-table loops in a leisurely way is to adopt a tree. Or a hen. Agritime, in the province of Bolzano, Italy, hires out apple trees and grapevines. Whoever adopts a plant follows through the cultivation process during the year, joins in the harvest, and receives the fruit. A similar arrangement is offered for hens and their eggs.

Some people prefer to get their hands dirty. Urban family vegetable gardening has been regaining popularity in Great Britain, where numerous local associations hire allotments to people who want to work their own piece of land, even in the major urban centers, and gather the fruits of their labors. These associations are linked through the National Association of Allotment and Leisure Gardeners.[46]

A growing number of cities promote themselves as slow cities—even if we reach them quickly. Citta Slow, the Slow Cities movement, was founded in Italy in 1999 following the success of the Slow Food movement. Citta Slow advises city managers to promote the quality of hospitality as a real bond between visitors and the local community.[47]

Slow food, slow trams, slow cities: These are more than passing fads. Demographic change seems certain to diminish further the demand for acceleration. People live more slowly as they get older, and we would do well to note that more than half of all adults in Europe and the United States are over fifty. By 2100, one-third of the world's population will be over sixty. This group is bound to influence time regimes. Two-thirds of disposable consumer income will held by this age group—and it's a group that tends to appreciate quality more than quantity. "Slowness is fundamental to quality," says industrial ecologist Ezio Manzini. "To appreciate quality, I have to take time. With a glass of wine I have to smell it, look at it, I have to take my time to drink this wine. Even beyond that, to be able to understand that is a good glass of wine, I had to do something before—to learn, to spend time in study."[48]

Downshifting is also changing patterns of work. The average number of hours worked per year has been falling in most rich countries over the past decade. In recent years, 20 percent of Americans, a very large number, reported that they had made voluntary lifestyle changes that resulted in their earning less money, such as changing their jobs, quitting work, or going from a full- to a part-time job. And these were not only the old. Juliet Schor, who has pioneered research into downshifting, finds that these downshifters tended to be more young than old—indeed, they are disproportionably found in the eighteen- to forty-year-old range.[49]

Business shows some signs of a return to slowness—thanks in large part to a revalorization of time as an element of trust. During the dot-com years, it was thought that "disintermediating" people from business processes would improve efficiency and reduce costs. The theory of eco-nets, agoras, aggregation, value chains, distributive networks, and so on was that as networked communications dissolved inefficient ties to people and place, companies would access different suppliers, procure new items, and so drive down prices. But experience has shown that relationships based on the development of mutual trust through time remain the vital essence that makes markets work. Social ties and personal relationships that have developed slowly through time have proved to be as valuable as brute speed in many industries that experimented in disintermediation.

Journalist Lee Gomes of the *Wall Street Journal* chronicled the struggles of one family-owned food distribution business in Oakland, California, that matches buyers and sellers in the eighty-billion-dollar-a-year food produce industry as it toyed with an e-commerce model. Gomes described a vivid scene that featured "six salespeople in a small noisy office, buying and selling produce using telephones, fax machines, and 20-year-old software on a recent-model IBM minicomputer about the size of a small refrigerator." The dot-com proposition was simple: Use Web technology to build an automated business-to-business exchange—and banish billions or even trillions of dollars of inefficiencies. More speed seemed a prime target in a sector whose prime rule is "Sell it or smell it." It turned out that the main assumption behind the Internet exchanges was wrong: The technological workhorses already in use were efficient enough and had little to gain from the Internet. "I could sell ten times more produce by just getting on the phone and hustling than I ever could on a website," said one trader Gomes interviewed. As Gomes wrote at the time, "the abrupt leap from old-fashioned personal relationships to the ruthlessly competitive world of electronic exchanges was more than many could handle. The boosters failed to balance the cost efficiencies of electronic transactions against these personal relationships."[50]

The Nemawashi Factor

Modern organizations need to learn quickly about changes in their core technologies and also about shifts in their environments. Fast perception —being quick on the uptake—is vital. But when it comes to action, different tempos can apply. As my friend Kayoko Ota once told me, the Japanese refer to the creation of trust through time as *nemawashi*. Originally a horticultural word that means "to turn the roots" prior to replanting—or, by implication, "laying the groundwork"—nemawashi has come to mean the process by which groups in Japan develop the shared understanding without which nothing much gets done.[51] This matters to businesspeople in Japan because if trust has been established between people, it takes less effort to reach a consensus in regard to any issue. As I show in chapter 6, on conviviality, dialogue and encounter are the inescapable basis of trust in our relationships with one another, and technology-enabled disintermediation can support but not supplant that time-based fact. I'm not sure nemawashi is uniquely Japanese; many recent surveys report that stress and unhappiness have increased among office workers in the West during the same years that "disintermediation" and other forms of automation have been on the increase. Time is a key issue for the information society—but perpetual acceleration is not a given. The accelerated innovation of new tools is of diminished importance if the quality of relationships among the people who use them is where the real value resides. Trust accrues through time and is built during encounter and interaction between people; it cannot be digitized, and it cannot be rushed. "People will only pay for what is scarce, personal, customized, tangible, nonreproducible," says Esther Dyson, one of the wisest of the Internet gurus; "intellectual value is often simply the presence of other people, specific ones, interacting casually or formally or both. The key success factors are presence, time, attention ... what you sell is interaction with your company."[52] Social capital takes time to grow. Local knowledge cannot be imported from somewhere else in a Boeing 747.

From Velocity to Virtuosity: Design Principles for Speed

Acceleration weighs us down. Always on means seldom free. But the design challenge now is not to design slow systems to replace fast ones. "Braking" measures, such as reducing speed on highways from 120 to 90 kilometers per hour, or reducing the beats in music from ninety-eight beats per minute to sixty, simply substitute one inflexible regime of control for another. A return to "natural" time is not an option. The coming of computers and networks has seen to that. We have filled the world with complex systems that won't function without clocks and schedules. It's too late, now, to get rid of them. We have to be smarter and more flexible than that.

A combination of natural and machine time is feasible if we imagine technical systems as an infrastructure that we use, but are not controlled by. Jeremy Rifkin, in *Time Wars*, anticipates a variegated "temporal spectrum" with empathetic rhythms on one pole and power rhythms at the other. "Those aligning themselves with the power time frame are committed to the values of efficiency and speed that characterize the 'time is money' dogma of the modern industrial age. Supporters of the empathetic time frame argue against these artificial time frames and seek to redirect human consciousness towards a more empathetic union with the rhythms of nature."[53]

We cannot delete technology from the world, but it is within our powers to reverse-engineer the spatialization of time and to separate time, speed, and distance. One way is to change the word "faster" to "closer" in our design briefs for cities and transport systems. In chapter 3, I show how wireless communications, in combination with modern logistics systems, make it possible to reduce the distance between people who need things and people who can meet those needs. Dynamic resource allocation—in which the resource may be a power drill or a drill sergeant—is the basis for a speed-time situation better adapted to the rhythms of individuals.

The design challenge is not to slow everything down, but to enable situations that support an infinite variety of fast and slow moves—at a rhythm dictated by us, not by the system. Ivan Illich described the speed issue as a prison, out of which there is no exit, when it's presented as an either/or choice: "We discuss fast and slow, endurable and destructive speed. We fantasise about becoming 'slowbies.' We speak of the good life as a slow life. But it's not about being fast versus being slow. It's about being Here, being Now, being—and that is the English word—Quick. You know what the word 'quickening' meant: the first kick of a baby in the belly of a woman. 'Quickening' meant: coming alive, quick. We might be already beyond the age of speed by having moved into the age of—and I say the word with a certain trembling—'real time.' The move toward real-time is one way out of the world of speed."[54]

Slowness does not have to be a drag on innovation. Products and services that incorporate selective slowness, and that are consistent with economic growth and continued technical innovation, are already being developed.

Slow Wash

A project by Whirlpool exemplifies multiple-speed design. Few industries are as competitive and no-nonsense as the white-goods industry, with its do-alike and look-alike refrigerators, washing machines, dryers, and the like. But Whirlpool Europe's ambitious design director, Richard Eisermann, was determined to rethink the clothes-washing process as a whole, including aspects of its "social speed." In Project F, the notion of washing as a social event is emphasized, and a notion of "clean" has emerged that involves more than just hygiene or a process for eliminating dirt. "Clean" is linked to a feeling of well-being. "We all feel the need to slow down sometimes, to tune into natural rhythms, connect more fully with our actions, add quality to our experiences," Eisermann told me. "When we spend time over a task, it shows. If we take things slowly, and step outside set schedules and routines to seek independent cycles, we find continuity."[55]

Project F is informed by insights into new ways of living explored by Francesco Morace, a Milan-based researcher. Morace is fascinated by "the new domesticity." His investigation into the changing social contexts in which we wash clothes began with an open exploration of the washing process and of new relationships among products, spaces, and humans involved in it: "Container + Water + Detergent + Agitation = Clean." Teams of designers then proposed scenarios for every aspect of the process. Tactile, organic forms, inspired by the body, emulated the softness of human touch. Nanotechnology was exploited in semitransparent, iconic shapes to provide a "waterless approach to washing." And hydroponic purification of water was coupled with fuel cell technology to provide a "slow wash" approach called BioLogic, based on natural principles of regeneration and efficiency. Nature transforms sunlight, carbon dioxide, water, and nutrients into action: plant germination, growth, and the production of oxygen. It is a slow, steady process, but it is auto-regenerative and chemically efficient. Morace explained that "BioLogic is a design that embodies a sense of care. Being based on cyclical principles, it grants the necessary time for system regeneration while keeping harmful by-products to a minimum."[56] BioLogic uses phitodepuration (a technique to clean used waters, which are first separated according to their different origin, that relies on aquatic and earthly plants—and time—rather than on strong chemicals and speedy but energy-guzzling electromechanical processes) with hydroponic plants to renew wash water and fuel cells for power. A self-contained receptacle containing clothes is low to the ground and emphasizes the "garden effect": One tends to one's wash as one would tend to one's garden. Instead of a single wash drum, the wash load is distributed to a number of wash pods, allowing for continuous, overlapping cycles. Loads of various sizes can be simultaneously accommodated, and washing can take place as the need arises. A pod may be easily removed, loaded, and replaced at any time. Rather than remaining an isolated event in a more or less anonymous box, washing recaptures its lost significance and becomes part of an ongoing process that can take place anyplace in the home. In this way, BioLogic creates space, rather than just occupying it. The sound of gently flowing water, the scent of the plants, and the glow of lights: All make for a product experienced through the senses and emotions.

Fluid Time

Another project, Fluid Time, is an infrastructure to enable multiple speeds in a variety of services. Most of us pass many hours a week waiting for things to happen: waiting to see the doctor, waiting for a bus to arrive, or waiting for a package to be delivered. Waiting occurs when our personal time schedules do not coincide with the schedules of the people and services with whom and with which we interact. Because both people and services are in constant flux, precise appointment times are not the most useful means of coordination. When people are provided with continuously updated time information about a service or appointment, the activity of waiting becomes more tolerable. With accurate time information, people can adjust their behavior accordingly and take control of how they wish to spend their time. The unpredictable nature of events requires a more flexible system of time than the published schedule.

Fluid Time, which was conceived by Michael Kieslinger at Interaction Design Institute Ivrea, in Italy, explores the creation of a wireless-based service structure that links people to dynamic, personalized time information about public services and private appointments.[57] Using the capacity of pervasive computing networks to deliver real-time information to remote locations, the service delivers accurate time information where and when people need it. The project investigates a new way of interacting with time; instead of arranging appointments in reference to the clock, Fluid Time users flexibly arrange and adjust their appointments by coordinating their own schedules with the availability of the services they are seeking. By connecting people to critical time-based information, the service supports flexible time planning according to personal needs. By accessing data in real time, the system delivers accurate information about when and where a desired service might be available.

Accurate, dynamic information has a dramatic advantage over traditional static schedules. A system that accesses information in real time should be able to deliver accurate information about dynamic services. Fluid Time works with the unpredictable nature of events, constantly updating users with the most recent, most accurate time information on the availability of services such as transportation, delivery, or health. Relevant, personalized information is an important characteristic of the service. Users should not have to search through dozens of train schedules if they are only interested in a single line. Similarly, they should receive truly personalized information about their doctor's appointments, dry cleaning, and other services. As companies compete for the attention of their customers, they are discovering that more information is not necessarily better. People need information that is relevant to their unique situation. New technologies such as 3G and Bluetooth enable the delivery of such demand-responsive, location-sensitive information.

The potential markets for Fluid Time–type platforms is enormous. To take just one example: A better time regime is a key factor in the modernization of costly public services, which account for up to 65 percent of the economy in industrialized countries. A 2004 survey by Britain's National Health

Service has identified five "key dimensions of patient experience"—and time and speed issues dominate. The top two issues are, first, waiting times for appointments and access to services, and, second, time given to discuss health and medical problems face to face with health care professionals. A third priority, safe, high-quality, coordinated care, includes a need for after-hours calls as a major determinant of satisfaction.[58]

Time Literacy: From Velocity to Virtuosity

All cultures have something to learn from others' conceptions of time. The reasons for this are partly technological—but mainly cultural. It took in-dustrialization, and in particular technological developments between the 1870s and World War I, to make everyday mobility technically possible: better roads, trains, and steamships, and later cars, buses, and airplanes. But it took the culture of modernity, a culture of speed, to make mobility *desirable*. The same is true today. A more balanced temporal regime will not emerge on its own. Multiple tempos—some fast, some slow—can coexist, but they have to be desirable, and they have to be designed.

Tempo design does not need to start from scratch. Different temporal regimes than our own already exist in some cultures; we can learn from and reuse them. In Israel, Levine found, time is taught as a subject.[59] An elaborate set of time-teaching exercises is designed to train children from developing countries to adapt to Israel's mainstream pace of life. The children are taught about different conceptions of punctuality and learn to "translate" appointment times depending on the culture of the person making the appointment. They study the rules of the waiting game and are taught to distinguish between work time and social time.

Another project designed to help us live in the present while also being aware of the (very) long term is the Long Now Foundation, which is developing a ten-thousand-year clock. One of its architects, Stewart Brand, explains that the clock is designed to change the ways we think about time. "Civilization is revving itself up into a pathologically short attention span. The trends might be coming from the acceleration of technology, the short-horizon perspective of market-driven economics, the next-election perspective of democracies, or the distractions of personal multi-tasking. All are on the increase. How do we," Brand asks, "make long-term thinking automatic and common instead of difficult and rare?"[60]

Tempo Design

Music has always helped us find a balance between fast and slow, event time and clock time, up time and down time. Ragtime, the English writer Charles Leadbeater reminds us, marked the start of the acceleration of music to match the acceleration of industry: "jazz was followed by boogie-woogie, rock and roll, disco, punk, techno and house—the latter racing along at 200 beats a minute."[61] We make music as a response to tempo—but also to regulate tempo.

The introduction of the metronome into music marked the first clash between technology and culture around the issue of speed. A young colleague of Ivan Illich, Matthias Rieger, discovered that in preindustrial times, musical tempo was provoked by the setting—a special event, a place, a type of work or action. Work songs were related to the rhythm of the work; the tempo of dance music to the acoustic of the place and, of course, to the mood of the dancers and musicians. Tempo indication began to be used only in the early years of the seventeenth century. Composers started to use Italian time words like *adagio* ("at ease"), *allegro* ("cheerful"), or *presto* ("quick"). These time words did not, at that point, refer to an externally prescribed, measured time that could be expressed by units per minute. Although the metronome became common in the early nineteenth century, other nontechnical ways to give hints for the right tempo persisted: One was the use of the musician's pulse as a measure—a method first mentioned in the sixteenth century by an Italian monk named Zaccini. The metronome itself, which was invented in 1812 by the Dutch technician Nicolaus Winkler, shocked Beethoven when he listened to the first performances of his music that followed his metronome indications. "He tried to change [the prescribed settings] several times," says Rieger, "but finally—and he was not the only composer—he came to the conclusion that the usage of measured tempo made no sense in music."[62] Rieger's account of the tension between externally measured tempo and instinctual tempo then shifts from Beethoven to belly dancing and a story about a young drummer (who narrates the story), his teacher Ali, and a belly dancer called Abla:

"This is very interesting," Ali said to me with a sly smile. "Come on, take your drum and let us try to reflect on the concept of 'speed' with the help of Abla. Take your drum and just play a simple rhythm. Abla will dance with you. See if you can get the right tempo with the help of the metronome." So I adjusted the metronome at 60 minims per minute, and started to play. I immediately recognized that something was wrong. Abla moved, but not at ease. She really had difficulties in following my drumming. Drum and dancer did not harmonize. "Stop!" Ali shouted, "you are wrong." "Yes, I know," I said. "It seems to me that Abla just started to hate me. Shall I play it a little bit slower or faster?" "No," Ali replied, "you should not play faster or slower, you should play right. I know," Ali said. "Following the machine is the best way to play exact, which also means to be always wrong. There cannot be a fit, as long as you look at Abla from the machine's point of view."[63]

3 | Mobility

Shortly after the near miss on the Languedocienne between me, the Opel, and the tomatoes, I arrive in the Aubrac, the highest and least-populated region of France, to join La Transhumance. This ancient springtime festival dates back to the eleventh century. Farmers shepherd beautiful brown cows from their winter quarters up to their summer grazing meadows. The cows are garlanded with flowers, and their steady gait sets off a beautiful cacophony of ringing bells. The leisurely procession halts every few kilometers at fields full of food stalls and musicians. Cows and cowhands are refueled. At the end of the day, the cows are released into meadows filled with wild flowers, and the farmers are released into an all-night party.

It would have been nice to stay, but I had to catch a plane. At Nîmes Airport, the tempo of my life quickens—and its quality plummets. As I enter the air travel system, unpleasant forces come into play, and I yearn for the pastoral tempo of La Transhumance. Sadly for me, that's not an option. But it is also not an option to ignore the mobility question. The world and its goods are on the move—but modern mobility is unsustainable. As a system, mobility is locked into a mode of perpetual growth in a world whose carrying capacity is limited. Modern movement has also transformed the ways we experience "here" and "now" and "there" and "next."

The status quo policy—"predict and provide"—promises increasing travel (of people and goods), forever, but using new technologies and integrated systems to make mobility more efficient. A second design strategy is mobility substitution—doing things at a distance that we would otherwise move to do. But mobility substitution is an added extra, not a viable alternative to mainstream mobility. The only viable design option, as we shall see, design strategy three, is to design away the need to move and foster new time-space relations: from distance to duration, from faster to closer.

Why Mobility Matters

Modern mobility comes with a price, but the price tag is seldom visible, and we seldom pay it—or not directly. Its costs are hidden. Not only is transport expensive in time and money to the user, but it involves such external costs as accidents, traffic congestion, air pollution, climate change, noise, and hidden infrastructure costs. In Europe, these add up to more than 6 percent of gross domestic product (GDP).[1] As global systems, air, rail, and road travel are greedy in their use of space, matter, and energy. The city of Los Angeles, for example, which is owned by the car, is a city of paved surfaces. The surface area of its road network, at 1,400 square kilometers, is far greater than that of its city center, at 880 square kilometers. Air travel is just as bad.[2] London's Heathrow Airport, the world's busiest in terms of international passengers, covers twelve hundred hectares, an area four times the size of London's Square Mile financial center.[3] It's a moot point whether either of these plots of land is productive in a sustainability sense, but at least the money people seem to need far less space to do their thing.

There is no international agreement on how to measure the matter and energy burden imposed by aviation, but a clever organization called CLiPP (Climate Protection Partnership), which sells "climate tickets," reckons we should all pay roughly 6.5 euros (8 dollars) per hour flown in order to fund projects that foster the use of renewable energies or more efficient uses of energy.[4] Aircraft manufacturers have promised to halve pollution from their aircraft by 2010—but air traffic as a whole will probably triple by then, meaning that the environmental impact of aviation will rise 50 percent.[5] In Europe, where five hundred million passengers fly a year, and there are already twenty-eight thousand flights each day during the peak season, fewer than 8 percent of Europeans have ever been in an aircraft.[6] Traffic growth seems bound to overwhelm any per-passenger resource efficiency gains the industry might achieve.

One hundred years since the first manned flight, roughly four hundred commercial flights operate each day in India. That sounds like a lot, but in the United States, with one-fourth of India's population, there are forty thousand flights a day. If India were to emulate the U.S. economy, as its leaders say they intend to do, today's four hundred flights would rise four-hundred-fold to one hundred sixty thousand a day. Promoters of low-cost air travel in India are salivating at that prospect, but environmentalists pray that far fewer of the 5.5 million Indians who now take the train each year will take to the skies as the economy grows. Eurocontrol estimates, conservatively in this context, that air passenger numbers will double by 2015.[7] Predict-and-provide thinking drives plans for new airports and more planes. The National Aeronautics and Space Administration (better known as NASA) has developed scenarios under which the number of aircraft departures in the United States would increase—from today's thirty-seven million (including general aviation) to five hundred million a year.[8] Does that sound sustainable?

We Europeans are proud of our high-speed trains and believe them to be far more environmentally friendly than aircraft. But we're wrong. High-speed trains are not a light alternative. A total of forty-eight kilograms (about a hundred pounds) of solid primary resources is needed for one passenger to travel one hundred kilometers by Germany's high-speed train. Life-cycle researchers at Martin Luther University used materials flow analysis and life cycle analysis to study the construction, use, and disposal of the system's rail infrastructure. They measured everything: the running costs of train retrofitting factories, the gasoline used by passengers getting to the station, even the provision of drinking water. They added these to numbers for the carbon dioxide emissions, cumulative energy demand, and so on to derive a "material input per service unit," or MIPS, for train service. The energy demands of the traction process—actually moving the train—dominate the system's life cycle, but the construction of tunnels and heating rail track points during winter also impose a significant cost.[9]

Cars do more environmental and social damage than air and train combined. In 1950 there were 60 million of them in the world; by 2000, when I started writing this book, their number had grown to 535 million.[10] We are now traveling 50 percent more than we did twenty years ago as a result. The average German citizen now drives fifteen thousand kilometers a year; in 1950, she covered just two thousand kilometers. But few car owners have a choice in the matter. Much of this travel involves commuting and work-related travel that we cannot avoid.

The time costs are severe. One hour of mobility a day over a working year of 220 days adds up to a vacation missed of five to six weeks. Add in the money you have to earn to do this commuting and the costs are higher.

"Time is money, we are told, and increasing mobility is a way of saving time," says economist John Whitelegg, "but how successful are modern transport systems at saving time?" If air travel, or commuting by car, is any guide, the answer appears to be: not very.[11]

In fact, the faster we go the less time we feel we have. Intrigued by Ivan Illich's time analyses in the 1970s, the German sociologist D. Seifried coined the term "social speed" to signify the average speed of a vehicle (and its passengers) after all sorts of hidden time costs are factored in. So in addition to "getting to the airport" time—and waiting time once you get there—Seifried reminds us about the time spent earning the money to go on the journey in the first place. Some urban designers have introduced the concept of time planning to take account of these hidden costs of travel. Air travel purists, wedded to the fantasy that air travel denotes fast and efficient mobility, face worse disillusion ahead. London's Gatwick Airport has developed a forty-million-dollar airport theme park whose target is one million people a year—"travelers" whose only destination is the airport itself.

Only a small proportion of the growth in car use during the past fifty years has come from people transferring to the roads from public transport. According to a British expert, Mayer Hillman of the Policy Studies Institute, for every passenger mile "lost" by public transport because of people's moving to transport by car, twenty-five car user miles are added by geographically spread patterns of activity: urban sprawl, distributed production, modern logistics, taking children to distant schools. Says Hillman, "Car-based journeys cannot be replaced by public transport, however much money is thrown at it. Rail travel, for example, accounts for only 1 percent of all journeys in the United Kingdom. If we are to minimize the ecological depredations of excessive fuel use, we have to end the 'further, faster' culture. The transport sector should receive less money, not more."[12]

As we saw in chapter 2, despite the perpetual expansion of time-saving travel, many of us feel more pressured by the lack of time than before. "We may travel at greater speeds, but we work, eat, sleep, and play in much the same proportions as before. We simply do these things farther apart from one another," explains John Whitelegg.[13] Spending time on distance, we travel billions of miles by train and plane for our work, and more again on vacation. Everyday shopping is highly transport intensive: Traveling to shop usually takes far longer than doing it. On average, a Stockholm family saves two and a half hours for every delivery of groceries made by teleshopping—that's ten hours a month for the average family.[14]

Predict-and-provide planning persists in part because its negative consequences have not been seen or felt. From the crest of a hill on that stretch of the Languedocienne motorway I was traveling in France, I could see about three thousand trucks. But they were the visible part of a much bigger flow of traffic: Thirty thousand trucks pass along that road every day. The volume of goods transported by road between Spain and Portugal and the rest of Europe, I later discovered, had more than tripled during the ten years before I made that trip.[15] The volume of this vast flow is expected to grow as new EU member countries in Eastern Europe, and those of the Maghreb Region of Northern Africa, are plugged into the supply web. A similar pattern is found around the globe. Throughout the world, but on roads that I could *not* see from that hill, 244 million containers are moving around, or standing in yards, or waiting to be delivered, at any one time. If all these containers were placed end to end, the line would stretch to the moon and back eight times.[16] Their contents account for about 90 percent of the world's traded cargo by value.[17] In other words, 85 percent of all the goods and materials in the world are not in factories or shops, but moving, or waiting to move—on the road, in the air, or on the sea.[18]

Moving all this stuff around is a huge industry in its own right. Business logistics costs in the United States amount to more than 10 percent of GDP.[19] Oil companies are criticized for waste, but they are but one set of actors in a mobility industry that employs armies of planners and consultants, transport engineers and road builders, vehicle designers and car manufacturers, and myriad small firms making everything from gas cans and crash barriers to road signs and the sandwiches sold at gas stations. Millions of people are employed in hotels, airports, and railway stations. Mobility is probably the world's largest market for high-tech equipment and software, too: Logistical networks, of the kind that enable the flow of goods that I saw on the Languedocienne, could not exist without the Internet.

Logistics is the nerves and blood vessels of today's overweight economy. In industries ranging from electronic components, consumer electronics, mobile phones, personal computers, and pharmaceuticals to fashion, food, and cars, logistics capability can make the difference between success and failure. The average car contains ten thousand different parts, for example, and bad logistics in regard to the production of those parts can mean expensive products sitting idle for up to one hundred days in a field. Parts manufacturers are working hard to reduce that idle time, but their task is complicated: At Ford's Toronto plant, which produces fifteen hundred Windstar minivans a day, logistics company TPG orchestrates eight hundred deliveries a day from three hundred different parts makers. Parts are loaded onto trucks at the point of supply in prearranged sequences in order to speed unloading at the assembly line. Loads arrive at twelve different points along the assembly line without ever being more than ten minutes late. It takes two hundred computer-wielding operations planners to orchestrate the ballet.[20] The more the movement, the less the waste.

Many firms aspire to build "only to order" (OTO), rather than guess what will be in demand and then supply it from accumulated stocks. Obsolescence—products' becoming unsellable before they reach the market—can account for 40 percent of inventory carrying costs. Eighty percent of toy sales, for example, occur in a period of just forty-five days, the Christmas period, so a lot of work goes into improving the visibility of inventory throughout the supply chain.[21] A popular metaphor is that of a retail "glass pipeline" that affords an enterprise total visibility of products: the ability to identify, in real time, where inventory is and how much of it exists. This kind of visibility is expensive: It takes major investments in systems for enterprise resource planning, transportation and warehouse management, tagging, tracking, tracing, and communications technologies to improve visibility and, ideally, control and responsiveness.

The use of radio frequency (RF) tags and the Internet is significantly improving supply chain management. Taken together, RF tags and software agents are revolutionizing inventory control in manufacturing and distribution. Transponders on product packages can communicate with devices in factories or warehouses, enabling companies to know precisely where things are in space at any given time. Organizations such as Daimler-Chrysler and Southwest Airlines are using early versions of intelligent agents to cut logistics costs still further.

Logistics is the incarnation of real and virtual worlds combined. In logistics, information technology, data, and stuff are as one. Companies that once ran fleets of trucks now run fleets of information systems, too. Companies like FedEx, United Parcel Service (UPS), and Deutsche Post World

Net (DPWN, formerly DHL) proclaim that "delivery is just the beginning of what we can do for your business." They have transformed themselves into "consolidators" or "integrators" of multiple flows of stuff, information, and money. They have become proficient, too, in supply chain management, brokerage services, trade financing, reverse logistics, critical-parts distribution, global freight, e-commerce tools, online tracking, and package delivery.[22]

Modern logistics enables supply chains to become supply webs. Hau Lee, director of the Global Supply Chain Management Forum at Stanford University, says the perfect supply system "is an intricate network of suppliers, distributors and customers who share carefully managed information about demand, decisions and performance, and who recognize that success for one part of the supply chain means success for all." The problem is that companies do not always want to share information. That's where chief information officers (CIOs) need to step in and help manage the flow of information and build trust among business partners, according to Lee.[23]

Modern logistics, although undeniably impressive, is a smart answer to the wrong question. Logistics analyzes and optimizes the supply chain for a company and so creates value—but at a cost to the rest of us. In addition to the energy consumed, logistics consumes huge amounts of space and equipment. The total supply of short-term warehouse space increased from 6.1 to nearly 6.5 billion square feet between 1999 and 2000 alone.[24] Faster movement of people or goods requires much greater public investment in transport systems. More logistics, however efficient, will make things worse if it is dedicated to shifting stuff further, faster. Rather than long-distance patterns of movement at accelerating speeds, local patterns of activity are a better destination.

Design Strategy 1: Think More, Drive Less

The overwhelming majority of modernization programs around the world aspire to improve existing mobility systems through the better integration of the transport systems already in place. Increasingly, European planners now treat car, rail, air, and ship as complementary—not competing—modes of transport. Airlines, for example, are happy to displace passengers from some short-range flights onto rail; I can already buy a single code-sharing ticket from Amsterdam to Montpellier in which the first leg of my journey is by air on Air France, and the second is on a high-speed train that leaves from a platform underneath Charles de Gaulle Airport. The purpose of transport system integration is predictability. Systems such as Zurich's "clock-face pulse timetabling" ensure that passengers have a high degree of certainty about interchange between modes, and a high enough service frequency, to make the psychological leap from private to public transport. The Zurich model has been adapted by Toronto, which boasts that its transport system is "like New York, but run by the Swiss."[25]

In the Netherlands, planners hope that transport telematics will make it possible to reduce so-called vehicle hours (the time spent by vehicles in traffic) by 25 percent. A key concept in Dutch policy is the multimodal or "chain" approach. The idea is that information systems will help me work out the best combination of walking, bicycling, private car, train, bus, plane, or boat for making a particular journey before I set off. Right now, individual transport information systems are pretty good—train and bus websites are reliable and reasonably easy to use—but they don't work well together. The next step is to connect systems in such a way that I will enter the beginning and end points of a journey—in place and in time—and be offered a menu of ways to complete it.

Online timetables and route planners are static. Mobility is more dramatically enhanced by dynamic systems based on the actual position of vehicles, passengers, and goods in real time. Organizing the supply of incoming parts and outgoing goods can account for 10 percent of a company's costs, so it pays to be good at it. But the just-in-time requirement imposed by supermarkets and the distributors of short-life products is another driver of mass mobility. The trend is for food to be delivered in smaller but more frequent quantities to each distribution point. When researchers at the Swedish Institute of Agricultural Sciences studied movement among bakeries, wholesale butchers, wholesale florists, and distribution firms in the country's Uppsala region, they had to measure and correlate an immense number of variables: the times required for loading and unloading, driving, and stopping at different distribution points; when engines were running or switched off; the weight of goods at each destination; distance, speed, and road conditions; the geographical location of manufacturers, distribution points, and stores; and emissions into the atmosphere. Based on deliveries among Uppsala's shops, restaurants, schools, and day nurseries, the study compared actual journeys made with the best routes as calculated by computers.[26] The results were startling. It was found to be possible to reduce the total distance covered by 39 percent, the number of vehicles by 42 percent, and the number of journeys by up to 50 percent. Otherwise stated, it would be possible to reduce the vehicle fleet from 19 to 11.[27] Based on these numbers, a project to implement these techniques on a wider scale has started in the commercial center of Uppsala. One of the project's partners—Skandia, a large haulage company—is rethinking its entire business model based on joint loading, coordination of delivery rounds, alternative fuels, most effective use of vehicles, and a new transport management system. Together, these changes have already delivered savings to the company of 20–25 percent. Future steps promise to bring even bigger savings. Sweden's Institute for Transport Research, having compared different distribution concepts, calculates that it should be possible to improve the efficiency of deliveries by a factor of six.[28]

In Norway, the transport company Tollpost Globe has started to implement a comparable system. It's a complex business. When a driver has to make multiple deliveries or pickups in one journey, there are thousands of ways to arrange the route. If a vehicle has to carry out fifty tasks in a day, there are in theory as many as 10^{65} different ways to schedule them. Tollpost Globe set out to make a system that would include these variables in managing traffic for the three thousand individual vehicle transport operations in Oslo on a daily basis. It connected its global information system, a database of addresses, and a mobile network provided by Telenor. Each individual item that is collected or delivered is marked with a bar code (soon to be replaced by RF tags). Each box is scanned by the driver into a handheld terminal, which in turn is connected wirelessly to the network. The traffic management system contains up-to-date information on the location of each vehicle. On average, each vehicle caries out seven jobs per hour, and an average of nine minutes separate each task. Therefore, no information in the system is more than four or five minutes old. This dynamic planning has reduced distances traveled by at least 25 percent.[29] Logistics systems match objects to space, to moving vehicles, and to other data, in real-time. As I reiterate throughout this book, these systems have enormous potential to lighten the ways we use time and resources in all sorts of contexts, not just in mobility.

But making mobility more efficient will not resolve our core dilemma: mobility will not stop growing of its own accord, yet perpetual expansion of mobility is unsustainable. That assertion is not just the opinion of green activists. A recent report by twelve global automotive and energy companies concluded that if today's mobility trends continue, the social, economic, and environmental costs worldwide will be unacceptably high.[30] Historical data suggest that, throughout the world, personal income and traffic volume grow in tandem. The average North American earned $9,600 and traveled 12,000 kilometers in 1960; by 1990, both per capita income and traffic volume had roughly doubled.[31] Another way to measure mobility is in terms of distance traveled per passenger. The average distance traveled by each of the Earth's inhabitants in 1950 was 1,334 passenger kilometers—equivalent to a daily commute of 3.6 kilometers per person. By 2000, that number had grown to 4,781 kilometers per year, or more than 13 kilometers per person per day. If the world does get steadily richer, and mobility rises continuously pro rata, traffic volume in North America will rise to 58,000 passenger kilometers per person per year by 2050.[32] The travel time budget is typically between 1.0 and 1.5 hours per person per day in a wide variety of economic, social, and geographic settings. The difference is that the resident of an African village will spend much of that time walking, whereas by 2050, if nothing changes, I will often be sitting in a high-speed train. The average North American will spend most of her 1.1 hours of travel time in 2050 in a car—much as she does now.[33]

These trends look impossible to change until one remembers that everyday mobility is a recent phenomenon. We have been commuting, driving to shops, or traveling on business or on vacation only for the last hundred years. There is no evidence that long-distance mobility is a basic human instinct. I return to this important point later.

Design Strategy 2: Mobility Substitution

An alternative to predict and provide, mobility substitution, once seemed promising. Many of us thought that so-called telepresence—traveling on highways of the mind—could replace the highways of traffic jams, pollution, and road rage. The arguments seemed persuasive during the 1990s: Matter is more expensive than energy; energy is more expensive than information; it is almost infinitely cheaper to move information than people or things; so why not fly less and communicate more? Why go in person when you can e-mail, or call, or videoconference? Nicholas Negroponte, founder of MIT's Media Lab, immortalized this approach as "atoms to bits." In Doors of Perception conferences during these years, when our conference themes were words like "speed," "lightness," and "flow," we too promoted the idea that a combination of fast information and slow matter could provide a way out of the mobility dilemma.

But dematerialization didn't happen. On the contrary, as we have seen, the Internet hugely accelerated the physical movement of people and stuff. It became possible to do things outside the company that were once done inside—and so we did. The Internet has done more to increase road traffic, particularly of goods, than all the truck manufacturers put together. The same goes for people. The Internet did not replace business and recreational travel, it stimulated us to travel more. New business models accelerated the process. Value webs, in which networks of suppliers work together within a single process, entail a lot more movement of stuff.

Being There

If the aim of travel were simply to exchange information, then we wouldn't bother doing it. The trouble is—to state the obvious—that's not why we do it. It's that mind-body business: Experientially, there never will be a simulated alternative to actually "being there." The world's telecommunications companies (telcos) have still not absorbed this fact. On the contrary, they continue to spend vast amounts of money and bandwidth in the expectation that demand will explode for systems that reproduce as closely as possible the sensation of "being there." At one of Germany's huge national computer laboratories (now known as the Frauenhofer-Gesellschaft), one research team harnessed together a whole row of superfast Thinking Machine computers in order to increase the perceptual depth of its virtual conference room. The engineers' idea was to re-create as closely as possible the experience of sitting around a conference table—only with the people opposite you being located in different parts of the world. I remember the director of the institute at the time (this was 1994) proudly showing me a huge radio dish on the back of a truck that was parked outside his office. He told me he had his own dedicated satellite channel ready and waiting for the teleconferencing system to be deployed.

Other presence researchers have built face-to-face teleportals that involve wearing a headset that incorporates a projective display and stereo video cameras. Such systems allow participants to view 3-D, stereoscopic, video-based images of the faces of remote participants, local participants, and a room that blends physical with virtual objects that can be manipulated. A tracker, composed of markers worn on the body, is used to record the position of the users. One company developed 3-D whole-body scanners that took hundreds of thousands of measurements of the human body in just a few seconds. In Europe, a project called Populate planned to develop a service, using this technology, in which likenesses of people—avatars—would represent people in "inhabited information spaces." The idea was that your humanoid avatars would be captured in avatar booths, similar to the way you can get your passport photo taken in booths in railway stations today. Having digitized your whole body, you would be able to send it out onto the Internet on your behalf, where it would meet and hang out with other avatars. The project was nicknamed "Immortality 'R Us" by fellow researchers.

Hiroshi Ishii at MIT's Media Lab is a leading critic of "being there"–ness as a strategic aim of telcos. Ishii points out that the human eye has something like forty million receptors in it. Many millions more receptors are to be found in our ears, up our noses, in our skin, and on our tongues. (There are dense clusters of receptors elsewhere on the body, too—but this book has a family readership, so I will not dwell on those.) Even if you could capture the smells, sounds, tastes, and feel of a place, digitize them, and send them down a wire, you'd still never get near the sensation of "being there." Why? Because we humans are not so dumb. Our minds and our bodies are one intelligence.

Tele-Hugs Won't Do It

"Most of what we experience, we can never tell each other about," says the Danish science writer Tor Norretranders. "During any given second, we consciously process only sixteen of the eleven million bits of information that our senses pass on to our brains [see table 3.1]. Subliminal perception—perception that occurs without conscious awareness—is not an anomaly, but the norm. Most of what we perceive in the world comes not from conscious observation, but from a continuous process of unconscious scanning, our senses having been censored so that our lives can flow more easily. In other words, the conscious part of us receives much less information than the unconscious part of us. We experience millions of bits a second but can tell each other about only a few dozen." Humans, says

Table 3.1
Information flow in sensory systems and conscious perception

Sensory system	Total bandwidth (bits/s)	Conscious bandwidth (bits/s)
Eyes	10,000,000	40
Ears	100,000	30
Skin	1,000,000	5
Taste	1,000	1
Smell	100,000	1

Source: Tor Norretranders, *The User Illusion: Cutting Consciousness Down to Size* (New York: Viking, 1998).

Norretranders, are designed for a much richer existence than processing a dribble of data from a computer screen. There is far too little information, he concludes, in the so-called information age.[34] "Consciousness is our shallowest sensation," concurs the philosopher John Gray. "Being embodied is our nature as earth-born creatures."[35] The danger in our infatuation with digital communication is that we feel compelled to reduce all human knowledge and experience to symbolic form. As a result, we undervalue the knowledge and experience that we have by virtue of having bodies. Hubert Dreyfus, another philosopher, puts it more poetically: "Telepresence is an oxymoron. Tele-hugs won't do it."[36] When we persist in trying to substitute virtual experiences for embodied ones, we end up with the worst of both worlds. Digitization speeds the flow of data, but impoverishes our lived experience.

Face-to-face communication is not the only type of communication that counts. The telephone, after all, is a form of virtual realty—and it's a powerful medium that delivers a satisfactory sense of connection to billions of people everyday: POTS, they call it in the trade—or "plain old telephone service"—and POTS has been a workable mobility substitute for three generations now. But like the Internet, although it substitutes for some mobility, it stimulates a lot more.

There are more interesting tasks for design than the use of brute bandwidth to achieve "being there" verisimilitude. The communication quality of cyberspace can be enhanced by artful and indirect means. In a project called The Poetics of Telepresence, British designers Tony Dunne and Fiona Raby looked at the potential fusing of physical and telematic space. They were inspired by the social science of proxemics, which looks at how different spatial relationships—standing close, standing apart, eavesdropping—change the tenor of the ways we communicate. Dunne and Raby asked themselves, why should videoconferencing always be face to face? and developed alternative scenarios. Dunne and Raby asked, why limit contact to speech, or sight? Why not use radio to trigger heat devices remotely? In one such scenario, each person sits inside a box in which the weather of the other person's country is represented. Temperature is highly evocative of the body: To re-create an intimate atmosphere of copresence with another body, why not make the area one is occupying warm? I particularly like their idea of a "hot air" button on my telephone that would enable me to politely let the person at the other end know she or he is talking nonsense.

Big telcos tend to emphasize "purposive" communication. The result is all those ghastly television advertisements that feature dynamic business-people making deals over mobile telephones. But in addition to the subliminal consciousness described by Norretranders, a lot of important social communication is informal and happens by chance. Just as in the brain, intense activity takes place in liminal parts of the cortex that researchers barely understand but know are important, so too in offices, space designers now perceive the water cooler or coffee machine to be about as important as the boardroom or personal desk as a communication nexus. Wondering why similar serendipitous spaces could not also be enabled in cyberspace, Dunne and Raby came up with telecommunications moments that allow people to "bump into" other people in distant spaces.

Design researchers have looked at other aspects of indirect and low-bandwidth, but nonetheless valuable, communication. During face-to-face communication, our body acts as a medium that transforms our internal emotions into external signals: actions, expressions, gestures, postures, attitudes, and voice intonation. Other physiological manifestations such as blood pressure, heart rate, and pupillary responses also work more than we realize—but mainly in proximity through direct physical contact or special monitoring devices. In a project called Faraway, designers at the Interaction Design Institute Ivrea in Italy looked at long-distance communication between loved ones who are physically distant, but emotionally close. The idea was to increase the sense of presence of a loved person across distance—but indirectly. The team explored what happens when gesture, expressions, heartbeat, breathing, and alpha and beta rhythm information are incorporated into long-distance communication via objects that pulse, glow, and murmur. The Faraway team used heat to help participants experience the warmth in one application, DistantOne: A sender activates a "bean" by touch that heats up and sends a signal to another bean, held by another person located at a distance, which also heats up. Another application, Heart, allows someone to share his or her heartbeat with another in a similar fashion.[37]

Could there be electronic crowds? Could virtual networked contexts also substitute for mobility of groups? A project in Europe called eRENA (Electronic Arenas for Culture, Art, Performance and Entertainment) focused on the development of information spaces inhabited by such groups. In trials, audience members, as well as performers and artists, explored, interacted, communicated with one another, and participated in staged events. The aim of this dynamic crowd aggregation was to give hundreds or thousands of simultaneous participants a sense of sharing the same space. eRENA brought together digital artists, experts in multiuser virtual reality and computer animation, social scientists, broadcasters, experts in three-dimensional immersive video environments and other projected interfaces, networking expertise, spatial technologies, and novel artistic content. A market for online crowds big enough to justify the costs of the necessary technology and bandwidth has not yet emerged.[38]

Sometimes mobility to a place is physically impossible. Then substitute methods can work to a degree. One such place is the bottom of the ocean. It is possible to translate real-time sonar and acoustic tomography data into a visual display of undersea terrain and objects. A head-mounted display configured for 3-D sight and hearing allows the wearer to perceive images of whatever lies in the depths below the ship that carries him or her—the shape of the sea floor as transmitted by remote sensors beneath the ship. The Human Interface Technology Laboratory at the University of Washington is planning an acoustigraphics library that will contain objects such as fish that one can hear coming; the pitch of the associated sound becomes higher as the fish approach the participant and lower as they move away. Undersea technology used for submarine tracking by the military has been adapted for undersea resource management and underwater construction, maintenance, and repair.

Digital playgrounds are another situation in which we will tolerate impoverished forms of presence. We are willing to pay theme park operators a dollar a minute so that we can experience sophisticated simulations. This market (plus the military) is a major source of support for presence researchers around the world. These researchers are testing a wide array of different devices for interacting with virtual worlds: computerized clothing that recognizes physical gestures as commands; systems that track the movements of the body; trackballs and joysticks that allow movement of perspective; devices that allow interaction with 3-D objects such as a bat, wand, and glove; feedback devices that use force, pressure, or vibration; and remote-operation systems that translate human movements into the control of machinery. Today's head-mounted displays are bulky and have low levels of resolution, but developers promise that before too long, tiny microlasers will scan pictures directly onto the retina of the eye, thereby enabling us to see detailed virtual worlds with the comfort of sunglasses and the clarity of natural vision.[39] So-called fakespace systems will themselves be augmented by temperature, touch, pneumatics, trackballs with "contextual motor feedback," and various olfactory interfaces.

A displaced temperature-sensing system, which Dunne and Raby dreamed about in 1998, is currently being built. It enables you to feel the temperature of a remote location—real or unreal—as if you were there. With so-called haptic interface devices, a user can also feel the motion, shape, resistance, and surface texture of simulated objects. Telerobotic manipulators, which incorporate actuation, sensor, and control technologies, permit us to achieve dextrous manipulation in remote or hazardous environments. A company called Cyrano Sciences claims to be able to digitize smell.[40] And acoustigraphic environments now combine 3-D sound systems with stereoscopic head-mounted displays. Ambient and localized sounds are coordinated with graphical representations and with the movements of the participant. You hear the sounds of traffic in the distance and wind rustling the leaves of nearby trees. You listen to each fish tell a tale as it swims through a musical stream.

As computing suffuses everything around us, a new relationship is emerging between the real and the virtual, the artificial and the natural, the mental and the material.[41] But many design questions about the qualities we need to make the new hybridity work remain unanswered. Judith Donath, for example, who leads the Sociable Media Group at MIT's Media

Lab, counsels that technology that mediates our interaction with other people—chat rooms, e-mail, videoconferencing, etc.—still restricts the range of social cues that act as social glue and guide our behavior.[42] At the Doors of Perception office in Amsterdam, for example, eight of us work in two connected rooms. We have a great team that works really well together. What did not work well was a relationship a while back that we had with a writer working from home a few miles away. He was an excellent writer—a high-tech, PowerBook-toting, mobile-always-on nomad. We, of course, were excellent clients. But somehow, things between us did not "click." Despite endless phone calls and e-mails, we did not build up a momentum of understanding during a six-month editorial project. And the reason? He was not there, with us, in the office. That's all. No amount of immersive virtual environments or multisensory interfaces would have helped us click.

Another approach to mobility substitution emphasizes the decentralization of production: Send the acorn, not the tree. My favorite example concerns drinks. The weight of beer and other drinks, especially mineral water, trucked from one rich nation to another is a huge part of the freight flood that threatens to overwhelm us. But first Coca-Cola, and now a boom in microbreweries,[43] demonstrate a radically lighter approach: Export the recipe, and sometimes the production equipment, but source raw material, and distribute, locally.

Design Strategy 3: From Faster to Closer

Those of us who were enthralled by the potential of the Internet in its early years once hoped that teleshopping would replace trips to the mall, that air travel would give way to teleconferencing, and that digital transmission would replace the physical delivery of books and videos. Each has happened to a certain degree—but with technology serving as additions to, not replacements for, other kinds of mobility. The Internet has increased transport intensity in the economy as a whole more than it has displaced individual acts of movement. It continues to stimulate more mobility than it replaces in much the same way that roads built to relieve congestion often end up increasing traffic. Rhetorics of a "weightless" economy, the "death of distance," and the "displacement of matter by mind" sound ridiculous, in retrospect. There is an alternative. The speed-obsessed computer world, in which network designers rail against delays measured in milliseconds, is years ahead of the rest of us in rethinking space-time issues. Computer network design can teach us how to rethink the real-world mobility dilemma.

Embedded on microchips, computer operations entail carefully accounting for the speed of light. A 600-megahertz Pentium II processor, for example, executes one computing instruction a nanosecond; this is the time needed for a signal to move nine inches on a metal wire—and a leading-edge chip today houses as much as seven miles of wires. On the ground, network delays stem chiefly from the distances between Internet routers. Across the Internet, the average message flows through seventeen routers, and sometimes as many as forty. Many of these routers are thousands of miles—or tens of milliseconds—apart.

The problem the designers are struggling with is called *latency*—the delay caused by the time it takes for a remote request to be serviced or for a message to travel between two processing nodes. Another key word, *attenuation*, describes the loss of transmitted signal strength as a result of interference—a weakening of the signal as it travels farther from its source (much as the taste of strawberries grown in Spain weakens as they are trucked to faraway places like Amsterdam).

The inevitability of latency and attenuation prompt serious talk of a "light-speed crisis" in microprocessor design. Optical computing guru George Gilder, for example, says that "the chip faces a light speed crisis that requires a radical change in the time-space relations of processors and memories. Money will not change it: you can't bribe God."[44] The only way to combat the limits of light speed is by moving closer to the data—and moving the data closer to you. Hence the emphasis now being placed by network designers on geodesic distance. Gilder describes the Internet as a "computer on the planet. Like a computer on a mother board, it faces severe problems of memory access."[45]

The search for geometric efficiency now dominates all scales of information processing and distribution. This search has prompted the emergence of the *storewidth paradigm* or "cache and carry"—a focus on copying, replicating, and storing Web pages as close as possible to their final destination—at so-called content access points. If you go to retrieve a large software update from an online file library, you are often given a choice of countries from which to download it. The technique is called "load balancing"—even though the loads in question, packets of information, don't actually weigh anything in real-world terms. Choosing a nearby country will usually result in a faster transmission. Firms optimize the delivery of data to customers by storing lumps of popular and heavy data in caches sprinkled around the world. Akamai, a cache-and-carry market leader, maintains eleven thousand such caches in sixty-two countries. By monitoring demand for each item downloaded and making more copies available in its caches when demand rises and fewer when demand falls, Akamai's network can help to smooth out huge fluctuations in traffic.

Other companies have not given up on distributed computing. Kontiki's approach, for example, combines Akamai's cache-and-carry approach with smart file sharing similar to that in the system invented by Napster: Users' own computers, anywhere on the Internet, are employed as caches so that recently accessed content can be delivered quickly when needed to other users nearby on the network.

The light-speed crisis favors specialized distributed processors doing their work on location—the network's example of sending the acorn, not the tree. While investigating the subject of distributed computing, I received a flyer for a report called *Colocation: A TeleGeography Guide to Power and Space*. The explosion of global networks, opened markets, evolving information transmission methods, and competing information carriers has introduced a new problem: Where should the multitude of new carriers and content providers interconnect their networks? The book promised to identify and evaluate 350 "colo sites" in fifty cities around the world.[46] The cover price of the report was $1,795—so I cannot tell you where they are—but I am able to conclude that colo sites are the information equivalent of the intersections between road and rail networks, inelegantly named "transferiums" in some countries, which—like airports—are now being developed as destinations in their own right.

Where the Internet actually is, is in cities. Anthony Townsend, an urban planner at the Taub Urban Research Center at New York University, says that just as cities are often railway or shipping hubs, they are also the logical places to put network hubs and servers, the powerful computers that store and distribute data.[47] Cities are already vast information storage and retrieval systems in which different districts are organized by activity or social group. A mobile Internet device can become a way to probe local information resources. Distance between two points is one thing (and even that matters, according to Gilder)[48]—but where those points are still matters a lot. Says Townsend, "mobile devices reassert geography on the internet."[49]

The Law of Locality

People and information *want* to be closer. When planning where to put capacity, network designers are guided by the *law of locality;* this law states that network traffic is at least 80 percent local, 95 percent continental, and only 5 percent intercontinental. Between 1997 and 1999, for example, 30 percent of all U.S. Internet traffic never crossed the national infrastructure but stayed within a local metropolitan network.[50] Someone should have mentioned the law of locality to investors before they dumped some seventy billion dollars into projects for long-haul Internet infrastructure. Only a tiny fraction of these costly fibers are currently "lit"—as little as 3 percent by some estimates.[51] According to the research firm Probe Research, only 14 percent of the fiber-optic cable laid across the Atlantic to support Internet traffic may ever be needed.

This is not the "death of distance" that the companies who laid the fiber had in mind. The assumption driving the money spent on this long-haul infrastructure was that the need for more capacity on the Internet would grow exponentially through the widespread adoption of bandwidth-sucking applications such as virtual private networks and videoconferencing. The enduring popularity of the telephone is proof that high-value connectivity is not bandwidth-dependent. At the height of Napster's popularity, in 2000, the service was using about 5 percent of the available network capacity in the United States—but no other Internet-based service has ever come near that level of usage. High-capacity networks are a fabulous technology chasing applications that do not yet exist—and may never exist.

The designers of computer chips use another design rule that we can learn from: "The less the space, the more the room." In silicon, the trade-off between speed and heat generated improves dramatically as size diminishes: Small transistors run faster, cooler, and cheaper. Hence the development of the so-called processor-in-memory (PIM)—an integrated circuit that contains both memory and logic on the same chip. Savings of energy and speed efficiencies operate at all scales of network topology. By using a decentralized architecture, Napster saved six hundred million dollars in storage costs and over six million dollars per month in bandwidth expenses, according to Bear Stearns analysts Chris Kwak and Robert Fagin.[52] No single software application hosts all the critical data in a particular company. No single media outlet produces all the good news analysis. And no network operator controls all the access points or all the users. When our systems take advantage of the power of the network the gains usually make business sense.

This design principle—"the less the space, the more the room"—is nowhere better demonstrated than in the human brain. Edward O. Wilson describes the brain's custardlike mass as "an intricately-wired system of a hundred billion nerve cells, each a few millionths of a metre wide, and connected to other nerve cells by hundreds of thousands of endings. It comprises the equivalent of one hundred billion squids linked together. Overall the human brain is the most complicated thing in the known universe—known, that is, to itself."[53] Information transfer, Wilson explains, is improved when neuron circuits, filling specialized functions, are placed together in clusters. Examples of such clusters so far identified by neurobiologists are sensory relay stations, integrative centers, memory modules, and emotional control centers. "The ideal brain case is spherical, or close to it," Wilson says. "One compelling reason is that a sphere has the smallest surface relative to volume of any geometric form—and hence provides the least access to its vulnerable interior. Another reason is that a sphere allows more circuits to be placed close together. The average length of circuits can thus be minimised, raising the speed of transmission while lowering the energy cost for their construction and maintenance."[54]

Conclusion: Imagined Geographies

Increases in mobility have a negative impact on the environment, deplete resources, are inefficient, and wear us out. Modern mobility even makes us fat. Cities in which people drive to work, school, and the food court contribute significantly to obesity.[55] We seem to be locked into a vicious cycle in which increased mobility both causes and is driven by geographically spread patterns of activity. In planning for mobility, we don't even consider pedestrian time as an alternative: People walking around in a city don't get counted as travelers. Bizarrely, nonmotorized forms of mobility such as walking, biking, or boating are excluded from the most influential databases, thereby skewing wildly policy considerations of the best mobility mix. And we use time gained by speed in order to travel further. We don't choose explicitly between more mobility or less—we simply build the components, or the infrastructures, that we think we'll need in the future. Small actions can have big effects. Once we get it into our collective heads that predict and provide is a hopeless way to deal with mobility, and revalorize the here and now, we'll be motivated to start looking for alternatives and try out small alternative steps. One alternative is all around us, ready for inspection. This system is the result of 3.8 billion years of iterative, trial-and-error design—so we can safely assume it's an optimized solution. As Janine Benyus explains in *Biomimicry*, biological communities, by and large, are localized or closely connected in time and space. Energy flux is low, distances proximate. "Nature doesn't commute to work."[56]

The chicken breast packets in my supermarket in Amsterdam bear a photograph of the Swedish farmer who rears the birds. He is leaning on the wooden fence of an attractive-looking farm. Behind him are blue sky and green trees. The label recounts a little story about the town where the farmer lives. Before you ask: No, they don't show a picture of the ex-chicken itself—but I'm nonetheless intrigued. What's going on here—why am I being provided with this background information? It's a packet of chicken, not a package holiday. My questions contain their own answer. The farmer's locality has become as much a product as the chicken's leg. The legs of dead chickens look and taste pretty much the same, and it's a challenge to make each one look attractive and different. Human beings and places, on the other hand, are different from one another. Associate your product with nice people, and a nice place, and it should do well.

My chicken-in-a-context is an example of how the focus of both business and social innovation is shifting from locomotion—sourcing things in poor places and shipping them to rich ones—to locality. Authenticity, local context, and local production are increasingly desirable attributes in the things we buy and the services we use. Local sells, and for that reason is a powerful antidote to mobility expansion.

But design to enhance locality is easier said than done. Localities contain a lot of nature, for example, and nature is the result of millions of years of iterative, trial-and-error design. Biologists describe as *choronomic* the influence on a process of its specific context. Choronomy adds value, but often in ways we do not yet understand. Janine Benyus counsels humility in the face of how little we know about even small natural locations. "There are four or five thousand species of bacteria in a pinch of ordinary soil—most of them, species we don't yet have a name for, still less an understanding of how we might need them."[1] Social contexts, too, are more complicated the closer you look. The kind of design that focuses on the shape of buildings or that draws thick lines across maps with a felt-tip pen, reconfiguring whole neighborhoods at a stroke, is not well-suited for local situations. The lesson is that design for locality is not about a return to simplicity; it involves dealing with more complexity, not less.

Locality matters not just as a place to sell things, but as a medium of innovation. Social contexts, for example, determine the ease with which new ideas, trends, and social behavior spread through populations. "Once you understand that context matters," writes Malcolm Gladwell, "you realize that specific and relatively small elements in the environment can serve as Tipping Points."[2] Disregard for context is one of the main reasons, for me, why the new economy failed. Dot-commers promoted "anytime, anywhere" over and above the here and now—and we didn't buy it.

As I explained in chapter 3, globalization brought with it numerous assertions that economic power is less and less rooted in a place. Distance is dead, geography is obsolete, the pundits declared. They argued that sophisticated distribution and logistics systems, computer-integrated manufacturing and design, and direct marketing have changed what it means to design, produce, distribute, or sell a product or service. Investor pressure to reduce costs, more or less regardless of the consequences, increased pressure on companies to move production around constantly in search of low-cost materials and cheap labor.[3] As the distance between the producers of products or services and their users grew as a result, activities that used to be centralized downtown were steadily dispersed. Two geographers, Stephen Graham and Simon Marvin, described this phenomenon as "splintering urbanism."[4]

Many cities, persuaded that they were now in competition with one another, embraced the concept of marketing. Some started to think of themselves as brands. At first, many were persuaded that snappy communications were the key to success; these places spent lavishly on logos, slogans, and corporate identities. Many of these campaigns were banal—"Glasgow's Miles Better," "EuroLille," and the like—but advertising and design consultants did good business peddling these surface treatments, which persist to this day. According to Philip Kotler, a marketing professor, some 10 percent of business-to-business advertising—a vast amount—is now spent on place marketing.[5]

Much of this money is spent badly. There's a big difference between selling soap and making sense of a locality—but many place marketers don't get it. The promotional literature they produce for clients tends to be backward-looking and sentimental; it represents places as culturally homogeneous—even when they're not and don't want to be. Charles Landry, director of Comedia, one of the first consulting firms to take a multidimensional approach to place development, reckons that 85 percent of place brochures have a heritage or pastoral theme on their cover: people in historic costume, knights in armor, gentle country peasants, local fisherfolk enjoying a pipe at dusk with their dog on the quayside.[6] "Identity has become a commodity," he says; "diversity or distinctiveness are edited out, and a predictable bland mix of facilities and attractions is promoted for every area."[7] Some of the people running cities now realize that communication campaigns will not work unless they are accompanied by genuine improvements to the product. The features that really matter to inward investors, it turns out, are the local economic and political situation, the availability of financial incentives, the particular location and physical communications, telecommunications infrastructures, the quality of the labor force in the area, and the availability of education and training to upgrade it. Cities are also looking afresh at the quality of life they can offer incoming workers and their families and have begun to emphasize the natural environment and local cultural activity as important competitive assets.

Societies of the Spectacle

"I believe that a desirable future depends on our deliberately choosing a life of action, over a life of consumption. Rather than maintaining a lifestyle which only allows to produce and consume—a style of life which is merely a way station on the road to the depletion and pollution of the environment—the future depends upon our choice of institutions which support a life of action."[8] That was Ivan Illich, in 1973. Thirty years ahead of the rest of us, Illich argued for the creation of convivial and productive situations and localities—including our cities. A sustainable city, Illich foresaw, has to be a working city, a city of encounter and interaction—not a city for passive participation in entertainment. Sustainable cities will be postspectacular.

The trouble is that place marketers are not alone in missing this point. Cultural producers, too, are stuck in a point-to-mass mindset. I attended a meeting in Amsterdam on the subject of "hosting." The invitation posed an interesting question: "What is the relationship between art biennales and their host cities?" Many international art power brokers turned up for this meeting, which was hosted by an organization called Manifesta. At the meeting, the curators and critics and producers seemed to be most interested in "viewers" and "audiences" and "publics." It dawned on me, as I listened to the art world's heavy hitters in action, that art has become most attractive to the interests it once ridiculed. The tourism industry loves art because its events and museums are "attractions." Property developers love art because a bijou gallery lends allure to egregious projects. For city marketers, an art biennale bestows an aura of intelligence on a city. Planners are bewitched by the idea that if they can only lure the "creative class" to their city, their place will become more glamorous. "Our events are not summer camps," pleaded Franco Bonami, director of the Venice Biennale. Bonami invited more than five hundred artists to that year's event. But he did not mention one single word about what, if anything, these five hundred people had to say—or why the rest of us should care. After two hours I had to leave. "Hosting" felt like a sales meeting for Saga Holidays.

So then I went to Japan where Prada, which at the time was said to be 1.5 billion euros in debt, had lavished 87 million dollars on a new Herzog and de Meuron–designed store in Tokyo. "Shopping," a public relations person gushed in the press, "is the fundamental purpose of cities today." In a busy Tokyo street the new store's Plexiglas exterior, which is like bubble wrap, certainly stood out—and so it should, for that much more. A creative consultant named Christopher Everard told *The Economist* that "by using iconic architects, the label is building brand equity."[9] (Everard's firm is called InterLife Consultancy. I e-mailed him the suggestion that he change its name to "Get A Life Consultancy"—but he has not replied.) For me the Prada project smelled like the last days of Rome.

My desolation at this sad consumerism was not diminished by a visit on that same trip to Tokyo's Roppongi Hills tower, an eight-hundred-thousand-square-meter giant that had just opened when I was there. No expense has been spared by Yoshiko Mori, its developer, to compensate local people for the sacrifice of their old neighborhood to progress and creativity. Several traditional features from old Roppongi had been retained, I was told, including a Japanese garden, a Buddhist temple, and a children's park. When I visited Roppongi Hills, these human-scale traces of old Tokyo proved elusively hard to find, hidden among the development's two hundred shops, seventy-five restaurants, and a zillion square feet of office space and apartments. But at the top of the tower, spiritual compensation awaited: the Mori Art Museum (MAM). A who's who of the global art establishment—including Nicholas Serota from the Tate Gallery in London, Glenn Lowry from the New York Museum of Modern Art, and David Elliot, MAM's British director—had joined this lavishly funded enterprise. The museum opened with a biting and critical look at the modern society that begat it. The show was called "Happiness: A Survival Guide for Art and Life." Only people with a "community passport" were admitted to this Xanadu of art-as-happiness. The passport, curiously, closely resembled a credit card.

"Tourism—human circulation considered as consumption—is fundamentally nothing more than the leisure of going to see what has become banal."[10] Guy Debord wrote that more than forty years ago, in *The Society of the Spectacle*. He would not have warmed to Roppongi Hills. In much the same way that tourism kills the toured, too much culture-as-spectacle dilutes diversity and desolates its host environment. Cultural "attractions" are like genetically modified food: bland, tasteless, and a threat to the ecosystem.

Tasteless Creatives

Best-selling author Richard Florida calls them "the creative class." Former U.S. Labor Secretary Robert Reich called them "symbolic analysts." Management guru Peter Drucker dubbed them "knowledge workers." British policymakers talk about the "cultural industries." Whatever the term for them, there's a lot of them about—30 percent of the U.S. workforce, by Florida's reckoning. A new survey of boom towns in North America attributes these cities' success to the presence of the creative class—public relations specialists, communication analysts, advertising sales agents, and the like. I have an instinctive aversion to the concept of a creative class, mainly because of the implication that anyone who is not a "creative" is not, well, creative. The survey is probably most useful as a checklist of places the rest of us uncreatives—who do "routine commoditized tasks"—can avoid like the plague.[11]

This is not to deny that the economic case for the creative industries is strong. After all, designing spectacles is big business, and tourism is a huge one. One trade fair and exhibition, called Exp, announced itself as "The Event That Defines the Experience Industry." For bewildered first-time visitors, Exp conveniently divided its global industry into four domains: corporate visitor centers, retail, casinos, and museums. Exp promised to show visitors "how to gain a greater share of your guest's discretionary time and disposable income"; how to "destroy the myth that great experience need [sic] huge budgets"; and "how to surf the generational shift." The website for the exhibition did not mention a session on how to speak English, but so-called experience designers (in Europe, they tend to be called "interaction designers"), undeterred, flocked to Exp.[12]

In some places, sport is replacing culture as an attractor in urban regeneration. Paris, in its bid for the 2012 Olympics, says the role that investment in sports infrastructures plays in the Games of the twenty-first century will be "comparable to that played by industrialisation at the end of the 19th century." Claude Bébéar, chairman of the Paris Olympic Committee, does not think of sport as kicking a ball around a field. He thinks about twenty-million-dollar sponsorships and about the well-being of those who provide the spectacle. His plans for a sporty Paris, celebrated in a lavish and immense book, feature a boulevard dedicated to sport, bordered with hotels to lodge journalists, an international media center, a superdome, and the Olympic pool. Private road lanes, of the kind Stalin pioneered in Moscow, and a travel time of twelve minutes from bed to track are promised for athletes and officials. If the bed-to-track journey proves too taxing, an electronic games and Internet center will be provided to "help athletes relax and get in touch with the outside world."[13]

It's Alive

Thankfully, there are alternative ways to animate a locality. The world of live performance remains resolutely opposed to the society of the spectacle. Theater people understand that what matters most in a postspectacular setting is activity and interaction. Tony Graham, Director of the Unicorn

Children's Theatre in London, looked at more than a hundred buildings before deciding to commission a new theater on the River Thames.[14] "We are moving back to the amphitheatre model which thrusts the stage into the body of the audience," Graham told me. "Audiences today don't want trickery, special effects and illusion. They want to see things as they are, without artifice." And as Peter Brook has said,

It is not a question of good building, and bad. A beautiful place may never bring about an explosion of life, while a haphazard hall may be a tremendous meeting place. This is the mystery of the theatre, but in the understanding of this mystery lies the one science. It is not a matter of saying analytically, what are the requirements, how best they could be organized—this will usually bring into existence a tame, conventional, often cold hall. The science of theatre building must come from studying what it is that brings about the *more vivid relationships between people*.[15]

Many people in theater question whether new buildings are needed at all. Big theaters, in particular, tend to sap energy out of productions and money out of producers. Some producers have taken literally to the streets in so-called promenade and site-specific theater. In Chaucer-like journeys, players and audience move together around cities, through forests, up mountains, or into resonant but abandoned spaces. In the age of the rave, street-level events are everywhere: festivals, concerts, corporate events, church pageants, and fashion shows vie with each other to occupy the streets.

In Europe, where theater people are leading the way to a sane policy for space planning, the term "territorial capital" is now being used to describe the "hard" and "soft" assets of a region. Hard assets include natural beauty and features; shopping facilities; cultural attractions; and buildings, museums, monuments, and the like. Soft assets are all about people and culture: skills, traditions, festivals, events and occasions, situations, settings, social ties, civic loyalty, memories, and the capacity to facilitate learning of various kinds. Turning the notion of territorial capital into a policy or a design program is a challenging task. EU countries are committed formally to the worthy ambition to enable a "European knowledge economy" by the year 2010. The problem is that these countries understand what the knowledge economy means in different ways. A British company, Local Futures, is therefore developing a regional economic model structured around human capital as the main determinant of growth, competitiveness, and employment. Calling this model a regional economic architecture (REA), Local

Futures models the geography of the knowledge economy in terms of the demand and supply of skills at the regional and subregional levels.[16]

As a design criterion, territorial capital means that successful cities need to be complex, heavily linked, and diverse. For the writer Will Hutton, just as local knowledge and information was key 150 years ago, when there were eighty different steps in the button-making industry, so, too, complex local knowledge and linkages are key today if you are a software, media, care, or educational enterprise.[17] This picture confronts smaller localities with a dilemma. They cannot easily offer the same density and complexity of knowledge skills that a large metropolis can. The metropolitan centers have their own problems, it is true, but they will always win on diversity, which is a key to evolutionary success. So how are the smaller ones to compete?

Chain Gangs

The answer lies in webs, chains, and networks of cities and regions. By aggregating their hard and soft assets, collective cities—multicentered cities—can match the array of functions and resources of the metropolitan centers while still (in theory) delivering superior social quality. The ability of small cities to offer a context that supports intimacy and encounter—what the French call *la vie associative*—is where small-city webs will win out over the big centers.

Multicity networks are not a new idea. They date back to the thirteenth century when, in the Hansa League, more than seventy merchant cities collaborated for their common good in order to control exports and imports over a wide swath of Europe. A powerful network of trading partners, with its own accounting system and shared vocabulary, the Hansa League became one of the major economic forces of the Middle Ages. At one stage it controlled much of Scandinavia, the Baltic states, northern Germany, and Poland—and outposts can be found even today as far away as Scotland and the Basque Country.[18] Hanze Expo, the League's modern incarnation, links the Baltic Rim—St. Petersburg, Tallinn, Riga, Rostock—to northern Germany and Holland. One part of this link, Estonia, has pronounced itself to be the Hong Kong of the Baltic.

Architects and spatial planners started thinking about clusters in the 1960s. The eminent architect Christopher Alexander first argued in the

1960s that in designing on a large scale, "we must look at the links, the interactions, and the patterns."[19] Networks are important because they are a means of building and enriching social capital. I discuss social capital, as something we might design, in chapter 6, but my point here is that the living links that connect people and localities help social capital accumulate. Urban planners need to pay as much attention to social networks as soft infrastructure as they do now to the hard infrastructures of roads and railways.[20]

For networked, multicentered localities to succeed, different kinds of territorial and social capital need to be linked by a combination of physical and informational networks. This integration of hard and soft factors is complex. For one thing, planners and policymakers have been joined by a variety of new players in a game they used to play on their own. Privatized network industries, such as railway companies, airports, electricity suppliers, and telecommunications operators, all want a say in planning discussions. So, too, do citizens. With growing confidence and sophistication, citizen groups are demanding that social agendas—such as social inclusion or environmental sustainability—be factored into planning processes. A nonprofit technology organization called The Open Planning Project (TOPP) argues that information about public places is as important a public good as the physical places themselves. TOPP advocates a free, distributed, and open geographic information infrastructure and is developing new ways to enhance the ability of all citizens to engage in meaningful dialogue about their environment. One of TOPP's projects, a collaborative weblog called DigitalEarth.org, is conceived as a shared public online space for talking about the environmental information infrastructure. The site includes technology and tools to help citizens deploy geographic data, environmental models, and visualizations.[21] The spread of open planning is a profound challenge to planning and design professionals. They are torn between the increasing complexity of the systems they have to deal with and the demand that people be put first.

The complexity of the new multiscalar, network-based groups of cities, combined with constant acceleration of the factors influencing their development, demands a more dynamic approach, and new tools, from designers. The Dutch architecture firm MVRDV (the letters stand for the names of its partners) has developed a family of software programs called

The Regionmaker as one way to help designers of cities and regions cope with the new demands.[22] "We keep getting asked to make 'visions' for cities and regions," Winy Maas, a principal of the firm, told me, "but we want to base these on real data, not just our imagination." The design challenge, for Maas, is to represent complex data about regions and cities visually, in order to provide a space in which the different actors now involved can explore options together.[23] The Regionmaker, developed by MVRDV initially for a project called RhineRuhrCity,[24] orchestrates a variety of existing information sources and flows—demographic data or outputs from geographical information systems (GIS) (or geomatics, as they are also called). The Regionmaker supports maps, study charts, and access to databases; imports and exports images and video feeds from helicopters or satellites; connects to the Internet; and uses computer-aided design (CAD) drawings. Maas and his colleagues plan to add to the system information on the movement of people, goods, and information. A housing subroutine will develop scenarios for optimal housing designs. A calculator will optimize natural light in built spaces. A function mixer will propose optimal mixtures of activities according to economic, social, or cultural criteria. The long-term aim is for the system to become a decision support environment in a more proactive and critical sense. "We could add an *Evaluator*, or an *Evolver* that can suggest criticism of the input we make," speculates Maas.[25]

Deciding who gets to use these new tools is itself a design action. The principle of open planning is that nonspecialized actors and stakeholders are involved in the creation process, not simply as yes-no responders to precooked proposals. MVRDV's system has the potential to enable municipalities, citizen groups, and planners to "compose" an optimized mixed neighborhood—but they have to be invited to do so and shown how. All of this takes commitment and time.

Multicentered places, as a response by smaller localities to the magnetic power of big centers, are cropping up in many regions of the world. In India, for example, P. V. Indiresan, a noted innovator of new concepts for rural development, has taken MVRDV's network thinking several steps further. He is developing plans for "virtual cities" among clusters of India's seven hundred thousand rural villages.[26] Special rural development zones (SRDZs) will be connected in a loop by a sixty- to eighty-kilometer-long circular road and state-of-the art communications via wireless local-loop communications. In these connected communities, a central market might be located in one village, a hospital in another, an industry in a third, and so on—to form a distributed economic web combining real and virtual elements.

Mediascapes

In his book *Digital Ground*, writer Malcolm McCullough explores the ways that communication technologies modify our perception and use of space. The high-rise building was made possible by elevators and, less obviously, by the telephone (which enabled a large organization to occupy several floors efficiently).[27] Could the mobile phone have an impact of similar magnitude on the functioning of social networks and, thence, on the ways we think about and inhabit localities? Wireless access to the Internet increasingly renders the whole city—not just its buildings, equipment, and furniture—an interface.[28]

Many large companies perceive locality to be the next big thing. For industry, "location" denotes a new opportunity to display and sell things. But as is so often the case, artists and design researchers are way ahead of them in the originality of their thinking and experimentation. Researchers at the Interaction Design Institute Ivrea in Italy, for example, think the mobile phone can function as a kind of remote control that activates interfaces in our surroundings in urban and public space. You head for a bus stop knowing that your bus will arrive in four minutes. Once there, you summon up your personal Web page on one of the bus stop's display panels. (J. C. Decaux and Viacom Outdoors manage tens of millions of such urban surfaces: They can run the infrastructure.) Or why not use the printers in automated teller machines (ATMs) to print out copies of text messages sent to your mobile phone? Among more than forty scenarios for using the phone in conjunction with public space developed by the Ivrea team is Sonic Hub, a street bench that doubles as a private communication space. When a person is called, he can sit down on a Sonic Hub bench and continue his call through the bench speaker system, rather than through the phone.[29]

Another unexpected application of mediascapes by media artists is called *collaborative mapping*. This is what takes place when GPS devices track the routes users take—and the information is shared or collectively developed.

Handsets allow users to "geo-mark" a location and then send details to other people, who then can use their own handsets' positioning capabilities to go to that spot. A wealth of data about places lies in the heads and lives of ordinary people—but it is not accessible knowledge. In experiments called *wireless graffiti*, augmented-reality technologies connect locations, people, media, and objects to unlock the "living memory" of a place. In one experiment in Amsterdam organized by the Waag Society, people walked around the city carrying devices, and the system plotted their routes. Amsterdam Real Time, as the experiment was called, was a joint venture with the city's municipal archives, which looks after the city's historical documents, including old maps. The long-term potential of the Waag installation lies in overlaying different movement patterns on one another and in being alerted, as one wanders round, to a historically interesting episode. Public physical spaces become "containers" for traces of fragmentary personal histories.[30] Digital graffiti or wireless graffiti have the potential, in time, to be attached to any object on Earth with an accuracy of a meter of less. Such a scenario—dubbed WorldBoard by Jim Spohrer, an Apple researcher—is about putting information in places or, to be precise, associating information with a place so that people perceive that place as if they were really there. "This is in some senses bigger than the world wide web," says Spohrer, "because it allows cyberspace, the digital world of bits, to overlay and register with real space, the analogue world of atoms." Spohrer describes WorldBoard as "a proposed planetary augmented reality system that facilitates innovative ways of associating information with places. Its short-term goal is to allow users to post messages on any of the six faces of every cubic meter (a hundred billion billion cubic meters) of space humans might go on this planet."[31]

The idea intrigues a lot of people, but it is not entirely clear, as yet, to what questions digital graffiti might be an answer. To date, the enabling technologies described here have been used mostly for tracking parolees and FedEx packages. In Europe and the United States, navigation systems in cars are popular. And in Hong Kong, a matchmaking service connects singles in the same neighborhood whose dating profiles match.[32] Other social uses of user-generated locational content include marking a picnic spot or a meeting place at a music festival. Business uses include a construction site manager's indicating where a consignment of materials should be unloaded.

At most industry presentations on technology of this type that I've ever been to, someone demonstrates a restaurant review service that enables reviews contributed by previous customers to be accessed by somebody outside the restaurant who is wondering whether to eat there. Many designers and media artists are convinced that there must be more to collaborative mapping than having lunch. In Europe, a concerted attempt to innovate imaginative location-based services was made by more than a hundred research institutions that participated during the late 1990s in projects that explored the notion of "territory as interface"—new forms of social communication in homes, museums, streets, cafes, cars, and schools.[33] Research and design teams divided into two groups. One, dubbed "Connected Community," looked at new interfaces and interaction paradigms aimed at the broad population. These included "computer support for real life": thinking of ways of augmenting everyday activity rather than replacing it with a synthetic virtual one. Projects with the theme "territory as interface" considered the whole territory of the community as interface and thus the relationship between real physical spaces and augmented ones. Researchers looked at ways to enable active participation, to make it just as easy for people to create and leave traces of information as it is to access that information on the Web. A second group of projects, under the rubric "Inhabited Information Spaces," looked at ways to design and populate virtual environments in which "digital crowds" could gather to participate in art and entertainment or to learn things. Scenarios involved broadcast television linked to interactive local content; new sensorial tools for children to use to tell stories and share experiences; wireless devices for connecting children and parents; wearable agents; interest-based physical navigation devices; public information systems around a city; techniques to map and visualize information flows in a community; interfaces for specific users; avatar-inhabited television; way finding; exploration and social interaction within information spaces; and new forms of social interaction such as collective memories and oral-digital storytelling. Roger Coleman, who develops new service ideas for seniors at the Royal College of Art in London, draws a parallel with architecture:

We know that the way you design buildings affects the relationships people have within them. The way they relate to each other, and the shape of physical space, affects the shape of relationships. Information has the same kind of potential in reverse. This opens up a new dimension of design—the aesthetics of relationships.

Relationships mediated by the things we design are really quite different; we knew that from our history of using telephones—but the internet adds another, rather strange, dimension that we are only beginning to understand.[34]

Resource Ecologies

For me, the most important potential impact of wireless communication networks—or mediascapes, as IT firms dub them—will be on the resource ecologies of cities. As I explained in my discussion of logistics in chapter 3, wireless communications connecting people, resources, and places to one another in new combinations on a real-time basis are enabling the growth of demand-responsive services. Combinations of demand-responsive services, location awareness, and dynamic resource allocation have the potential to reduce drastically the amount of hardware—from gadgets to buildings—that we need to function effectively in a city.

Taxi systems are demand-responsive services, to a degree. The old model was that you would ring a dispatcher, the dispatcher would offer your trip to all the drivers via a radio circuit, one driver would accept the job, and the dispatcher would send that driver's taxi to you. A better way has now been introduced in many cities: You ring the system, the system recognizes who you are and where, it identifies where the nearest available taxi is, and it sends that taxi to you. This is dynamic real-time resource allocation in action. Now: Replace the word "taxi" in the preceding description with the word "sandwich." Or with the words "someone to show me round the backstreets of the old town." Or the words "nerd to come and fix my laptop." Or the words "someone to play ping pong with." Likewise for those who have something to offer or information to provide, as opposed to needing or wanting something. Suppose I feel like helping out in a school and hanging out with kids for a day. I might have some time free, or make good sandwiches, or know the old town like the back of my hand, or know there's a ping-pong table in Mrs. Baker's garage that the Bakers never use. What do I do? I can call the system, or the system can call me. A city full of people can now be seen as a live database, full of knowledge, time, and attention—incarnated in human beings—that any of us might use. Louis Kahn talked about the city as a "place of availabilities";[35] with wireless networks and search technologies, the potential becomes actual.

Most of us are potentially both users and suppliers of resources. With networked communications we can access and use everything from a car to a portable drill, only when we need it. As noted in chapter 1, the average power drill is used for ten minutes in its entire life. Most cars stand idle 90 percent of the time. The principle of "use, not own" can apply to all kinds of hardware: buildings, roads, vehicles, offices. For more or less anything heavy and fixed, we don't have to own it—just know how and where to find it when we need it. Imagine there's a kind of slider on your phone. You set it to "sandwich" and "within five minutes' walk," and you use those search parameters (ideally including a real-time customer rating system) to grab a bite to eat. You don't need to go far to get fed; you just need to know how to find what you want to eat.

If the postspectacular city is to be well endowed with social capital, then the most useful use of location-aware communication devices is probably to enable person-to-person encounters. Marko Ahtisaari, a future-gazer at Nokia, says that enabling proximity—getting people together in real space—is a strategic focus for his company. "Mobile telephony might seem very much to do with being apart, but proximity is one of the killer applications of wireless communications," he says.[36]

Public Space

Could mobile phones do for cities now what parks used to do and re-create a sense of shared space? It looks as if the two could help each other. When a group called New York Wireless identified more than twelve thousand wireless-access hotspots (zones in which one can access the Internet wirelessly from one computer) in Manhattan alone and put their locations on a website, the result was a new layer of infrastructure, says cofounder Anthony Townsend of New York University's Taub Urban Research Center. "But no streets were torn up. No laws were passed. This network has been made possible by the proliferation of ever more affordable wireless routers and networking devices."[37] A "wireless park" soon followed. Bryant Park became the first park to install a dedicated system that provides coverage throughout its entire footprint.

This period in the history of infrastructure resembles the time, at the end of the nineteenth century, when electricity was the great new technology of the moment. Then, too, the private sector electrified major population centers—but left most of America, which was harder and more expensive to reach, in the dark. Recognizing that electrification was critical to their economic development, thousands of communities that were not large or profitable enough to attract private power companies created their own electric utilities. As Jim Baller, a U.S. expert on municipal wireless, has noted: "Most of these communities found that they could provide for their own needs better and at far lower cost than the private sector could or was willing to do." Today, approximately two thousand public power systems continue to exist and thrive in the United States, providing, says Baller, significantly better service at substantially lower prices than investor-owned utilities provide.[38]

Many municipalities are considering providing free broadband communication access in much the same way that they provide free roads and town squares. Brussels, for example, has deployed twenty hotspots as part of a larger project to bring broadband access to the entire city. (Some policymakers in Belgium want to make train travel free, too.) New York City Council has also embarked on a sweeping change in the way the city buys and utilizes telecommunications services on the principle that high-quality wireless communications have become one of the ways people evaluate the technical quality of a city's infrastructures. Even tiny Bhutan, a kingdom in the Himalayas, has completed a pilot project to use wireless and Internet-based voice telephony technologies to deliver communications services to rural areas.[39]

According to the group Wireless Commons, "A global wireless network is within our grasp." Wireless Commons has been founded to accelerate the spread of community-based, unlicensed wireless broadband initiatives. The group says that low-cost wireless networking equipment, which can operate in unlicensed bands of the spectrum, bridges one of the few remaining gaps in universal communication: "Suddenly, ordinary people have the means to create a network independent of any physical constraint except distance."[40] (Esme Vos, editor of MuniWireless.com, a website that provides reports on municipal wireless and broadband projects, says it can cost a town of four thousand people as little as twenty thousand dollars to deploy a wireless network.) "Technical problems are the least of our worries," says Wireless Commons; "the business, political and social issues are the real challenges facing community networks." Hardware and software vendors need to understand the business rationale for implementing open technical solutions. Politicians need to understand why universal access to open spectrum is important. Citizens need to understand that the network exists and how to get access.[41]

When the Internet and wireless communications first made the news, some architects and urbanists wildly overreacted. "Bandwidth has replaced the boulevard: five blocks west has given way to the mouse click," gushed Lars Lerup, dean of the architecture school at Rice University. "After thousands of years of bricks held together by mortar, the new metropolis is toggled together by attention spans. To understand the city, we must see it as a volatile gas and no longer as an inert solid."[42] After that initial exuberance, it's now clear that wireless communication networks are an additional layer of infrastructure—not a replacement of the physical city.

A wireless infrastructure, unlike hard and heavy roads and buildings and bridges, is malleable. Jo Reid, who is involved in a project called Mobile Bristol in the United Kingdom, talks about "drag-and-drop mediascapes."[43] In Britain, more mobile phones are used among homeless people than among the general population,[44] and Bristol Wireless is the initiative of a group of underemployed information technology professionals loosely based in Bristol, England, who proposed the idea of a wireless community local area network.[45] They had determined that rapidly emerging wireless technologies meant that even the most deprived communities would be able to create cheap wireless infrastructures that they could use. Ad hoc networks and reconfigurable radio networks provide a digital canvas over a whole city, a tapestry into which rich situated experiences can be painted and in which new commercial ventures explored. As you walk through the city, a diverse range of digital experiences such as soundscapes, games, and other interactive media bring the city alive in new ways. Researchers at Trinity College Dublin have developed an ad hoc wireless network called DAWN (the Dublin Ad Hoc Wireless Network) that supports instant messaging, Web and phone applications, e-mail image attachments, and more. Project leader Linda Doyle talks of "a network that comes into being on an as-needed basis. It grows, shrinks and fragments as nodes join and leave, or move in and out."[46]

Rural Locality

In rural areas, the hope for services enabled by wireless networks is that they will slow down urbanization by improving the living standards of people on the land. Already in industrialized agriculture, farmers have been able to reduce their use of nitrogenous fertilizer by 34 percent by using GPS and accurate field-mapping and data-gathering techniques to apply chemicals only where they are needed. There have been additional fuel savings from reduced spraying of crops and the reduced use of unprofitable land. Take-up of these services has been slow in Europe because farms tend to be smaller and have less capacity to invest in sophisticated communication systems. One solution to this cost obstacle is for agrochemical and fertilizer suppliers to create a service package that includes these smart services rather than just sell bulk chemicals.[47]

But the big opportunity for mediascapes is in countries such as India, in which hundreds of millions of people live in rural localities and farming remains small scale. Distribution networks are already extraordinarily effective in India, even without technology, but ITC, one of India's largest trading conglomerates, is deploying a system called Soya Choupal that connects rural farmers, information, products, and services, to remarkable new effect. Soya Choupal is a service designed to provide physical service support through a Choupal Sanchalak—himself a lead farmer—who acts as the interface between computer terminal and the farmers.[48] Srinavasa Rao, who leads the Soya Choupal agricultural business, explained to me that a *choupal*, traditionally, is where farmers meet to share news and information. Through the Soya Choupal Web portal, which is in Hindi and other local languages, farmers can access the latest local and global information on weather and scientific farming practices as well as market prices at the village itself. ITC claims that the system enhances farm productivity, improves farm gate price realization, cuts transaction costs, and facilitates the supply of high-quality farm inputs and the purchase of commodities.[49]

The basic cost of providing conventional telephone and Internet connections in India is about 750 dollars per line. An operator would require a monthly revenue of about twenty-two dollars to break even on that line. As a monthly payment, this figure is affordable to barely 3 percent of Indian homes—and these are concentrated in large cities. To resolve this dilemma, a system called nLogue uses wireless local loop (WLL) technology to provide multifunctional access to a network of kiosks. n-Logue facilitates relationships among hardware providers, nongovernmental organizations (NGOs), content providers, and local governments. Rather than directly promoting and maintaining countless WLL networks, nLogue is developing a network of local entrepreneurs to provide front-line implementation and services to local subscribers. These local service partners (LSPs) set up access centers in small towns and rural areas that provide simultaneous Internet and telephony access to subscribers within a thirty-kilometer (nineteen-mile) radius.[50]

In India, Sparse Area Communications involve combinations of satellite and fixed or wireless local loops, with relay stations and devices powered by solar panels, deployed to connect even isolated communities. When I visited the Centre for Knowledge Societies in Bangalore, a researcher described walking for three hours up a hill to a village that was inaccessible by road. When he arrived, he discovered that children in the village were all computer literate—and one showed him a PowerPoint presentation. I wasn't sure then, or now, that finding a PowerPoint presentation at the top of a mountain represented progress. The more heated debate among communications designers concerns whether proprietary systems like Soya Choupal and nLogue are compatible with the ideal of an open-systems society.

"The trick is to think and act rural," advises Ashok Jhunjhunwaller, a promoter of the electronic kiosks that are transforming connectivity in rural India. Even if individual farmers do not own a PC or handset themselves, 85 percent of India's seven hundred thousand villages now have functional access to some form of connectivity. Many hundred millions of people use the country's million-plus public call offices (PCOs), and PCO revenues currently account for an astonishing 25 percent of India's total telecom revenues. A remarkable man named Sam Pitroda came up with this idea of "an entrepreneur in every street," and since he first outlined his vision to me in 1995, it has been has been realized in vast areas of the country.[51] Pitroda's PCO innovation had relatively little to do with technology; it was mainly a business brilliant business model: first, to aggregate demand, and second, to scale the service rapidly by involving existing local entrepreneurs. Jhunjhunwaller is hoping to leverage similar scalability dynamics, optimistic that kiosk systems as an enabling infrastructure should make it possible to double average incomes in rural India from today's two hundred dollars per year to four hundred.[52]

From Far to Deep

In chapter 3, I told you about the law of locality used by telecommunications network designers to allocate capacity. As I noted earlier in this chapter, much of the world's GDP is highly localized. Local conditions, local trading patterns, local networks, local skills, and local culture remain a critical success factor for the majority of economic activity in the world. Especially if we steer them in that direction, mediascapes can improve the resource efficiency of the places we live in.

Big business is already using mediascapes to shape the evolution of localities. Locational data and demographic models are used by Starbucks and McDonald's to site new stores. Huge volumes of point-of-sale information are mined to help firms like WalMart tune the placement of wares, even inside stores. My proposition is this: The same kinds of software and data that enable WalMart to locate its huge stores can be repurposed to optimize local-area service ecologies. Flows of resources can be shaped that minimize the movement of people and goods. New parameters can be introduced into open planning systems—for example, that 50 percent of produce in a shop or railway station should be local or have traveled no more than fifty kilometers from where it was grown.

Local-area service ecologies can be further enhanced by referral and ratings systems. Position index databases, social navigation, quick messaging, local polling on handheld or worn devices: All these have the capacity to combine depth with lightness in economic life in a locality. A similar approach could optimize the siting of decentralized educational facilities, too.

Participatory Place

In Tokyo, cement trucks sport the slogan "Begin the next." When you buy cellophane tape at the corner shop, the bag carries a slogan: "Perhaps we are at the beginning of a new renaissance." Honda's Dio motorcycle sports an entire text on the faring that declares: "Movement: The City is a 24 hour stage where we act out a life. Be it day or night, we go out anytime looking for something new." Hardly surprising that they call Tokyo the "sea of desires": Its citizenry revels in continuous change and innovation.[53] Change—and multiple and changing cultures—are what cities are about. But this makes it hard to come up with design criteria.

The other downside of mediascapes and urban networks is although we can't live without them, they are not stable. In recent times urban-network collapses have become more frequent and more alarming. A seminar in the United Kingdom, "Urban Vulnerability and Infrastructure," featured the Montreal ice storm, the Auckland power blackout, the gas attack on the Tokyo underground, the Sydney drought, the California energy crisis, the Chicago heat wave, the failure of Hong Kong airport's freight system, the September 11 attacks, and the Lovebug virus. Said the organizers:

As seamless and 24 hour flows and connections become ever-more critical for capitalist urbanism, so massive political, discursive and material resources are being devoted to try and reduce the supposed vulnerabilities that these systems exhibit to collapse, malfunctioning, or attack. Huge resources and efforts are now being devoted by States, infrastructure corporations, the military, urban infrastructure agencies, and corporate capital to reducing the supposed vulnerability of telecommunications, transport, logistics, transaction, electricity, and utilities systems to technical failure, sabotage, natural disasters or the failures caused by the reduced built in back-up that often comes with liberalised markets. The glaring fragility, and low reliability, of many computer-mediated communications and infrastructure systems is a particular focus of concern.[54]

The danger with control mania is that it precludes bottom-up social innovation. Openness is vital if we are to answer an important question: When traditional industries disappear from a locality, what is to take their place? In Spark![55] I helped multidisciplinary design teams from five countries, together with local officials and citizens, conduct design scenario workshops in five very different European locations: Narva-Joessu in Estonia, Cray Valley in London, Forssa in Finland, Valdambra in Italy, and Nexo in Denmark. In these five locations, groups of twenty to thirty people would do a crash investigation. Mapping and notation of local knowledge would record what kinds of value reside in the locality. Technical types would explore what roles new communications technologies such as wireless and GPS play in new services for these places and would debate how to understand boundaries between devices and networks, infrastructure, content, equipment, software, space, and place. But content questions were uppermost among all the disciplines involved. Nexo, on Bornholm in the Baltic Sea, for example, is one of dozens of Baltic and European fishing ports in which industrial fishing has become unsustainable. Our multidisciplinary team decided that the Bornholm Rooster, a superior kind of chicken, should be a star product on what it christened "Food Island"—along with the legendary white salmon, a ghostly creature that passes quietly by this misplaced Danish island (it sits between Sweden and Poland) only in the winter months. (This desolate but fertile spot was the location for the final workshop at the Spark! conference.)

An Icelandic designer, Halldor Gislason, has also looked into the ways designers can help rejuvenate localities devastated by the loss of fishing but where assets remain: harbors, keys, boats, fish factories, etc. In one town in the north of Iceland, where the trawlers have all been sold off, Gislason developed a new kind of cultural tourism that features whale watching and an exhibition space dealing with timber boats and Viking sailing technology.

These experiences have taught me that among the success factors in design-for-locality projects, the most important are a real-world context; a service orientation; a requirement to connect actors in new combinations and exploit network effects; and above all, an insistence that the incoming project team work with local people and ensure, where feasible, that expertise is left behind after the project ends. This kind of bottom-up design is not easily reconciled with security-driven control of networks.

The beauty of projects like Spark! is that they help citizens perceive their own locality through fresh eyes. The most valuable service designers and artists can provide a locality may therefore be to help it develop a shared cultural vision of the future, but not to design that future for it.

Design-Free Zones

As with networks and infrastructure, so too with localities: Too much of our world is just too designed. Too much control over networks is detrimental to the social innovation upon which our future fortunes depend. It is welcome to note, therefore, that several European cities are contemplating the protection of design-free situations, or free zones, in which planning and other top-down, outside-in improvements will be kept at bay to make space for the kinds of experimentation that can emerge, unplanned and unexpected, from wild, design-free ground.

It's tough for planners to embrace a phenomenon that flourishes because it is *not* planned, and free-zone promoters face tough opposition from both security and health and safety officials, who hate the idea of places outside their control. (Tickets for the Burning Man Festival in Arizona include the disclaimer that the buyer may suffer injury or death.)

We can learn a lot from the free-form approaches to urban design that flourished in situations in which the state was collapsing. A project called Wild City: Urban Genetics involved a group of designers called Stealth in street-level research undertaken in Belgrade over a number of years. The city experienced an abrupt change from centralized to atomized growth as the result of a decade of crisis and a United Nations embargo in 1992. As the state and its institutions collapsed, individual initiative led to innovation in literally every urban domain, from commerce to housing production and public services. The new, nonregulated structure that emerged flooded the public realm and, in the designers' words, "superimposed a layer of mutants on the existing city." Mapping the interactions between nonregulated processes (street traders moving into spaces vacated by defunct official businesses) and existing city fabrics (the green market or a department store), Stealth has developed tools to map actors and forces that previously did not figure in urban design notation.[56]

This research into urban genetics focuses on the evolutionary, time-based character of nonregulated transformations. It is a practice of discovering the inherent logic of emergent processes, based on the assumption that the result is often more sophisticated than a conventionally designed one. Through this experiment, a set of tools and a specific methodology have been experimentally developed for visualizing, monitoring, and to a certain extent, predicting spatial and organizational changes over time. Stealth's objective, in the longer term, is "to point out the undiscovered potentials of specific locations."[57] As the Wild City researchers put it, the city itself acts like a wild garden, as an "incubator of new urban forms. The paradigm of 'wildness' emerged through non-planned and scarcely regulated processes. In the urban domain, these processes feature a remarkable degree of innovation. They lead to possibilities for redefining institutional participation in the creation of urban space."[58] Wild City provides empirical evidence that an adapt-and-provide focus on the adaptation of existing infrastructures to serve new purposes can work.

Conclusion

The list of challenges facing the design of the places in which we live is daunting. In chapter 1, I explained that the ecological footprints of cities appear to be unsustainable. In chapter 2, I described the many indications that constant acceleration is wearing us, and our institutions, out. In chapter 3, I described the costs we incur for spending more time on the move than on being there.

In this chapter, I have looked at the often malignant impact of place marketing on the identity of regions and cities. I have shown that powerful but bland retail chains threaten to turn our homes into "clonetowns" and that far too much money is being spent on point-to-mass buildings in which we are supposed to pay and gawk at culture and sport performed by others. Overlaying it all is a layer of technology-based systems that we depend on but that are overcomplicated and fault-intolerant. These systems and networks occupy far too much of the attention of our planners and urban designers, whose high-level thinking causes them to operate in an ever-more-abstract realm. All these trends are antithetical to the open, collaborative, bottom-up design promoted in this book.

These challenges look daunting, and they are. But the beauty of the metaphor of tipping points is that in a context of complex systems and constant change, even small actions can have a powerful, transformative effect on the bigger picture. Thinking local and thinking small is not a parochial approach, and it is not an abdication of responsibility for the bigger picture. On the contrary, we will get from here to there by a series of small, but carefully considered, steps.

We have to live somewhere, and if nature and social history are any guide, that somewhere is local. Proximity and locality are natural features of the economy. Most of the world's GDP is highly localized. Around the world, the vast majority of small and medium-sized companies operate within a radius of fifty kilometers of their headquarters location. Local conditions, local trading patterns, local networks, local skills, and local culture are critical success factors for the majority of organizations.

5 | Situation

In May 1993 I arrived in Amsterdam to start work at the Netherlands Design Institute, where I had been appointed its first director. Builders were already on site at the Fodor Museum, on Keizersgracht, which was to be our home—so I cannot claim to have been involved in the project from the very beginning. But when I first met the architects Jan Benthem and Mels Crouwel (the same architects who take care of Schiphol Airport), our roof was off, the foundations were laid bare, and most of the internal space and infrastructure still had to be designed. A full year remained before we were due to open. Following that rather alarming first site visit, I had six years of on-the-job training in the design, commissioning, and use of a new building. During that period, we designed and built a new knowledge-based organization, too—also from scratch—a "think-and-do tank" whose objective was to reframe the way we perceive and use design. In the course of those six years, the building as a space and the relationships it supported interacted in powerful ways—most of them positive, some negative. The experience taught me that a focus on space constrains the design of a workplace. The word "situation" better encompasses social factors.

Our building was frequently criticized for being too stiff. It isolated us from the real world and from one another. It was beautiful and a pleasure to be in—but because of the way the circulation of people worked, we seldom bumped into one another or visitors. When we resolved to try to loosen up the building, we discovered that it was not an easy space to change. We tried dozens of ways to make our space smarter and more interactive: video art installations, tricks with screens and doorbells, dynamic information screens, flashing lights, sound sculptures, kinetic art. You name it, we considered it. In the end, the single most important change we made was to move two "front of house" human beings from the back of the building to near the entrance.

My conclusion, after several years of enjoyable experimentation, is that much office design deals expertly with many different, interrelated elements, including spatial layout, lighting, furniture specification, material finishes, technology services, and catering provision; but it does not deal well with the subtleties of social interaction. Architects and office equipment designers are usually intelligent and well-informed people. During many years as a design journalist, I enjoyed numerous interesting conversations on the subject with leading practitioners. But at the end of the day their job—and the business model that enables them to do it—is based on the supply of new buildings, desks, chairs, or lights.

My skepticism about office and workplace design was reinforced by the year I spent helping the Museum of Modern Art in New York develop a show called Workspheres. I was a member of the advisory group for this big-ticket production about the future of the workplace. As a public event, Workspheres was an immediate smash hit—"off the charts" in the words of one expert on what's in and hot in that febrile town. There were more people at the press preview than attend the public openings of big art shows (or most of the events at the institute I led in Amsterdam at the time). The private view was a heaving, black-clad throng that contained everyone who was anyone in New York architecture and design. As one leading journalist wrote at the time, Workspheres "falls just short of greatness; modernity is back at the Modern."[1]

The trouble was, for me, that this smash-hit show told a story about the future of workplace design that was more or less the opposite of the one that really matters. Workspheres contained a glittering collection of products—but the story it told was all about gadgets and tools. It was full of beautiful objects for isolated, narcissitic, and inward-gazing individuals. The most gorgeous desks, chairs, lights, pens, personal digital assistants (PDAs), and laptops were on display. Little was said about the future content of our work: its purpose and meaning, how we would do it, where we would work, and when—and above all, how—we might redesign it. If gadget-filled Workspheres was "the new modernity," as the journalist had declared, it was a dispiriting prospect.

Workspheres was mounted at a time (this was in 2001) when hard questions had started to be asked about all the physical assets owned by organizations. In the extreme view, ownership of any kind of asset other than information is a liability. For Bill Mayon-White, a professor at the London School of Economics, the physical assets owned by most corporate giants represent "an albatross hanging around their necks."[2] Companies gain flexibility by *not* owning physical assets, by concentrating on ownership of intellectual property and moving that around. A big part of the impetus to such thinking has come from the Spanish economist Manuel Castells, who wrote evocatively about the networked economy as a "space of flows."[3]

The constantly changing flows of people and ideas that characterize a dynamic learning organization, and the quality of interactions with other people and communities and customers, are more important than the boxes we meet in, the chairs we sit in, or the keyboards we punch to communicate with. If innovation is a *social* process that involves complex interactions among individuals, communities of practice, and customers, then fostering these complex interactions—designing the *context* of innovation and learning—brings so-called soft aspects of workplace design to the fore. The keyword here is minds in the plural—and in particular the innovative capabilities of groups. Learning happens best when people participate in different communities of practice. The best collaboration environments provide the opportunity to meet, share ideas, discuss, and learn from one another's experiences. We need to interact in them, not pose in them.

Design does not take place in a situation; it *is* the situation. As planners, designers, and citizens, we need to rethink our spaces, places, and communities in order to better exploit the dynamic potential of networked collaboration. Gadgets, furniture, and high-design buildings are of modest value, at best, in this context, and the solution to high-tech environments is not to add more tech. Learning relies on personal interaction and, in particular, on a range of peripheral, but nonetheless embodied, forms of communication. Technology obscures these kinds of liminal communication more than it enhances them. Understanding, relationships, and trust are time-based, not tech-based. I cannot recall ever having an intelligent conversation in a smart room.

For Nobel laureate Murray Gell-Mann, innovation is an "emergent phenomenon" that happens when a person or organization fosters interaction between different kinds of people and disparate forms of knowledge.[4] Designing the context of innovation and learning is therefore about fostering complex interactions, not about filling up spaces with gadgets. Anything that impedes the free flow of interactions among individuals hinders innovation.

Aborigines dream in the vastness of the outback. Dream time for modern man takes place in high-tech offices. "We no longer have roots, we have aerials," goes the urban legend, and telecommunications companies promote "anytime, anywhere" as a value. Life in systems-rich environments is understudied. Social scientists research endlessly the impact of television or the computer on behavior, and interaction designers study people in control rooms, air traffic control towers, and the like, but behavioral investigations of life for the rest of us in shopping malls, departure lounges, and other highly designed environments are rare. This is a significant gap, because these spaces have transformed the way we experience "here" and "now" and "there" and "next."

Some designers have become bored with gadgets and are learning now how to map the way communications flow in different kinds of communities. These "maps" do not just focus on so-called purposive communication—letters to the bank, calling a taxi, a project meeting—but also embrace social and cultural communications: the many ways people build relationships, articulate their needs and fears, and interact informally with friends, family, careers, officials, and so on. Traditional workplace design emphasized the individual worker and his space and equipment. The Walt Disney Company employs "imagineers" to animate its supremely artificial environments; we are beginning to see something similar emerge in the offices of knowledge-based companies: "office clowns," "animateurs," "show business impresarios," and others whose role is to generally liven the place up.

Lost in Space

A lot of my work involves travel, and I have often pondered my curious state of mind while engaged in modern movement. As well as being thresholds between land and air, modern airports are gateways to complexity. Through them, we enter the operating environment of global aviation, one of mankind's most complicated creations. But in airports and other large spaces, although we are isolated from the rhythms of the natural world, we remain ignorant of how this artificial one works. The result is to reinforce what philosophers call our ontological alienation, a sense of rootlessness and anxiety, of not quite being real, of being lost in space. Aviation is typical of the way the whole world is going: saturated with information and systems, complex but incomprehensible, an exhilarating human achievement and a terrifying prospect at the same time. It's time design came to grips with these ambiguous features of our technology-filled environment.

Different kinds of space affect the way we think and feel. Building plans, of the kind you find in an architect's office, say almost nothing about the quality of our interactions in complex technical spaces like transport hubs or high-tech offices—the operating environment within which space, electronic signals, and people interact with one another continuously on a global scale. An immense global system determines what architects would call the *program* of an individual airport building. As we saw in chapter 3, aviation is a vast system. The world's airlines now carry one-sixth of the world's population—more than one billion passengers—on scheduled flights. As I write this, three hundred thousand people are in the air above the United States alone. They're in a uniquely space-out office.

The world's aviation system, of which airports are one component, is distributed not just in space, but also in time. Its earthbound infrastructure is linked into a complex operating environment, or aviation space. Airports exist at the intersection of airways—the space through which aircraft pass—which are densely crisscrossed, in three spatial dimensions and at different times, by the routes planes are flying, have flown, and will fly. Aviation space is saturated with electronic information from humans and machines, chattering out directions to thousands of aircrews—and onboard computers—at any one moment. The fact that people—passengers, aircrews, ground staff, air traffic controllers, and the like—are part of the system, too, adds to the complexity.

As we saw in chapter 3, these huge flows of people and matter and information are increasing in volume and power at an increasing rate. The biggest international airport hubs—the United States alone has thirty—are like giant pumps that greatly increase flow through the whole system. Phenomenal costs land on those places that wish to join the hub club. Once road and rail links, baggage-handling systems, air traffic control systems, and so on are factored in, the capital cost of an international airport can quickly exceed a billion dollars. That's a high-end office rent.

Planning a big transport hub is like designing a city with more than half a million inhabitants. But it's not like living in one. A big hub handles more than a thousand airline movements a day, and the ground traffic generated by all the associated workers, passengers, well-wishers, cab drivers, and so on is also enormous.[5] Frankfurt's airport, with a workforce in excess of forty thousand, is the biggest single-site employer in Germany. London's Heathrow employs fifty-five thousand people directly—meteorologists, air traffic controllers, pilots, cabin crew, cleaners, caterers, check-in staff, baggage handlers, engineers, firemen, police, security guards. Another three hundred thousand or more people are employed by myriad suppliers—all those van drivers and sandwich makers. Airports are also the world's largest employers of dogs.

Costs on this scale are sustained because airports and railway termini have become large multinational businesses in their own right. Less than 50 percent of Heathrow's earnings come from landing fees or servicing aircraft. Commercial activity on the ground is one of the main sources of airport revenue, and hence one of the main drivers of airport design. Transit passengers *not* flying spend an average of thirty-five dollars a head at Heathrow's hundreds of shops, restaurants, hairdressers—and four caviar bars. Heathrow is also the largest market for Havana cigars in the world—including Havana.

Powerful commercial and network operation agendas drive the way both space and time are designed. In the old days, when airports and transport hubs were conceived as transport utilities—if only for an elite—engineers and operations people would have regarded an idle passenger as evidence of system inefficiency. Not today. Mobility is just one of the products on sale at a modern interchange. To commercial managers, "passenger discretionary time" or "dwell time"—the time spent by passengers killing time between journeys or between links of a journey—is a sales opportunity. The management of dwell time to optimize commercial yield is one reason—traffic jams are another—that throughout my lifetime, the proportion of time I have spent in the air on a journey has steadily decreased.

The design of work and the experience of mobility are merging. In today's networked economy, many people spend their lives doing projects to earn a living; they do not necessarily have jobs. For project workers, life on the road has replaced the daily commute to an office. The growing amount of business carried out across national boundaries in the new economy has fueled demand for meeting rooms, exhibition and showroom facilities, business centers, and other non-travel-specific facilities—inside, next to, under, and on top of most new airports and railway stations. Transport interchanges have replaced science and business parks as the epicenter of business real estate.

These multiple programs and agendas—operational, commercial, political—are one reason these places feel strange. Cities have inhabitants, but in transport hubs, everyone is transient. "When public space becomes a derivative of movement," says the writer Richard Sennett, "it loses any independent experiential meaning of its own. On the most physical level, these environments of pure movement prompt people to think of the public domain as meaningless.... [They are] catatonic space."[6]

What is going on, when these great modern spaces have this effect? Any space, including artificial space, affects our minds and our bodies. But artificial environments shield us from phenomena like climate, and particularly daylight, whose cycles in the natural world expose us physically to the reality of constant change. In an optically static environment, like an airport, mall, or lobby, the body is physically desensitized from its sense of time. In "The Poetics of Light," the American architect Henry Plummer observes that "our very sense of being is based on an experience of process, activity, and movement. We seem to find an image of our own existence in the changing lights of the natural world."[7] Moment-to-moment mutations of light also provide what the philosopher Henri Bergson called "lived time" and Ernst Cassirer "a consciousness of sequence."[8] I was reminded of this when, wandering slack-jawed around Anchorage's airport en route to Japan, I accidentally stepped outside into an Alaskan night. It was literally like waking up from a dream. Startled by the cold, dank, spooky Alaskan air, I lost my bearings for a moment. Where was I? Nature, the real world, seemed alien. Luckily, a blast of noise, and the warm embrace of kerosene fumes, reminded me where I was.

Lived time, natural time, cold, dank, spooky Alaskan air time stands in stark contrast to the so-called objective time of clocks and departure times in high-tech, systems-filled spaces. According to the psychologist David Winnicott, loss of temporality is a feature of the psychotic and deprived individual in which the person "loses the ability to connect the past with the present." The bridging of the present into the past and into the future is, says Winnicott, "a crucial dimension of psychic integration and health." So there you have it. Systems-rich spaces, by scrambling your mind-and-body clock, create the preconditions for psychosis.[9]

The implications of this for our technology-filled world are serious. According to IBM, growing complexity means that the number of IT workers required globally to support a billion people and millions of firms connected via the Internet—possibly within the next decade—may be over two hundred million, a number equivalent to two-thirds of America's population.[10] That figure—two hundred million to keep our systems going—could be a grave underestimate if levels of stress and anxiety continue to grow and continue, as they do now, to keep people away from work. In Britain, days lost to stress, depression, and anxiety doubled in just five years during the late 1990s, and since then over half of all employees have seen increased absenteeism due to stress.[11] Stress-related absenteeism is one reason why staff shortages at British Airways in 2004 left travelers in long lines, people sleeping in the street, and heated exchanges between customers and check-in staff at several airports. A spokeswoman at the time said staff shortages were the result, too, of unusually high staff turnover: Twice the usual number had quit.[12]

The penetration of systems-based design into public space is also bad for the body politic. Innovation thrives in conditions of diversity, not efficiency, and spaces designed for a single function—be it movement, sport, entertainment, or culture—are unlikely to foster innovation. This is why old-style cities remain unmatched as sites of creativity: Diverse peoples and cultures are crammed into them in a most undesigned manner. Monofunctional zones, gated communities, and themed districts all exclude the opportunity for surprise encounter and combination—the urban equivalent of the mutation and adaptation that determines evolutionary success in nature.

This is also why corporate research laboratories are often so bad at social or service innovation. Many corporate labs are designed and function as gated communities, isolated physically and experientially from the messy real world. Dark reflective glass often intimidates the visitor on arrival; as often as not, you have to sign a nondisclosure agreement before even being let in the door. (I was once late arriving to give a talk at an IBM campus because guards with ferocious dogs would not let me in. The theme of my talk was "transparency in design.")

Designing Situations

Systems-rich situations pose three main challenges to a designer wishing to improve the experience for their users. First, there are the contradictory operational and commercial agendas to deal with; second, the designer has to tackle the impact of complex artificial environments on our physical and mental states; and third, the design and remaking of these spaces never stops—indeed, the rate of change is accelerating—so that the project-based model of design is inappropriate.

The contradictory agendas of transport nodes are by themselves an intractable problem. The architect is one of the few people—along with the planner and the economist—who grapples materially with space as a totality. Everyone else looks after a little piece. Amsterdam's Schiphol Airport is "run" by five people—but they do not direct what the fifty thousand people who work there do. The job of those three or four people is to manage the interactions among the many conflicting agendas of those involved in the airport's operation. In such a context, the chances of an architect's imposing a coherent and stable design solution are small. We will return to the consequences of that in a moment.

The second challenge—that of artificial space which isolates us from the rhythms and sensations of nature—can at one level be tackled by something simple, like letting in fresh air (as any parent, opening a child's window at night, knows intuitively). Window manufacturers are doing a huge song-and-dance about the fact that their latest high-tech products, some of which are being used in airports, can actually be opened. Even where windows remain sealed, letting in daylight is now a requirement in airport design.

Perceptual confusion is a harder design nut to crack. Countless modern writers, from Karl Marx, to Baudelaire, to Richard Sennett, whom I quoted earlier, have written about the alienation we feel in modern places. Urban anxiety is part of our culture. Psychologists who study the phenomenon have discovered the importance of what they call "situated understanding"—a clear mental picture of an artificial environment, which contributes to one's mental health. An anthropologist, Lucy Suchman, brought the attention of a whole generation of human-computer interaction researchers to this topic in a 1987 book, *Plans and Situated Actions*. Suchman argued that that people do not just follow plans, such as those made by architects or systems designers, when acting in the real world; rather, human action is deeply situated and interactive with the context.[13]

When it comes to giving us a clear mental picture of our environment, a situated understanding, high-tech, systems-serving spaces don't. In most of them, one is situated in a box, and it feels like it. Eero Saarinen's TWA terminal in New York once had a particularly strong impact on the public imagination; it became for many critics a symbol of modernity. Today, Saarinen's masterpiece at Kennedy Airport has all but disappeared from sight. You glimpse it every now and again, cowering between lumpish great buildings like a lost child in Times Square.[14] Transport and urban planners, swimming in a sea that keeps on rising, find it hard not to think in terms of boxes. Boxes contain lots of space, they can be packed together, and they stack up nicely, like Legos, when you need to expand. The result is usually functional, bland, and easy to get lost in.

Creative architectural solutions do not necessarily improve the user's experience. Roissy Terminal 1 at Charles de Gaulle Airport in Paris, for example, is a design monument to system complexity and flows—and is a nightmare to use. I must have been through the terminal forty times, but it is still disorienting as I glide down its capillary-like tunnels into the featureless aorta of the main building. It's like being in a Jacques Tati movie, or in one of those exhibits in a zoo in which ants crawl up and down transparent tubes from one nest to another. The experience is typical of any building that serves the system, rather than the system's users.

Architecture lacks a pleasing spatial language for flow-based contexts of this kind. One apologetic designer, Bernard Tschumi, put his finger on the problem: "Three thousand years of architectural ideology have tried to assert that architecture is about stability, solidity, and foundation—when it is the very opposite. Like modern scientific knowledge, buildings are constantly on the verge of change."[15] Another design diagnostician, Donald Schön, concluded that design is now increasingly taking place "beyond the stable state."[16] And Rem Koolhaas, the architectural high priest of all that is big and fast in today's world, finds that architects are confronted by "arbitrary demands, parameters they did not establish, in countries they hardly know, about issues they are only dimly aware of. More and more substance is grafted on starving roots."[17] Koolhaas the critic understands the problem, but Koolhaas the architect can't do much about it. His design for Euro-Lille, in France, celebrates space, change, and movement—but does virtually nothing to give passers-through a cognitive sense of place. You feel like one of those tiny humanoid figures architects use to decorate their models: sleek, but blind. (Architects frequently complain that the architectural models they make for competitions cost them tens or even hundreds of thousands of dollars to make. But a one-tenth scale model of a person standing can be purchased for seventy-five cents—far less than the five dollars it costs to buy a model car at the same scale.[18])

Some system hubs do try to make their spaces interesting. Schiphol, for example, installed a Jenny Holzer artwork in one particularly vapid void. Cryptic words and phrases flow up and down a twenty-meter-high digital display. Holzer no doubt spends a lot of her life staring at departure boards, and her piece is strong, clearly conceived, and well-executed. But the result is pitiful in the context of Schiphol as a whole. Phenomenologically, her piece is powerless to communicate amid the not-so-silent roar of people, movement, and information that pervades the rest of the airport. Confronted by ten thousand other signs and screens that battle for one's attention, the artwork is struck dumb.

Hub designers have a clear priority: to control and optimize flow. They devote all their energies to controlling one's movement in a particular direction at a particular time. The signs they deploy are the design equivalent, for humans, of those metal strips on the floor that guide robots around automated factories. And they can work. When I arrive back at Schiphol from a trip, the design quality of the banks of video information screens and those large yellow signs are a reassuring pleasure. If one is going to be processed by a system, better to be processed by an elegant, even beautiful system than by a bad one. But even Schiphol's signs are losing their perceptual potency as the space around them expands remorselessly. A sign pointing to "D" meant a lot when Pier D was a corridor, as it was ten years ago. Today, Pier D is continuously gaining width and height; it has become a bloated plaza in place of a tunnel. "D" has become a place rather than a direction.[19]

To be a designer in the space of flows is like King Canute facing the tide: No individual has the authority to improve our experience of systems space. Some operators make their facilities cleaner, easier to use, and mildly more humane than others. Sometimes they hang art on walls, or put sculptures in concourses, or fountains in lobbies. But apart from the fact that most concourses are semiotically stronger than most art, this is not really the point. The fundamental logic of hubs—their basic operating software—is to process passengers, not to enlighten us.

The design of multimodal, multifunctional, multitemporal transport intersections is particularly advanced in the Netherlands. It's a small and densely populated country in which infrastructure projects have become epicenters of extraordinarily complex spatial and building design processes.[20] Increasingly, in the design of these complex places, high-tech simulations and physical structure influence each other. "The diagramme functions for us as a sort of mediator in between the object and the subject," says the architect Ben van Berkel of UN (United Net) Studio, a new-generation design practice that uses diagrams for the proportioning of information—to represent visually, and where possible in real time, variable phenomena for a specific location such as climate, budget, construction processes, orientation, and activities. Van Berkel describes as "deep planning" the process by which his team scans a site for its flow structure. "These scans reveal its real problems and potentials," says van Berkel; "the flows of the physical movements of people and goods reveal the relations between duration and territorial use." The typical product of deep planning is a situation-specific, dynamic, organizational structural plan, using scenarios, diagrams, parameters, formulas, and themes, that encompasses the mapping of political, managerial, planning, community, and private relations.[21]

Movement studies are the cornerstone of design proposals made by van Berkel and his colleagues. A project like Arnhem Central exemplifies the convoluted type of public construction that takes place when multiple networks and systems converge at one place. A multitude of designed activities is concentrated in a forty-thousand-square-meter site: central concourse, underground parking for a thousand cars and five thousand bicycles, tunnel, shops, offices. Six different transport systems converge on the station area. Every weekday, fifty-five thousand travelers move through the location as they transfer from one system to another. Designing these perpetual-motion environments involves combining physical circulation with the experiences people may have along the way.

It's not enough to design for pure movement: The designer has to build in spaces, activities, and intersections where people will leave the flow. Pure movement can be bad for business. Jan Benthem, who with his partner Mels Crouwel is the master architect of Schiphol, told me with glee about the time when the commercial people insisted an area of seating be removed to make way for a row of shops. The result was the opposite of that intended: Revenues per square meter in the new shops, and in existing ones next to them, actually decreased after the redesign, which, as it happened, had created a kind of canyon through which passengers rushed like white water in the Rocky Mountains—too fast to stop and shop. The seats were put back. Flow designers like Jan Benthem and UN Studio have learned from such experiences to pay attention to what they call "kaleidoscope moments"—the turns in flows where movement is tighter or more compact, or where they cross over other flows. "Obstacles to flow can be functional, and add value," says van Berkel.[22]

Situations and Meaning

I have spent thousands of hours of my life in transport hubs and airports. I have visited countless high-tech offices and studios. I have had a beginner's hands-on experience in the design of the building for knowledge-based institute. I have worked with the world's most powerful cultural institution on an exhibition about workspace design. My conclusion? Gadgets and tools are of modest importance, at best. Creating community is only marginally about technology. What matters is the copresence through time of bodies and the emergence of shared meaning as we interact with each other in meaningful activities.

Neither of these processes is much enhanced by mediation or locomotion. Spaces oversaturated with media actively harm them. What matters in situation design is the meaning and purpose of what we're there to do. I learned this lesson a few years back when I arrived in New York to meet my daughter Kate for a vacation. She seemed her normal, sunny self, but as we chatted in the lobby of her mother's hotel, we noticed a lump behind her ear. It did not hurt, Kate said, but we resolved to see a doctor just to check. It was a weekend, there was no house doctor on call, so we were advised to go to the emergency room of St. Vincent's Hospital a block away.

A gothic scene awaited us. There were armed guards at the door. Drunks and junkies lolled on the benches of the waiting room. A half-naked lunatic was running around. And most of the staff in the large, gloomy space wore bright pink face masks. Kate, who was six at the time, watched this all with great interest. Her parents were petrified.

We were seen rather promptly by a nurse, and then by a doctor. She took one look at Kate's bump and said she had to be admitted. Within an hour she was in a children's ward on an intravenous feed of industrial-strength antibiotics. She had mastoiditis, an infection of the bone behind the ear. Increasingly stronger drugs, and then combinations of them, did not work. Kate's temperature soared above one hundred and stayed there. The mastoiditis begat bacterial meningitis. It looked—and was—very bad indeed.

And the doctors were unsure what to do. Two different teams were involved: pediatrics and surgery. The pediatricians wanted to stick with the drugs; the surgeons said drugs would never cure the infection and wanted to operate. Both groups of doctors consulted endless charts and test results, but they examined Kate a lot, too. People looked at her eyes, or her hands, or would lay a hand gently on her head. In Kate's cubicle, the medical people were gentle and respectful, but out in the corridor, and back in the staff room, they would argue, constantly. They would pore over crumpled printouts from online research someone had done earlier. They would look at the endless test results. Boy, did they argue. For us, as parents, these arguments added to our terror. In Britain, senior hospital doctors, and especially the godlike consultants, barely speak to parents, let alone share their doubts with them. At St. Vincent's, we were involved in every twist and turn of their perplexity and concern.

In any event, the drugs never worked, Kate got weaker, and the decision was made to operate. A team of twelve people spent eight hours clustered around a hole in Kate's head less than two inches wide. Whatever it was they did, it worked. They saved her life, and I had had a crash course in collaboration, tacit knowledge, and work design that I would not recommend to anyone.

So what did I learn? The first thing Kate's story taught me was that the flesh and blood of the doctors and nurses was just as important as Kate's flesh and blood. Medical knowledge is embodied. Having formal knowledge in your head is not the same as having it in your fingertips. Doctoring is a physical and fleshy thing. We therefore need to design work situations that enhance tacit and embodied knowledge, rather than pretending that they do not exist or do not matter. The other thing I learned at St. Vincent's was that matters of life and death foster great collaboration and that this collaboration can take place in featureless corridors lit by neon and lined with beige linoleum.

"Place is not given, it is made," the writer Malcolm McCullough reminds us.[23] Interactions in a place create and add value to it for the interactants. That value never reaches a final equilibrium but remains constantly in play—from the routine of domestic microtransactions such as buying a quart of milk to the vast flows of capital markets. Context and situation were vital to craft in preindustrial times. The settings of shop and studio reified work practices, and props, supporting tools, and work process configurations—which had evolved through time and continuous improvement—embodied intellectual capital.[24] The same simple lesson is true today. The best situation for work, the most efficient and effective method of conveying information within a development team, is face to face.

Computing and software professionals recognize this fact in the fast-growing Agile Alliance, whose "Manifesto for Agile Software Development" includes these words:

We are uncovering better ways of developing software by doing it and helping others do it. Through this work we have come to value

Individuals and interactions   over processes and tools

Working software   over comprehensive documentation

Customer collaboration   over contract negotiation

Responding to change   over following a plan.[25]

I once talked to a group of computer scientists about "the thermodynamics of networked collaboration." I chose this phrase as the title of my talk because we human beings are social creatures. Our networks and communities need the time, energy, presence, and participation of real people to flourish. Human systems need inputs of human energy to do well. Everything else—the Internet, agents, wireless, gadgets—is contingent. They're support, not the thing itself. So when designing systems, services, infrastructures—and work itself—we should ask whether our design actions will enable or disable human agency. Embodiment is a killer app. Whatever it is that we design, it's better if we design people in, not out.

Whole nations now worry about their social lives. There's a growing awareness that social ties are fundamental to wealth creation, economic growth,
and competitiveness. As we saw in chapter 1, four decades of growing environmental awareness have taught us to value natural capital as well as
industrial capital. Now social capital—defined as "networks, together with
shared norms, values and understandings, that facilitate cooperation within or among groups"[1]—is also on the agenda. The worry is that although
some people may be getting richer in money terms, economic progress
damages the ties that hold society together. Social capital is harder to measure than industrial or natural assets; it also seems to be delicate and hard
to exploit, like a rain forest most of whose secrets remain undiscovered.
But social capital interests governments because they see it as a possible
solution to the care crisis. Turnover in the "third sector" or "support
economy" is huge—65 percent of GDP by some estimates. Expenditures
on health care, disability allowances, retirement and pensions, survivors'
pensions, family and child benefits, unemployment, and other forms of
social support play a major role in the budget of modern states—and the
amounts keep rising: Health care spending is growing faster than GDP in
most rich countries.[2]

The financial situation is less extreme in so-called less-developed countries. The poorest nations spend two hundred times less per person on
health ($11) than do high-income ones, which average $1,907.[3] But rich
countries risk impoverishing themselves by spending endlessly on health.
Health care spending in the United States had reached 15.3 percent of
GDP by 2003, an amount equivalent to nearly five thousand dollars for
every single U.S. citizen. It all adds up to a two-trillion-dollar service

industry populated by a complex ecology of powerful interest groups: insurance companies, pharmaceutical companies, doctors, for-profit hospitals, and high-tech medical suppliers. Less powerful, but increasingly well-informed and organized, are the patients and their caregivers it's all supposed to be for.

Health and care industries are growing because people don't look after each other as much as they used to. We expect governments to provide support services instead. Governments don't like this. The provision of care costs a lot of money—and besides, the customer is never satisfied. Hence the growing interest among policymakers in ideas of social capital and conviviality. The case for conviviality is that if we were to take more responsibility for our own well-being, we might rely less on care as a service delivered to us by third parties—especially the state. Such a shift in emphasis—from delivered care to supported care—would enable governments to focus on the supporting infrastructures, collaboration tools, and social software for better connected communities by enhancing dialogue, encounter, and community in our everyday lives.

Weak social ties are bad for our health in a variety of ways. Recent studies have shown that psychosocial factors, such as lack of social support and depression, are important predictors of morbidity and mortality in patients with cardiovascular disease (CVD)—since 1900, the number-one killer in developed countries.[4] Extensive social networks appear to offer protection from the condition. The mortality rate for men with CVD is inversely related to the level of social connectedness.[5] "To the extent that psychosocial intervention can be shown to impact favourably on survival and recovery," argued one report, "the human and financial burden associated with heart disease can be reduced."[6] As far back as the nineteenth century, the sociologist Emil Durkheim had found a close link between incidence of suicide and the degree to which individuals are integrated in society.[7]

Health psychologists today have amassed considerable supporting evidence that a sense of social support is a buffer against stress and illness. Studies conducted in a number of countries have found that "a strong support system lowers the likelihood of many illnesses, decreases the length of recoveries, and reduces the probability of mortality from serious diseases. People with higher levels of support recover faster from kidney disease, childhood leukemia, and strokes, have better diabetes control, experience less pain from arthritis, and live longer."[8]

Wellware

Confronted by unsustainable rates of growth in expenditure, much of the health industry is looking to automation and technology for ways to reduce costs. Thousands of services connecting our bodies to networks are in development. For Richard Saul Wurman, who runs an influential conference, TedMed (Technology, Entertainment and Design, and Medicine),[9] on the subject, health care and technology are "the next convergence." TedMed covers everything from computer graphics and imaging of the human body through microlozenges that record their journey through the body, wearables of all kinds, visualization of blood, urine, and DNA, genomics, robotics, and nanotechnology, plus myriad information services designed to assist people in the planning of a healthy life.

I would be foolish to argue that technology has no place in health care. After all, as I recounted in chapter 5, modern medicine saved my daughter's life. If I were a paraplegic, I would welcome cyberspace as a working environment for doing things disallowed by my body right now. The often-grim aftereffects of stroke—a present risk to millions of people—are being alleviated by new technologies: If I could not properly see or hear, I don't doubt that sensory implants would be a godsend.[10] What I object to is not technology in health, but the overreliance on technology to do things that human beings can and should do better, and the false expectations raised by special-interest groups that should—and do—know better regarding what technology can do and what it can't do in the realm of health care.

Communications technology and simulation are prominent in high-tech scenarios for health. Health care industries already spend the better part of twenty billion dollars a year on ICT, and that figure is set to soar. One of the more extraordinary books I found during research for this book was the 1,276-page *Telemedicine Glossary*. This hefty tome lists 13,500 organizations and projects involved with health telematics; a single page lists thirty online journals and magazines. Other pages list six hundred telemedicine research projects with acronyms like KISS (Knowledge-Based Interactive Signal Monitoring System), DILEMMA (Logical Engineering in General Practice, Oncology and Shared-Care), ESTEEM (European Standardized Telemetric Tool to Evaluate EMG Knowledge-Based), CONQUEST (Clinical Oncology Network for Quality Standards of Treatment), WISECARE (Workflow Information Systems for European Nursing Care), PRE-HIP (Predicting

Clinical Performance of Cementless HIP Replacements), CLIFF (Cluster Initiative for Flood and Fire Emergencies), and HUMAN (Health Through Telematics for Inmates) as titles.[11] The last of these is about treating prisoners remotely. The mismatch between the innocuous-sounding acronym and its less-than-innocuous meaning is not untypical of the medical research world. Elsewhere, crisp young white people, their gorgeous bodies wrapped in microcircuitry, adorn the website for "New Generation of Wearable Systems for Health: Towards a Revolution of Citizens' Health and Life Style Management?," a trade conference. This vision of the future features physically immaculate people who don't look remotely in need of implantable health systems. These wearables are "to manage people with risk factors and prevent diseases through health status monitoring and life style management."[12] This sounds fine, except that the almost casual penetration of technology onto and into our bodies is happening without discussion of its consequences. I call this phenomenon *Borg drift*.

Borg drift is what happens when you add all these tiny, practical, well-meant, and individually admirable enhancements together and find that the picture begins to look creepy. As often happens, artists and writers were the first to spot broader consequences of these trends. Donna Haraway, in her celebrated "Cyborg Manifesto," observed that "late twentieth century machines have made thoroughly ambiguous the difference between natural and artificial, mind and body, self-developing and externally designed. Our machines are disturbingly lively, and we are frighteningly inert."[13] We are designing a world in which every object, every building—and every body—becomes part of a network service. We did not set out to design such an outcome, but that's what's coming if technology push proceeds unabated.

The pity of it is that spending money on technology like this does not appear to buy better health—or at least, not a longer life. The biggest spenders on health care, North Americans, die earlier than Japanese or Spaniards, who spend far less on health care.[14] Medicine has become a two-trillion-dollar industry, and the world's three-hundred-billion-dollar pharmaceutical industry turns out thousands of different drugs. But much of the world's population dies of the same diseases that killed people a thousand years ago: malaria, tuberculosis, and malnutrition.

A growing number of health professionals believe that medicine, as an institution, undermines health. When Ivan Illich wrote *Medical Nemesis* in 1976, he was dismissed as a crank for this celebrated polemic:

More and more people are convinced that, if they do not feel right, it is because there is something disordered inside them, and not because they are manifesting a healthy refusal to adapt to an environment or life that is difficult and sometimes intolerable. Adaptation to the misanthropic, genetic, climatic and cultural consequences of growth is now described as health. As sensible creatures we must face the fact that the pursuit of health may be a sickening disorder. There are no scientific or technological solutions to death. There is the daily task of accepting the fragility and contingency of the human condition.[15]

Illich was not antitechnology. He argued that self-care and the use of modern technology could be mutually supporting. But he warned that technology push in health may itself be a sickening disorder. "When people no longer have the need or desire to resolve their problems within the network of their own relationships, medicine becomes the alibi of a pathogenic society."[16] Illich concluded that we have thrust the bad things of life—old age, death, pain, and handicap—onto doctors so that families and society will not have to face them.

It took thirty years for Illich's ideas to gain mainstream acceptance, but in 2002 the *British Medical Journal*, a bastion of the medical establishment, called for a turning back of the "medicalisation of everyday life."[17] The journal, citing Illich and the biologist René Dubois as its inspiration, proposed that we redefine good health as "the autonomous personal capacity to master one's conditions of life, to adapt oneself to accidental modifications of one's surroundings, and to refuse if necessary environments that are not tolerable."[18]

Jean-Pierre Dupuy, who has studied the stress and burnout suffered by the medical profession firsthand, says that when doctors are asked to provide the impossible to patients, they do not gain power or control—they suffer: "The ability to cope with a series of profoundly intimate threats that all men face and will face—namely pain, disease and death—comes, in traditional societies, from his culture. The sacred plays a fundamental role in this. The modern world was born on the ruins of these traditional symbolic systems."[19]

Decentralization

Few health care professionals are ready to embrace ideas so radical as those of Illich, but the many actors in health and care are being urged to work in less-directed, more decentralized, and therefore less costly, ways. Hospitals should function more like supporting hubs, say reformers, than gigantic centers that deliver all services. A decentralized health system would connect, but not direct, midwives, alternative home care, birthing centers, the fitness industry, health clubs, health food stores, organic farmers and growers, people who offer inspirational workshops, biofeedback, and massage. "In re-defining health," says economist Hazel Henderson, "hospitals are bound to be much smaller, serving just the most acute and intensive cases. Even within the traditional matrix of medicine, healthcare will be forced into a more clinic-based and neighbourhood-based approach." Prenatal care, family planning, STDs, immunization, nutrition, eldercare—the medical parts of building a healthier community are all things that should involve a lot of people at the local level, she says.[20]

Health City

Amsterdam Medical Centre (AMC), one of Europe's largest hospital complexes, houses a vast array of activities having to do with patient care, research, and teaching. The building itself is like a medium-sized airport, only taller. Road, bus, and rail links intersect at this hub, and there are shops, restaurants, a university, and even a post office to service the eleven thousand staff members and eight thousand visitors who pass through each day. A multitude of actors is involved; untold thousands of actions and decisions interact with one another every hour of the day and night. Rather like the five-person team that "runs" Schiphol Airport, a three-person board "runs" the hospital: Its main task is to create a common platform, as well as shared agendas, working methods, and approaches, so that staff, partners, and suppliers can do their jobs. The institution strives to be as unbureaucratic as possible simply in order to survive: openness, teamwork, learning, continuous improvement, performance measurement, and accountability are the only ways that such a complex system can keep moving.[21]

Apart from the existence of huge centers such as AMC, the problem with decentralization is that it's an organizational answer to a conservative question—namely, how best to organize the existing biomedical enterprise. This is a systems-centered, not a person-centered, approach. A more radical approach would be to transform the logic of care into a patient-centered one and enable what software designers would call the commons-based peer production of wellness and care. In the language of health policy, this would be a shift from a biomedical to a biopsychosocial and epidemiological model. The aim would be to empower patients to take responsibility for their own well-being, facilitated by new forms of partnering and use of the Internet.

A commons-based model would still involve teams of physicians and nurses. One radically decentralized model already operating is Shahal Medical Services, an Israel-based company with fifty-five thousand patient-customers who suffer from the usual array of cardiac, hypertensive, and respiratory illnesses. The service also caters to elderly people and healthy people with a high level of health awareness. Shahal uses online and wireless services to organize therapy brought to the customer's home (or wherever the customer is). Customers measure body signals that are sent to a monitoring center that is open twenty-four hours a day. These data are linked to immediate consultation and advice based on symptoms, medical history, and further real-time measurements. The system is designed around proprietary software modules, a broad range of advanced end-user devices, and protocols for the setup and maintenance of home care telemedicine systems. According to writer Richard Normann, "The system creates new linkages between end-customer-patients, the monitoring centre, physicians, public authorities, and a fleet of mobile intensive care units." The Shahal system spans the real and the virtual in an integrated way.[22]

The use of the Internet by citizens to find health information is booming. Sixty million Americans troll the Net in search of health-related information, and research shows that nearly nine out of ten people want as much information as possible from their doctor—good or bad—so that they can participate in planning their own health care. Medical professionals increasingly involve patients in evidence-based medicine—the conscious, explicit, and judicious use of current best evidence in making decisions about the care of individual patients. Multidisciplinary teams of statisticians, health economists, academics, and health practitioners work increasingly alongside service users and caregivers to sift through available evidence and disseminate the results to clinicians. As Andrew Moore, editor of Bandolier, one of the most popular evidence-based sites in the United Kingdom, puts it, "There are six million research papers out there and most of them are bollocks. We're entering a new age of medicine where the doctor and patient forge a therapeutic alliance."[23]

Other kinds of decentralized care services offer sophisticated monitoring devices, tailored treatment plans, and personalized Web pages that store individuals' health care data and facilitate regular interaction with health care professionals. These Web-based health services encourage real-time patient feedback, provide online tracking to enhance treatment plans, and facilitate cost-effective patient monitoring.[24] Researchers at Accenture have developed an online medical cabinet that says things like, "Good morning, I have an allergy alert for you." Not only does the online medicine cabinet know about your allergies, it also monitors other aspects of your health and tracks whether you're taking the proper medication. It can also order drug refills when supplies run low and pass along details about your blood pressure to your doctor. According to Accenture, "By using a camera and face-recognition software, the cabinet can identify different persons in a household, and their special needs. For example, if an individual suffers from allergies or asthma, the Online Medicine Cabinet will provide information such as the day's pollen count, and remind that person to take their medicine. Sensors on prescription bottle labels allow the cabinet to identify each drug and alert consumers if they have taken the wrong bottle—or if it's the right bottle at the wrong time. This is vital, because at present, nearly one third of all hospital visits result from consumers not following their doctor's orders or taking the wrong medication."[25]

Support networks for less-glamorous conditions, such as mental illness, are also growing strongly. The Internet is helping to break through the isolation that often accompanies mental illness as well as providing a wealth of information on different disorders. David Batty, in the *Guardian*, describes how when one patient was diagnosed with borderline personality disorder, neither his family doctor nor the local mental health team could offer him much in the way of information about the diagnosis. But the man soon discovered that the World Wide Web was a prolific source of advice and information on his condition. "It's very difficult to explain the sense of relief that came with the information I was able to gather from the net," the thirty-two-year-old patient told Batty. "Yes, I had a serious mental health difficulty, but at least I could begin to get to grips with it. I soon realised millions of people the world over were struggling with the same behavioural problems. Suddenly I didn't feel quite so alone."[26]

Many mental health caregivers and sufferers from mental health disorders have set up websites to provide information and mutual support.[27]

One online user of a support service who runs an online mental health directory, Zyra, told Batty, "The internet is like Speaker's Corner in Hyde Park, except it has global coverage. It means that drug companies, professional organisations and government can no longer ignore service users." Mental health websites contain a wide array of information, news and discussion, user feedback on medication and side effects, alternative approaches, counseling, and therapy. Coping strategies for partners, friends, family, and colleagues are important features. Care is a time issue, not a technology issue. The biggest users of today's health systems are people with chronic conditions—those that are long-term, but not in need of instant attention. In Britain, 60 percent of consultations with family doctors relate to chronic disease management; in the United States, people with chronic conditions consume 78 percent of all health care spending. And yet health systems in these countries are configured to focus on *acute* illnesses—those with a rapid onset that follow a short but severe course. This mismatch between supply and demand is reflected in the results of a study to identify five "key dimensions of patient experience" carried out by Britain's National Health Service. The study found that time—not staying alive—is the most important factor for citizens: waiting times for appointments, time needed to access services, and time given to discuss health/ medical problems face-to-face with health care professionals. A similar pattern is found in the United States where, in 1997, doctors spent an average of eight minutes talking to patients—less than half the time they spent a decade earlier. "The average person with diabetes spends about three hours a year with doctors, checking prescriptions and general health. That same person spends thousands of hours a year self-managing their condition," say Hilary Cottam and Charles Leadbeater in their book *Health: Co-creating Services*.[28] Cottam and Leadbeater also point out that the largest health care provider in Britain—and bearer of the largest time burden—is not the National Health Service, but the family. Between 80 and 90 percent of health incidents are dealt with at home—from giving aspirin to a child to the long-term care of an elderly or sick relative.

Design for Our Future Selves

One of the greatest of human achievements—longer life spans for many of us—also worries policymakers. They calculate what it will cost the state if we live longer, and they fear that escalating social, welfare, and health care costs will soon be an intolerable burden on society. Business, for its part, either ignores elderly people or assumes that they are all dependent and infirm. James Pirkl, a leading expert on aging, is contemptuous of what he calls the "myth of senility," which states that all older people are either disabled, decrepit, senile, or locked away in nursing homes. Frail elderly people living in institutions, he points out, comprise less than 5 percent of the over-sixty population.[29]

The potential market for services that will enable us to live independently as we age is vast—but it's unclear who will pay for them. Elders control nearly two-thirds of disposable consumer income in developed countries, and people over sixty-five already control more than 77 percent of all assets in the United States, but no old person I have ever met wants to spend a penny on being "looked after."

The simplest way to think about design for old people is that "they" are "we." Pirkl uses "transgenerational" design to bridge the physical and sensory changes associated with aging—a process that most of us, after all, go through starting the day we are born.[30] The European Design for Ageing Network lists ubiquitous products that need to be modified to accommodate older members of the population: packaging that opens without the need to slice it (and, potentially, one's hand) open with a knife; clothing that is easy to wear and maintain but still looks good; chairs that are easy to get into and out of; houses that can accommodate changing space and equipment needs; clear signs and labeling on buildings, vehicles, and products in shops; cups, door handles, light switches, supermarket carts— the list is endless—that do not require the strength of a weightlifter, the eyesight of Superman, or the patience of Job to handle.[31] We all can benefit from the development of products that are sympathetic to the gradual decline in vision, hearing, and movement capabilities that will affect us as we age.[32] So there are practical reasons why elderly consumers are a good market for services and products that adapt to their changing needs.

The majority of product and service innovation for elders treat the symptoms of social isolation but not the causes. They are perceived as passive recipients of "aging in place" infrastructures. Intel, for example, is exploring "a variety of proactive computing applications that could assist the aging in the digital home environment. As the name suggests, proactive computing is designed to anticipate people's needs and take action to meet the needs on their behalf." The input for proactive computing applications is real-world data gathered by wireless sensors. According to its website, Intel Research Berkeley is developing tiny sensors or "motes" that can be used "to gather both behavioral and biological data for customized proactive health applications." Such proactive systems, the website continues, "will also enable adult children to assess the health and well-being of their aging parents remotely through private, secure Internet connections."[33] While Intel figures out how to immerse old people in sensors and motes, the Center for Aging Service Technologies (CAST) is focusing on the development of business models to pay for it all. CAST is developing strategies to "evangelize the potential of technology to transform aging services and the experience of growing older."[34]

Treating old people as a passive market for technology-based products and services is well-intended but short-sighted. A smarter approach treats elders as a knowledge asset to be exploited. Elders have and embody knowledge and insights that cannot be learned from a textbook, website, or business school. Søren Kierkegaard once reflected wistfully that he wished he had known at age twenty what it had taken him until the age of seventy to understand. Without being naïve about the demand among twenty-somethings for advice from oldies, the fact remains that older people who know a great deal can make excellent mentors on a wide array of subjects. "My child has red spots. What do I do?" The design question here—how best to access the time and tacit knowledge of older people—connects with another question: how to enable older people to be more "present" in their communities. Social contact is more important for people of all ages, not just elders, than first-aid systems and fancy wireless distress-call systems.

Life as a Spot

As I argued in chapters 2, 3, and 4, social fragmentation and personal isolation are among the more damaging consequences of the ways we organize modern time. Social capital and conviviality are also damaged by the ways we design our work. During the 1990s, the enticing rhetorics of a new economy promised us a rosy future in which, rather than salaried men and women, or wage slaves, we would be self-employed "portfolio workers." We would be actors, builders, jugglers, and stage managers of our own lives.

There would be no tedium and no drudge. Work and family life would be in balance. Our every working moment would be filled with meaningful projects and boundless creativity. In this paradise, we would live effortlessly as high-tech nomads.

The reality of Net work, for most of us, is turning out to be pretty much the exact opposite of those promises. A huge gulf separates the rhetorics of the information society from the logic, and hence realities, of the way it actually works. We are too busy working to look after one another.

Reality check one: We are not living in an information *society* but in an information *market*. In this market, three powerful economic forces—downsizing, globalization, and acceleration—are fragmenting the social fabric. Says writer Eric Britton: "Jobs, for one thing, are disappearing; a twenty-year-old today has little chance of selling a hundred thousand working hours to an employer in advance upon joining an organization."[35] As a result, tens of millions of young adults will labor at short-term tasks—"the project"—and change employer or client frequently. This kind of work—work that is marketed and sold as a commodity by intermediaries with names like Manpower—tends to be fragmented and atomized. Suppliers of the commodity languish near the bottom of the economic food chain in "spot markets" for "human resources." Human beings "count," in this new economy, in the same way that a sack of cocoa beans "counts": Free markets treat people as a cost, not as a value. Increased networking "unbundles" aspects of the employment relationship that once acted as social glue.[36]

Reality check two: Work today is bad for our health, both physically and psychologically. In a 2000 survey by the European Commission, nearly half of Europe's workers complained of physical health problems—posture discomfort, headaches, back pain, repetitive strain injury, and so on. Forty percent of all workers said they suffered from feelings of "high pressure, low control." Two-thirds said they "do not have jobs of high intrinsic quality." Fifteen percent experienced their work to be precarious, and one-third—in round numbers, a hundred million people—said they suffered from stress. Things are just as bad in the United States. Less than half of all Americans say they are satisfied with their jobs—the highest level of discontent since surveys were first conducted in 1995. The decline in job satisfaction is found among workers of all ages, across all income brackets and regions.[37] All recent studies of working conditions in the world's most prosperous regions make similar points: New-economy patterns of work lead to ill health and early mortality.[38]

Reality check three: New economy work leads to loneliness, disconnection, and a loss of identity. We tend to be judged by what we do, not by who we are—and that question is hard to answer when we're working on multiple projects and tasks—"spots" that are not connected, do not have a story, have no beginning, and no end. Spot markets for our labor fragment, atomize, and disconnect us from narrative. Singularity replaces connection and flow.

Convivial Work

Things look less bleak when you compare the time we spend unhappily doing projects with many of the activities that contribute to a convivial society that have never been packaged as jobs—meal preparation, shopping, laundry and cleaning, child care. Household work is part of health care provisioning, as the sociologist Ann Oakley has argued. Freshly cooked food, proper clothes, a clean surface and home, a dust-free environment, and a safe place where one can relax and sleep are essential necessities for healthy people.[39] Roughly half of all the labor hours in industrialized countries are spent on unpaid "nonmarket" work—so we're talking about half the economy in time terms. In terms of the value of nomarket production, estimates range from 33 to 84 percent of GDP, depending on the value metric and methodology used.[40] Many governments have begun to redefine development to include all costs and benefits, not just those measured in money, and to take factors like literacy, health, and environmental quality into account.[41]

Could we design some kind of online "farm-to-market" barter economy for the time we can and want to spend on care? There are interesting hints of what may indeed be a startling change. One of these is the growth of local exchange and trading systems (LETS). A wide variety of individuals and local businesses are discovering that it makes sense to receive payment in local barter currencies, which get called things like "bobbins," "acorns," or "beaks." What happens is that local people form a club to trade among themselves, using their own system of accounts. They compile a membership directory containing offers and requests—goods, services, or items for hire; these are priced in local credits. Members use the directory to contact one another whenever they wish. They pay for any service or goods by writing a LETS credit note for the agreed amount of local credit. The credit note is sent to the LETS accountant, who adjusts both members' accounts. Each member receives a personal account statement, directory updates, and a newsletter. From humble beginnings in the small town of Courtenay, Vancouver, LETS have spread to the United States, New Zealand, Australia, and Europe. Tens of thousands of people are participating in some four hundred local LETS around the United Kingdom alone; similar networks have been established in most European countries. All this despite the fact that, until recently, LETS have been completely manual, and people would sit for hours in each other's kitchens filling out ledgers and sorting little bits of paper.[42]

Some policymakers worry that the local tax base will be eroded if too many people start swapping tomatoes for baby-sitting—without recourse to (taxable) money in the transaction. Tax economists are even more worried about what might happen when the manual, grassroots world of LETS takes off on the Internet. The OECD calls this link the "missing network"; OECD research on the future of money uncovered substantial unmet demand for real-time peer-to-peer virtual payments as an enabling infrastructure for LETS.[43]

In the United States, one LETS-like scheme called Time Dollars is described by its founder, Edgar Cahn, as "a currency for rebuilding the core economy of family, neighborhood and community." Says Cahn:

The history of the past century or more is the history of the market economy taking over functions previously performed by the family, kinship groups, neighborhoods, and non-market institutions—because of seemingly superior efficiency. We have contracted out as many of the functions of the informal economy, the non-market economy, as we can. McDonald's now provides the meals; Kindercare the day care; public and private schools the education (such as it is); Nintendo the child care andentertainment; Holiday Spa and Gold's Gym the exercise; insurance companies the protection; Medicare and Medicaid the nursing care—and on and on the list goes.[44]

According to the Time Dollars website, the following four core principles underlie Time Dollars:

• Assets   "No more throw-away people. Every human being has the capacity to be a builder and contributor."

• Redefining work   "No more taking the contribution of women, children, families, immigrants, for granted. No more free rides for the market economy extracted by subordination, discrimination, and exploitation. Work must be redefined to include whatever it takes to rear healthy children, make neighborhoods safe and vibrant, and care for the frail and vulnerable."

• Reciprocity   "Stop creating dependencies; stop devaluing those whom you help while you profit from their troubles. The impulse to give back is universal. Wherever possible, we must replace one-way acts of largesse in whatever form with two-way transactions. 'You need me' becomes 'We need each other.'"

• Social capital   "No more disinvesting in families, neighborhoods and communities. No more economic and social strip-mining. Social Networks require ongoing investments of social capital generated by trust, reciprocity and civic engagement."[45]

Systems like LETS and Time Dollars begin to acknowledge and compensate people for the time they invest in care and convivial activities. Margrit Kennedy, a German pioneer, says LETS are "immune from local or international recessions, interest on debts, thefts and money shortages. The world money system can collapse; the dollar or DM [deutsche mark] can lose their value; unemployment may rise; but Time Dollars ... still function because they are guaranteed one hundred percent by work and by goods. The advantage of LETS is that it is limited only by the time and energy a person is prepared to invest."[46] According to Kennedy, between 10 percent and 30 percent of the world trade is barter trade. "Barter and exchange systems, specializing at a local, national or international level, have benefited greatly from the new information technology. The notion of a free exchange of goods and services ... is now much easier to implement where information travels fast to any place in the world."[47]

Noncash economic systems are, for me, where a genuinely new economy is being born. The dot-coms were a distraction from this much more profound transformation. If, as I have argued, a light and therefore sustainable economy means sharing resources more effectively—such as time, skill, software, or food—then economic systems for exchanging nonmarket work have got to be part of the answer. Nonmarket work includes much of the essential activity we have always undertaken to raise and educate our families, get fed, and look after one another. Half of all the labor done in industrialized countries is spent on unpaid work. The fact that this kind of work is not considered to be part of "the economy" is partly a problem for economists to deal with, but partly, too, a service design challenge that we can sink our teeth into.

Convivial Services

Networked communications and wireless networks can be repurposed as enabling infrastructures to help systems like local and complementary currencies, Ithaca Hours, Time Dollars, LETS, microcredit programs, interest-free banking, and other community-oriented monetary systems scale up.

These are not technology projects in the dot-com era sense of the word. Ben Reason, a service designer in London, reminded me that LETS grew strongly during the 1990s—the Internet decade—without themselves migrating onto the Net.[48] Reason, who keeps a close eye on social innovations emerging at a grassroots level, believes that the Mondragon cooperative in Spain and the KaosPilots business school in Denmark are also worth watching as new models that can have a big impact.

The world's telecommunications companies should be rejoicing at the news that the world needs these kinds of services. Communication, after all, is their business. But most telcos remain stubbornly fixated on the "purposive" or task-related communications of business. Business callers pay premium rates, which is why so many ads feature busy executives rushing around being, well, busy. Social communications, by comparison, tend to be a high-volume, low-margin business. Social communication occupies a large amount of time in our daily lives—about two-thirds of our conversational exchanges are social chitchat—but telcos don't understand social contexts and find it hard to shift the focus of their innovation from work to everyday life.

Everyday life contains many distractions. Humans are hard-wired to chat. The evolutionary psychologist Robin Dunbar believes that humans gossip because we don't groom each other. In studies of the social organization of great apes, Dunbar observed that these animals live in small groups and maintain social cohesion through almost constant grooming. Grooming is a way to forge alliances, establish hierarchy, offer comfort, or make apology.

Once a population expands beyond a certain number, however, it becomes impossible for each member to maintain constant physical contact with every other member of the group. Dunbar believes that we developed language as a substitute for physical intimacy.[49]

Social communication is overwhelmingly local, as well as personal. As I noted in chapter 4, much of the world's GDP is highly localized: The vast majority of small and medium-sized companies, for example, operate within a radius of fifty kilometers. Television images of global computerized dealing rooms tell only one part of the story of economic life. Local conditions, local trading patterns, local networks, local skills, and local culture remain a critical success factor for many companies and for most people.

It was in this context that an increasing number of European researchers have focused on new ways to enhance social communication among an extended family in the community. Gossip and informal communication —sharing jokes, teasing each other, asking what kind of day you've had— is an important part of everyday life. Most families also do a lot of communicating to organize and schedule shared resources: carpools and school runs in the morning, ferrying kids to sporting events after school, getting in touch for help with homework in the evening. A big proportion of the one hundred billion minutes of telephone calls made each year are short-distance; as I explained in chapter 3, network designers even have (and apply) a "law of locality." So the market for any service that adds value to local, intracommunity communications is potentially vast.[50]

Capitalist Care

Howard Rheingold says of smart mobs, in his book by that name, that they "emerge when communication and computing technologies amplify human talents for cooperation. The impacts of smart mob technology already appear to be both beneficial—and destructive."[51] Among the potentially destructive consequences of technology-enhanced cooperation is the commercialization of access and social ties. "People yearn for support to help them through life's complexities," say Shoshana Zuboff and James Maxmin in *The Support Economy*. "Distributed capitalism creates wealth from the essential building blocks of relationships with individuals." Zuboff and Maxmin write about investments in commitment and trust as if they were commodities on the stock market, and they have invented an economic axiom for capitalists: Their task is to "maximise realised relationship value. Today's individuals want to take their lives into their own hands and are ready to pay for the support and advocacy necessary to fulfill that yearning. Providing that support economy is the next episode of capitalism."[52] Another analyst, Chrysanthos Dellarocas, thinks it should be possible to make money by reengineering word-of-mouth networks and reputation systems. "In pre-Internet societies, word of mouth emerged naturally and evolved in ways that were difficult to control or model," concedes Dellarocas. But he goes on: "The Internet allows this powerful social force to be precisely measured and controlled through proper engineering of the information systems that mediate online feedback communities. Such automated feedback mediators specify who can participate, what type of information is solicited from participants, how it is aggregated, and what type of information is made available to them about other community members."[53] These steps are feasible technically, of course—but I don't buy the idea that word of mouth as a paid-for service will succeed in social situations in the same way it does on eBay.

Happily for the optimists among us, noncommercial collaboration is already a strong social trend among the Internet generation. Free software is but one symptom, although the most visible one, of a much broader social phenomenon—a new mode of production in the digitally networked environment that New York University law professor Yochai Benkler calls *commons-based peer production.* "We are seeing the emergence of a new mode of production," says Benkler, "distinguishable from the property- and contract-based modes of firms and markets. Its central characteristic is that groups of individuals successfully collaborate on large-scale projects following a diverse cluster of motivational drives and social signals—rather than market prices or managerial commands."[54]

Conviviality and decentralization go hand in hand. Although decentralization is a fashionable topic among today's Internet theorists, the issue was first promoted by progressive social thinkers such as Harold Laski from the 1920s onward. The difference is that Laski's generation did not have the Internet, and we do. The Internet gives us the capacity to design services and institutions that will give back to us the opportunity to organize our daily lives among ourselves—not by recourse to paid-for services.

Connected Communities

A network is not, per se, a community. A community embodies trust and social capital that develop through time as a result of embodied interaction between people. The Internet complements communities—it does not create them. Connections between people can be enabled by technology, but trust is dependent on the passage of time and the contiguity of bodies. As Pekka Himanen and his colleagues have written, "the tools and governance principles of the open source software community, in some modified form, could yield new approaches to community organization and problem solving."[55] To do this, we need supporting infrastructures that enable dialogue, encounter, and community. The collaboration tools and social software for these better-connected communities need to be designed. So how do we design support networks as effective ways to enable mutual support?

A number of researchers have been preoccupied with this question for quite some time. Eve Mitleton-Kelly, for example, a professor at the London School of Economics, creates connectivity netmaps of organizational communications—e-mail, telephone, instant messaging, etc.—in order to reflect real-world interactivity and coevolving patterns of connectivity over time.[56] The aim is to reveal unexpected linkages and connections—or gaps—within social networks. Another researcher, Valdis Krebs, has developed social-analysis software that maps social networking in academia and other domains. "Experts have long argued about the optimal structure of a person's professional network," says Krebs. "Some say that a dense, cohesive network brings more social capital, while others argue that a sparse, radial network, one that provides opportunities for innovation and entrepreneurial activity, equates to greater social capital." Krebs has constructed a links map of the so-called Erdős network (about a celebrated mathematician by that name) that shows both patterns—a densely connected core, along with loosely coupled radial branches reaching out from the core.[57]

These experiments in mapping social networks can be fascinating, but the conclusion I draw is that you don't design social networks as you would a railway or cable network. Social networks generally start out small and develop gradually. The modest design actions we might take to improve the efficiency of information transfer within a network are to create hubs, or add new links, to act as artificial shortcuts between otherwise distant regions. Mapping social networks and analysis of the topology of communication links within a network may help identify where such interventions are needed. Equipped with this information, managers or community stewards might be able to adjust network architecture, create clusters of linked individuals, or put together groups with complementary expertise.[58]

Link and Do

Design strategies for the creation of communities of practice have been considered by a number of leading organizations. Communities of practice are largely informal, voluntary, and self-organizing—like all communities—so it is a challenge for organizations to shape them. Etienne Wenger, an expert on the subject, cautions that "without an understanding of their dynamics and composition, community of practice initiatives can be wasteful, ineffective or even harmful."[59]

Social computing, coordination technology, community software, and "groupware" in this context are just that: tools. Tools for collaboration, such as the Internet, agents, wireless, and knowledge mining, are support for the process, not the process itself.

"All real living is meeting." Martin Buber's focus on dialogue and community marks him as an important thinker for service designers.[60] His fundamental concern with encounter as the basis for our relationships with one another and the world is a salutary antidote to technology push. Ivan Illich, too, was at first dismissed as a crank when he argued for the creation of convivial, rather than manipulative, institutions for learning, health, and care. As I noted in chapter 4, in French the word for these timeless insights—*la vie associative*—recognizes the importance of association in the widest sense of the word and the effect that such association can have both on the life of the individual and on the life of a village, town, region, or country.[61] In institutions such as churches, tenants groups, and youth organizations, people freely combine to produce goods and services for their own enjoyment. Many organize around enthusiasms ranging from swimming clubs to beekeeping societies and train-spotting circles, from allotment associations to antiques groups and basketball teams. These groups provide a sense of belonging and identity as well as a setting in which to meet and make friends with people.[62]

Throughout history, human beings have always established social communities, developed rules of social exchange, embedded their members in complex reciprocal relationships, and built social trust. We don't have to invent conviviality: It's already there.

My Last Rocket

My favorite shop in Amsterdam sells artistic funerals. All manner of caskets are shown: designer-chic ones, rustic-crafty ones, arty-weird ones. On the wall of the shop are photographs of processions in which people dressed up in strange, pagan outfits carry strange pagan objects on poles. My favorite item of all is a huge fireworks rocket, about six feet high, that has a container rather like a cookie jar hanging underneath it. One's ashes are put in this container, a loved one lights the blue touch paper—and whoosh: up-up-and-away you go. The rocket explodes several thousand feet up, and your ashes are scattered among the stars.

Everyday life, everyday death. The opportunities for service innovation are endless if only we shift the focus of innovation from work to everyday life. Many of the different ways we interact with one another can be improved by design. Edward O. Wilson, in contemplating the ultimate "consilience" of scientific knowledge and social science, has even furnished us with a list. Wilson unearthed a 1945 compendium, by the American anthropologist George P. Murdoch, that lists sixty-three "universals of culture" that had at that time been found to occur in hundreds of different societies (see box 6.1). These universals of culture are a gigantic "to do" list for service designers. Take one of these aspects of daily life, improve it, and figure out how to benefit from it in a nonmonetary way.

Box 6.1

George P. Murdoch's "universals of culture"

age grading	games	penal sanctions
community organization	gestures	personal names
cooking	gift giving	population policy
cooperative labor	government	postnatal care
cosmology	greetings	pregnancy usages
courtship	hairstyles	property rights
dancing	hospitality	propitiation of
decorative art	housing	supernatural beings
divination	hygiene	puberty customs
division of labor	incest taboos	religious rituals
dream interpretation	inheritance rules	residence rules
education	joking	sexual restrictions
eschatology	kin groups	soul concepts
ethics	kinship nomenclature	status differentiation
ethno-botany	language	surgery
etiquette	law	tool making
faith healing	luck superstitions	trade
family feasting	magic	visiting
fire making	marriage	weather control
folklore	mealtimes	weaving
food taboos	medicine	
funeral rites	obstetrics	

Learning as a Design Issue

You may remember the advertisement for an information services company that featured a water pipe, tied in a knot, over a person's head. A solitary drop of water dripped out of the pipe's open end. The ad's visual metaphor and accompanying text were about the removal of information blockages. A good information system, the ad seemed to suggest, will pour information into our heads, a bit like filling up a bucket.

Pipe-and-bucket thinking pervades policy that has to do with learning and education. The British government is even building a "National Grid of Learning" that will connect all schools to the Internet. It's a great political metaphor—knowledge for all, just like water or electricity. But it's an outdated model of learning. Learning is a complex, social, and multidimensional process that does not lend itself to being sent down a pipe—for example, from a website. Knowledge, understanding, wisdom—or "content," if you must—are qualities one develops through time. They are not a thing one is sent.

Content vs. Thought

Formal education is already crippled by too much content and too little time to think. By the early 2000s, no fewer than 270 different entities were in a position to send directives to English schools. The tap has been left running for so long that teachers and pupils feel like submariners in a disaster movie—afloat near the ceiling, struggling to breathe. As Ivan Illich understood thirty years ago, when he proposed the "de-schooling of society,"[1] the best solution to our many education dilemmas is probably to have less of it. But as Illich soon discovered, that's a hard approach to sell. Governments everywhere are convinced that in an age of accelerating change and increased technological complexity, the skill at learning of its people will distinguish one country from another. Education is universally perceived to be key to national competitiveness. Governments everywhere are looking for ways to give us more of it and to make it better.[2]

The febrile attention paid to education has spawned a boom in learning research. The world is awash in books, think tank reports, learning laboratories, institutes, and websites (and this chapter). Tens of thousands of intelligent people are learning about learning. At the Amsterdam University of Professional Education, research director Caroline Nevejan showed me a three-hundred-page document she had been given, written in execrable learning-speak, that evaluated no fewer than thirty different teaching methods and instruments. These ranged from "critical incidents method" to e-mail discussion lists, search engines, and "self-reflection instruments." (I decided at the time that the last of these must have been a mirror.)[3] Another university researcher I met had been asked to review the state of thinking on just one learning issue—assessment—and had to read ten years' issues of 160 different specialist journals to get up to speed.[4]

There may be too much of it, but this mountain of research has nonetheless delivered important insights. A consensus has emerged that learning is about the acquisition of new skills, including social ones—not just about the stockpiling of facts. People possess multiple intelligences, not just the formal ones measured by the intelligence tests and school exams that plagued me as a child. Social, physical, and emotional intelligences are important, too, we now know: We need to develop a combination of factual, process, and cultural knowledge to manage well in today's complex world. According to David Hargreaves, professor of education at Cambridge University, we need cognitive-intellectual skills, aesthetic-artistic ones, affective-emotional abilities, physical-manual skills, and personal-social skills.[5] For another eminent professor, Howard Gardner, professor of cognition and education at Harvard University's Graduate School of Education, the most important skills of all are so-called metacognitive skills—an understanding of guiding principles, of what really matters, and the ability to filter out the growing flood of stuff that does not. "We need to be able to formulate new questions," Gardner argues (writing with coauthor T. Hatch), "and not just rely on tasks or problems posed by others. We need the ability to learn in new ways, to evaluate our own progress, to be able to transfer knowledge from one context to another."[6] The new mantra is *learning to learn:* a range of skills—and the capacity to use them effectively—that will equip us to understand abstract concepts and complex systems and how to live among them and improve them.[7]

The research army has also discovered that we learn in different ways: when we listen to stories, when we do things with our hands, when we ponder deep questions on our own, perhaps in the bath. We learn when we participate in group projects in the real world. We learn when we make music and do art. All this is uplifting stuff when I think back to the learn-by-rote Latin lessons I endured at school. *Amo, amas, amat.*

Earning from Learning

There is a mismatch between the kind of learning prescribed by these enlightened experts and what many employers perceive to be their short-term needs. As a result of this mismatch, the school-to-work transition has become an increasingly difficult phase, and many employers now take their own direct training measures. These tend to be heavy on applied skills—and light on metacognitive ones.[8] We might reject the narrow focus of much corporate education, but it's partly our own fault as a society. We have filled the world with such unstable technology and clunky systems; these need to be looked after by people with limited horizons who do what they are told and don't ask too many questions. Call centers—to name just one among a thousand support functions in our technological culture—don't recruit people with metacognitive skills who look at the bigger picture. They need drones.

The widening gap between what formal education provides and what business thinks it needs has stimulated the emergence of learning as a market. This market also benefits from the fact that governments are looking for ways to educate more people to ever higher levels—but without spending more money. They therefore encourage private-sector investment in what is known in new-economy-speak as the "education space."

On paper, education, like health and care, is a vast market. Spending on learning by all organizations in the United States amounts to some seven hundred fifty billion dollars, or 7 percent of GDP. That's half what the country spends on health, but still a tidy sum. In France, Europe's highest spender on education, the number is closer to 25 percent.[9] Spending by all organizations worldwide is estimated to be two thousand billion dollars.

U.S. firms spend a big chunk of that total on internal training. The so-called consumer market for learning is also huge. Two hundred million North Americans take some kind of continuing education course each year, and nine out of ten adults aged fifty and over are actively seeking learning opportunities at any given time. These are remarkable numbers when compared to annual sales of tickets to sporting events in the United States, which total just ten million.[10]

The approach business has taken to the learning market has been to segment it. An influential paper by Jerry Wind and David Reibstein at Wharton Business School[11] divided education into discrete markets: child care and early education, K–12 or secondary education, postsecondary education, corporate training, and the consumer market. Another popular matrix divides learning into *content* (information technology, business skills, lifestyle, academic, customized), *services* (content distribution, consulting, implementation, e-commerce, community portals), and *technology* (learning management tools, digital portfolios, content creation tools, delivery platforms, collaboration tools).

There was a time when market analyses of this kind, combined with the huge financial numbers bandied around, greatly excited investors. There was talk of an "emerging electronic university," a ninety-billion-dollar "unified global marketplace for ideas," "Web-based knowledge exchanges," and so on.[12] One start-up, UNext, proclaimed that "the vast imbalance between the supply and demand for quality education provides an enormous, untapped global market. Countries, companies, and individuals that don't invest in knowledge are destined to fall behind."[13]

This bewitching vision enticed investors to pour billions of dollars of venture capital onto the e-learning bandwagon during the last years of the dot-com boom. A lot of this money went to so-called pure-play learning start-ups following a "land grab" or first-mover-advantage strategy. These start-ups thought it vital to own or control access to as much content as possible. "We are continually combing the Net to feed our growing database of 37,000 online courses," boasted the website of HungryMinds (now defunct).[14] Other start-ups proclaimed themselves to be "learning portals" through which all conceivable types of knowledge and learning would be accessed and exchanged. Blue-chip players were not immune from the frenzy. Columbia University invested tens of millions of dollars in Fathom, a learning portal, and recruited a consortium of fellow blue-chip academic institutions to join them; these included the London School of Economics, the New York Public Library, and the Universities of Chicago and Michigan. Industry gossip at the time had it that Fathom spent seventy-five million dollars building its portal website before the service was even launched.[15]

Most e-learning start-ups were inspired by a simple idea: They would make money by "dis-intermediating" disposable steps in the production process of learning—namely, people. They compared the people costs of education (which are up to 80 percent) with those in manufacturing (20–40 percent) and services (around 60 percent)—and concluded that it must surely be possible to produce learning in a more profitable way by automating the process.[16]

The e-learning investment bubble burst when, in 2001, MIT announced that it would put all its content online—and access would be free. The university further committed one hundred million dollars to a project called OpenCourseWare in which public-domain websites would be built for all of its two thousand courses. Lecture notes, problem sets, syllabuses, simulations, even videos of lectures would be put online. As Charles Vest, MIT's president, said at the time, "our central value is people, and the human experience of faculty working with students."[17]

The private sector was not uniquely to blame for a skewed vision of learning that prioritized prerecorded content over people. Visions of a vast, semiautomated learning machine still bewitch many politicians—not just entrepreneurs—and the world is replete with government-backed plans to "penetrate the schools" with new technology. A senior Dutch minister once told me confidently that with the Internet, "we can beam lectures from the best 10 percent of teachers to classrooms and do without the other 90 percent." The minister's dream reminded me of a joke I once heard in Hungary about the factory of the future. It will have only two employees, a man and a dog: The man will be there to feed the dog; the dog will be there to stop the man from touching the equipment.

Evangelists for computers in schools are perplexed that the computer revolution has moved so slowly. They observe that some areas of human activity—medicine, transportation, entertainment—have changed beyond recognition in the wake of modern science and technology. One institution that most definitely has not is school. MIT's Seymour Papert has a vision of a truly modern school in which the computer is as much part of all learning as the pencil and the book have been in the past. In Papert's vision, computer-based media would enable children to master areas of knowledge that would otherwise remain inaccessibly difficult. Self-directed work would allow an unprecedented diversity of learning styles and opportunity for students to learn to take charge of their own learning. According to Papert, American schools have acquired more than three million computers, yet resistance to progress persists.[18]

Anyplace, Anytime

When students are sufficiently motivated or lack alternatives, they indeed seem to be prepared to take online courses in significant numbers. The most widely quoted success story, University of Phoenix, has more than thirty-seven thousand enrolled students, and its parent company, Apollo, was valued at more than six billion dollars in 2002.[19] The university, which caters specifically to working adults, relies wholly on distance learning; the Internet and e-mail are its primary means of communication. Online classes in the school's master's of business administration (MBA) program (one of a number of degree programs it offers) are conducted in groups of ten to twelve students, most of whom complete their degrees without ever having met a fellow student. The university employs no full-time academics. Instead, an army of eleven thousand working professionals teach online in their spare time.

Far from being a cost-saving panacea, "anyplace, anytime" distance learning is not inexpensive to deliver. Distance-learning students will tolerate minimal human contact and low-bandwidth media such as e-mail if they have no choice, but they will not tolerate deficiencies in technical support, the quality of which can be a deciding factor for students shopping for virtual courses.[20] Colleges that take distance e-learning seriously have to offer late-night, weekend, or even twenty-four-hour-a-day, seven-day-a-week technical support. University of Maryland's University College, with thirteen thousand online students, spends two hundred fifty thousand dollars annually on technical support. As a result, distance learning is not particularly cheap. A three-year MBA program at University of Phoenix costs upward of thirty thousand dollars. Convenience rather than price is the big selling point for students.[21]

Governments that hoped to save millions on e-learning and dreamed of websites filled with course notes have been disappointed. But investment in e-learning continues at significant levels. This is especially true in business education—but as an addition to, not a replacement for, existing course activities. Harvard Business School (HBS) has invested millions of dollars a year in its website since the early 1990s. Larry Bouthillier, head of multimedia development at HBS during those years (and now the director of educational technologies and multimedia development), told a conference I organized at the time that "simulations, databases, statistical and industry analyses, are intensively used learning 'objects' among Harvard's MBA students and researchers."[22] ICT also deepens the learning experience, according to Bouthillier. Online cases, audiovisual material, and computer-based exercises are useful extras. "Online is a microcosm of the new working environment graduates will encounter when they leave," said Bouthillier; "our goal is the emergence of Harvard Business School as an integrated enterprise that organises and connects information, and people, in a dynamic and continuous way."[23]

The ambition to be an open, connected, and integrated enterprise is shared by many advanced companies throughout the world—but by relatively few learning institutions. For Charles Hampden-Turner, who works in both domains, "there is a more open system of learning in most businesses than in most universities." It is clear to business, he says, that knowledge has become too complex to be carried in the heads of itinerant experts: "knowledge is necessarily the shared property of extended groups and networks."[24] These learning networks need to be organized and looked after. Business schools like Harvard's are working hard to add value to—not substitute for—a central function of universities: connectivity among a community of scholars and peers. Their approach uses the Internet to bring people together—not the opposite, as with pure distance education. As John Seely Brown and Paul Duguid write in *The Social Life of Information*, "Social distance is not overcome by a few strokes of the keyboard. Learning at all levels relies ultimately on personal interaction and, in particular, on a range of implicit and peripheral forms of communication that technology is still very far from being able to handle."[25]

Corporate U

For many companies, sending staff to an Ivy League campus—with or without a state-of-the-art website—is not an option. So they are doing it alone. So-called corporate universities (CUs) are booming. There are almost two thousand in the United States alone. Few CUs have interesting curriculums, but the way they operate is often innovative and state of the art. Many corporate university staff don't do much formal teaching, for example, but spend most of their time in needs analysis, curriculum design, and selecting and managing relationships with outside suppliers. One leading player, Sun Microsystems, has implemented an online learning management system for every employee that is based on the latest thinking about "digital portfolios" and self-assessment. Sun's system supports a customized training schedule for each employee that is based on past experience, current role, and future aspirations. Employees at Unisys, too, sign up for courses through an online career portfolio and evaluate their skills and performance online.[26]

Companies have adapted more rapidly than most colleges to the changing demographics and expectations of learners. Nearly half of all entrants to higher education in the United States are now over twenty-five years old, for example, and a growing proportion of these learners are working professionals, ranging from accountants to zoologists, for whom continuing education is a professional obligation. Take doctors: A majority of U.S. states now require doctors to complete a designated number of hours of continuing education each year in order to renew their licenses to practice. Continuous updating of professional knowledge has become a cost of doing business for millions of people—but this is hard to sustain. The need to sell our time competes with the time we need to spend keeping our knowledge up to date.

The learning load on most technical professionals today is awesome. A typical network administrator or systems operator (SysOp), for example, has twelve feet of hefty manuals on the shelf behind her desk, each containing hundreds of dense typeset pages.[27] A new manual, in paper or digital form, accompanies each device and software package that enters the environment. Most of these have a short life expectancy—a couple of years at most—so new editions and new manuals arrive in a constant stream. I once described this alarming information burden to the head teacher of my daughter's junior school in London. The head laughed and took me into her office where, behind her desk, was a shelf filled with a row of fat ring-bound manuals, all in a row. These manuals contained the latest version of the national curriculum that every school in England is compelled by the central government to teach. On the floor, half-opened, was a box containing another six of these fat binders—updates, recently arrived from some kind of Learning Central, that the head teacher had to read and feed into her school's already overloaded curriculum.

Whether we are SysOps running databases or teachers running a school, distant planners and developers often overload us with precooked input. The result is a *paté de foie gras* effect: Overregimented teachers are forced to cram too much predetermined content into students who spend so much time learning that they have no time to think. It's a downward spiral. The more important learning becomes, the more demands we put on teachers and students within rigidly organized institutions.

When Illich proposed that we should "deschool" society, his idea was that we should use existing technologies and spaces—the telephone, local radio, town hall meetings—to create learning webs through which learners would connect with their peers and with new contexts in which to learn. "We can provide the learner with new links to the world," said Illich, "instead of continuing to funnel all education through the teacher." Illich was right then, and he is surely right now. But a huge gulf separates his vision of what learning could and should be like from today's reality.[28] Our educational institutions remain, in the words of David Hargreaves, "a curious mixture of the factory, the asylum and the prison."[29] A command-and-control model, based on long lists of the new skills we all need, simply adds pressure to an overloaded system and people inside it.

From Factory to Farm

A better design approach to learning is to shift our attention from outputs—courses taught, facts learned, certificates awarded—to the *inputs* of learning and, in particular, to focus on the interaction between networks and contexts. In chapter 6, economist Hazel Henderson talked about the need to decentralize health systems. Another think tanker, Tom Bentley of Demos, in the United Kingdom, says similar things in *Learning beyond the Classroom:* "We should think of learning as an ecology of people and groups, projects, tools and infrastructures"—and allow stakeholders in each situation to take care of content issues. We need to reconceptualize education, he says, as an "open, living system whose intelligence is distributed and shared among all its participants. Schools and colleges need to become network organisations, to establish themselves as hubs at the center of diverse, overlapping networks of learning which reach out to the fullest possible range of institutions, sources of information, social groups, and physical facilities."[30]

So how might such an ecology be designed? What design principles should we apply in the development of networked learning?

Design Principle 1: Time and Tempo

The first design principle concerns time and tempo. Of the many damaging pressures placed on learning ecologies, time is probably the harshest. A first design task is to relieve that pressure. Time is a valuable resource within a school or daily life, yet the ways in which it is organized are often standardized and come with high costs and wastage. We also focus the great majority of our attention on formal learning time—school and college—forgetting that between birth and age sixteen, 85 percent of our waking time is spent *out* of school. In the United States, to put time further into perspective, children aged nine to fourteen spend nine hundred hours a year in school—but fifteen hundred hours a year watching television. When a Dutch researcher, Jos Baeten, studied the 168 hours available in an eighteen-year-old student's week, he found that 16 were spent in formal lessons and 9 in self-study—which left 143 hours for other activities: 58 for sleeping, 20 for social and family commitments, 26 for relaxation, 14 for traveling, and 13 for eating and "pausing"; 10 hours were spent in paid work.[31]

On the basis of these numbers, perhaps Illich would have been pleased. It looks as if the deschooling of society is well under way. The problem is that policymakers see an opportunity to fill up more time with formal learning. Those hundreds of hours American children spend watching the box are under scrutiny as an opportunity for "edutainment." With the notable exception of *Sesame Street*, nothing much of interest has resulted. Most educational or edutainment television casts children in the role of passive consumers; it continues to be based on a point-to-mass model—only with tinier budgets than the soaps or reality TV that command far more of young people's attention.

Those fourteen hours a week spent traveling by Dutch students are another tempting target. Why not put e-learning on the buses or in their mobile phones? In Japan, this has already started. In a country whose commute times are among the longest in the world, Rikkyo University has launched a website accessible from i-mode phones. Students use the system to catch up on missed classwork, ask professors questions, and check for lecture cancellations. Text-messaging symbols—such as a smiling face or a broken heart—have started to appear in students' essays. In other educational applications of text messaging (or SMS, short for "short message system"), tutors send reminders and alerts to students on courses or send a daily message to learners, thereby providing them (as one e-learning website puts it) with "a daily dose of learning ... the message is pushed to the learners so that they don't have to actually go out and get it every day."[32]

Content push is the wrong way to design the use of learning time. Those hours do not belong to policymakers or to mobile phone companies. They belong to the students. Rather than fill up all time with prepackaged content, we need to make it possible for learners, of whatever age, to use their own time more flexibly and actively.[33]

New technology seems to work best when helping people interact across time, rather than across space. If students and teachers can access Web documents—or each other—at different times, they can escape the temporal confines of the classroom. For Seely Brown and Duguid, "Learning technology should be built around a conversational paradigm. The web has its own rules, rhythms, and speeds; new kinds of documents, and new kinds of interactions with students, are emerging."[34] Educational providers have started to offer thirty-minute "instant knowledge" options, twenty-four-hour cycles, and—perhaps learning from online computer games—courses that do not end. The best Internet tools, by common agreement, are an extension of—not a replacement for—face-to-face exchanges.

New links—facilitated by the institution—can be made between students on campus with time and no money and students off campus with money but no time. According to Carol Twigg, "In such a scenario, a student's university career would no longer be through a particular place, time or pre-selected body of academics, but through a network principally of their own making, yet shaped by the degree granting body and its faculty. A student could stay at home or travel, mix on-line and off-line education, work in classes or with mentors, and continue their learning long after taking a degree."[35] As I stated earlier, companies lead the way in reconfiguring space-time relations for training purposes.[36] Caroline Nevejan has developed a map (figure 7.1) to help her institution's twenty-two thousand students

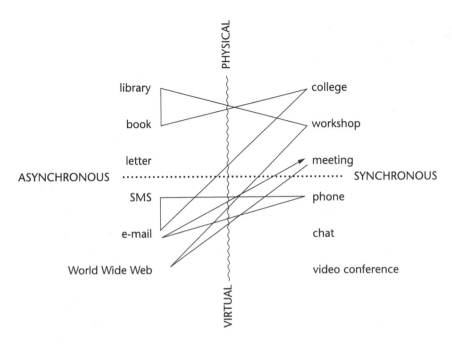

Figure 7.1
Time-lines. From Caroline Nevejan, *Synchroon|Asynchroon: Ondwerwijsvernieuwing in de informatiesamenleving* (Synchronous|Asynchronous: Educational Renewal in the Information Society) (Amsterdam: Hogeschool van Amsterdam, 2003), 40–41.

navigate the online/offline, synchronous/asynchronous modes of study that their course will in the future entail.

Design Principle 2: Place and Space

The concept of a "death of distance" made great headlines when Internet rhetoric was at its height. Its grandchild is the concept of "anytime, anywhere learning." This idea sounds attractive and uncontroversial—until one realizes that it describes a point-to-mass distribution model of learning that overlooks the significance of place and the localization of knowledge.

Learning depends on place, time, and context. An exclusive focus on schools and colleges as sites of learning and the distribute-then-learn model of e-learning both fail to exploit these more complex geographies of learning. As Seely Brown and Duguid emphasize in *The Social Life of Information*, a lot of what we learn is remarkably local: history, agriculture, politics, art, geology, viticulture, forestry, conservation, ocean science. A great deal of learning also takes place in what these authors describe as "an ecology of local or regional sites of professional excellence: research labs, hospitals, architects' and design offices, Web design studios, and the like—anywhere, indeed, that people gather together to work. Knowledge as it grows is necessarily social, the shared property of extended groups and networks."[37] All spaces, places, and communities that foster complex experiences and processes are potential sites of learning.

New geographies of learning need to be based on redesigned configurations of space, place, and network that respect the social and collaborative nature of learning—while still exploiting the dynamic potential of networked collaboration. We need to design the spatial configuration of education so that it connects communities and learners that, right now, tend to be separated from one another.[38]

Breaking down the walls that divide "school" and "work" and "home" entails challenging cultural and institutional changes—but it can be done. The municipal infant-toddler centers and preschools of Reggio Emilia in Italy, for example, are internationally recognized as a model of "relational space" planning in which buildings are relatively neutral in the use of colors, much like an art museum, so that the activities and work of the children become the focus of the space. (Documentation is central to the Reggio approach, and the architecture is designed to encourage playful encounters for the preschool students.) In Reggio the built environment is considered a "third teacher"—not only in the sense that it facilitates learning, but also because it explicitly acts as a connector that supports a networked, community-based organization and acts as a hub for the whole community. "In a relational space," says the noted Italian design researcher Giulio Ceppi, "the predominant feature is that of the relationships it enables, the many specialized activities that can be carried out there, and the information and cultural filters that can be activated within the space."[39]

The design emphasis in Reggio Emilia is on relationships, rather than on what the space looks like. Educational theories change faster than the buildings they are tested in. Many middle-aged Europeans went to schools built decades earlier whose windows were set purposefully high so that children would not be distracted by the outside world. I spent my own teenage years in buildings designed by a Victorian prison architect; his expertise with security and iron bars persuaded the founders of

Marlborough College that he was the ideal person to build a school for teenage boys. Maybe they were right—but I cannot recall being bothered by my school buildings one way or another. What I do remember (fondly, for the most part) are teachers and fellow pupils and some of the things we did together.

What matters most to all learners is activity, not architecture. We all deserve to spend time in safe, pleasant, and comfortable surroundings, rather than their opposite. Beyond that, most buildings will do. What learning needs most is a lot *more* space, as well as time, than it gets right now. There's no need to purpose-build huge numbers of schools and colleges. Fine calculations about square meters per child or the relative merits of discrete classrooms along corridors versus communal halls are secondary issues. We need double, triple the space we have now, for learning. The world is filled with abandoned or underused cinemas, gas stations, power plants, warehouses, and railway yards. We should commandeer them for learning. As I suggested in chapters 3 and 4, we can use the resource management systems pioneered in the logistics industry to combine learners and spaces in new ways and at new times.

Design Principle 3: Meaningful Projects

Metacognitive skills—judgment, understanding, the capacity to reflect—do not lend themselves to being taught by rote. Nor are they easy to download from a website. Active learning happens when we participate in projects that are meaningful to us and engage with the real world. We need to believe that the task we are about to tackle is important and meaningful. As Charles Hampden-Turner and Alfons Trompenaars so wisely counsel, we often overlook "the extent to which needed applications give meaningful zest to our work and learning: Without shared purposes and moral meaning, we end up with a culture of self-absorption and narcissism."[40] Those words resonate uncomfortably when I think about some of the projects I see during my frequent visits to universities and design and architecture schools. Projects that enable self-expression by the individual student, but are otherwise pointless, are depressingly common.

The design of meaningful projects is not easy—particularly if an instructor tries to do this on her own. A success factor for projects is that learners should help to design them. Precooked projects are usually uninspiring.

The most interesting phase of a project is setting it up, designing it, scanning the domain, framing the issues, specifying an action, seeking information and advice, planning the work, putting together the team. All these are design tasks, and they are best learned by experience. Designing and setting up a project can be messy, time-consuming, hard to manage—and won't go according to plan. Just like the real world.

Design Principle 4: Technology and Networks

When wiring up schools to the Internet fails to deliver instant, dramatic results—which is nearly always—politicians often blame teachers, whom they have long tended to regard as an impediment to technological modernization. The real culprits are policymakers who think of technology as a cost-saving cure-all. Serious budgets are persistently voted for the hardware of connectivity (computers, modems, and so on), but grossly inadequate resources tend to be allocated to content and process development—the what and how of learning in new ways. Education planners have persistently ignored the advice of their own software suppliers that 30–40 percent of any technology budget should be devoted to staff training and organizational development.

Outside education, larger companies reckon that their true ICT costs—when equipment, training, technical support, connectivity and hosting, software licenses, and so on are taken into account—are about ten thousand dollars a year per person. No government in the world invests that amount to support technology in schools. In the United States and Europe, head teachers and principals would count themselves lucky to have a technology budget of ten thousand dollars per school.[41] International Data Corporation has calculated that the total cost of ownership (TCO) for a school with seventy-five computers is $2,251 per year per computer, whereas for a comparably sized small business its TCO is $4,517 per computer, or more than twice that amount.[42] Tom Stewart, author of *Intellectual Capital*, puts the figure for business computing much higher: He states that the five-year costs of supporting a client-server computing network is $48,000 per person.[43]

The total amount spent on technology is not the most important point. I argued earlier that the main promise of technology does not lie in putting course notes and lecture transcripts online. That's the start, not the end, of the process. Technology becomes interesting when it facilitates new kinds of interaction among teachers, students, and the external world—and this does not need to be expensive. To get the most out of technology and networks, new skills and attitudes are needed—and these either are free or can be taught. *Search skills* are important, for example. With billions of pages and countless educational objects already on the Web, the skill of understanding how to search for things and how to evaluate online material is critical. The new learning economy values hits and links: Learning how to be found and how to link is also a core skill. Vital, too, are the *editing skills* students need as they find, evaluate, organize, and communicate all kinds of media assets: video, photographs, or computer files. Different ways to *share knowledge* and experience also need to be explored: file sharing, peer-to-peer knowledge exchange over the Net. File sharing is not just about music: It is more important as an infrastructure and a culture that enables collaboration and interaction among learners.

Design Factor 5: Testing and Assessment

Student-centered and self-organized learning is not the same as laissez faire. I'm continually impressed by the energy with which students search for new ways to assess and document their own progress. As lifelong learners, we all need systems of assessment that can provide us with feedback on our performance. Self-assessment places more responsibility on the student than assessment by others, but students are well aware that waiting for their institution and/or teachers to assess and guide their learning is not a promising option.

Some feedback can be enabled by technology. One of the most interesting uses of IT in education is digital portfolios of the kind already in use at ICT companies such as Sun. Digital portfolios provide an ongoing record of work that can be continually added to and reshaped.[44] Portfolios collect detailed information on the development of students over an extended period of time and serve as what Howard Gardner describes as a "record of growth": They can include the history of a specific project or a broader picture of progress over a longer period of time. According to Gardner, portfolios can be assessed (by instructors, but also by the learners themselves) against a variety of measures: the number and richness of entries, the degree and quality of reflection demonstrated, quantitative improvement in a technical skill, achievement of goals, and so on.[45]

The fact that a portfolio is created and stored digitally is not a big deal. I remember as a child being asked to keep a "commonplace book," and my own daughter today accumulates hardcover books containing project work, records of visits to museums, and reflections. Where "digital" can really add value is by leveraging the power of networks to enable peer assessment. For J. C. Herz, who studies the relationship between online gaming and learning, what underlies the dynamics of networked online environments is the process whereby individuals are evaluated and rewarded by the system itself, rather than by a specific individual. This process is perhaps most evident in massive multiplayer role-playing games (RPGs) like Sony's *Everquest*, Electronic Arts' *Ultima Online*, or Microsoft's *Asheron's Call*. For Herz, "the RPG game persona is the most fully dimensional representation of a person's accumulated knowledge and experience in the months and years they spend in an online environment."[46]

Design Factor 6: Mentors

Learner autonomy and self-organization are crucial ingredients in successful learning—if only for defensive reasons. Formal education systems are under pressure to teach more and more students—while at the same time being given smaller budgets per student to do so. When a government pays a school less than six thousand dollars per pupil per year, as is the case in Britain—an amount equivalent to two or three days' fees for a McKinsey consultant—quality face-to-face time between teachers and students will be minuscule.[47] The wise student does not wait to be taught. But in learning, self-organization works better when there's someone there to guide it. The best learning experiences, besides being codesigned by the people who have them, also benefit from good coaching, facilitation, feedback, and mentoring.

These are highly labor-intensive activities. Activity-based learning requires the presence, time, and attention of mentors in all shapes and sizes. For Theodor Zeldin, who teaches the art of conversation in a wide variety of contexts, "the most important skill, which underlies all creativity and all scientific discovery, is the ability to find links between ideas which are seemingly unconnected. Our life stories are dominated by the encounters we have had with particular individuals, and by our constant search for new encounters. Oxford normally describes itself as having 16,000 students and 2,000 staff, devoted to acquiring knowledge. But that is to forget its 130,000 graduates all over the world, busy acquiring experience, which is far more valuable than the donations they are constantly being asked for."[48]

Old people often have time to be mentors, and they usually know a lot. Søren Kierkegaard famously complained that his life would have made more sense had he known, as a young man, what he only discovered when he was old. In my own experience, young people crave feedback from any quarter possible; feedback from older people is appreciated not necessarily because it is better, but because it is better than none at all. After all, young people can be mentors, too. Families and communities are also important and influential places of learning. Many of us learn the basics about health, well-being, and key social skills at our mother's knee—or on the street.

The blockage is that learners and mentors do not easily or naturally meet each other. Teachers are surrounded by people, but they are often, distressingly, socially isolated. Classroom-bound, pressurized by timetables and the sheer numbers of students, they have limited access to the outside world. In the United States, only an estimated 12 percent of teachers have telephones in their classrooms provided by the school.[49] Our learning institutions tend to keep people out—or students in—when they should do the opposite.

At Oxford University, Zeldin is developing the idea for a Muse Hotel that would not content itself with providing beds in which tourists can recover from the exhaustion of staring silently at the historical monuments. Instead, those who stayed at the hotel would be able to sample what is most valuable in the university, notably the mind-stretching private tutorial. The logistics of connecting learners and mentors does not need to be complicated: Institutions simply need to create space and time and a business model for these connections, and the students will do the rest.

Design Factor 7: Mass Collaborative Learning

Mentors and intimate conversation are clearly important. But the complex challenges facing us will not be confronted unless we find ways to enable rapid, mass, large-scale learning, too. J. C. Herz's investigations of the on-line gaming world reveal numerous examples of networks in which profes-sionals—particularly those involved in fast-evolving technical domains—share information and experience. As Howard Rheingold confirms so cogently in *Smart Mobs*, we don't have to reinvent the concept of collabo-ration: It's in our nature as humans to collaborate, and this existing social characteristic is being amplified and accelerated by new communication tools ranging from data mining and ratings software to wireless devices.[50] A well-known example is Slashdot,[51] a website for technology news and discussion. Unlike that of a traditional technical journal, in which a small team of specialist writers roam the world's trade fairs and labs and then write articles about technology, the editorial content of Slashdot is cre-ated by its users. Any Slashdotter can submit a text or comment on one already there. Submissions to Slashdot are filtered and rated by moderators.

Despite the craze for "social software" and the growth of websites such as LinkedIn and Orkut that promise to revolutionize our social and pro-fesional lives, the Internet does not own mass collaboration. In all forms of learning, the best collaboration involves live contact, and this, too, can be designed. To give just one example, "OroOro" was a three-day event organized by Caroline Nevejan, research director of the Amsterdam Univer-sity of Professional Education, with its twenty-two thousand students and more than one thousand teachers. Nevejan was looking for ways to sup-port collaboration among teachers fatigued by years of forced continuous reorganization and by a government intent on pushing more and more students through the system. Many of the university's teachers were be-ing confronted by students who knew more about the technical details of their subject—for example, Java programming—than the teachers did. It was a recipe for demoralization. "My job was not to bring in yet more technology—we already had that," Nevejan told me at the time, "but to design processes that would enable our teachers and students to make better use of new tools." The aim of "OroOro" was to accelerate this new approach. Part symposium, part hands-on workshop, it enabled 1,000 teachers to explore together new ways to organize relationships between what—and who—we know.[52]

The lesson of projects like "OroOro" is that communities of practice can be designed—in this case, within a single institution—and they are not principally about technology. Communities of practice are defined by a common disciplinary background, similar work activities and tools, and shared stories, contexts, and values. They are not defined by the technology that helps them function. IBM, to its credit, has put hard numbers on the fact that communities of practice grow through time; they are not built with tech. It investigated communities of practice within several large organizations, including IBM, Scandinavian Airline Systems, World Bank, United Technologies, and British Telecom, and identified and priced four major cost drivers:

- the cost of participation time for community members (52 percent)
- meeting and conference expenses (32 percent)
- technology (10 percent)
- content publishing and promotional expenses (6 percent)[53]

Design Factor 8: Copyrights and Cryptolopes

In the flawed logic of early e-learning models, reinforced by government policy, teachers were treated as a discretionary cost. The opposite is nearer the truth. There is no limit to the number of teachers society could use, if money were no object. I once spent two weeks learning Dutch in a language school in which every lesson was one-to-one. Despite being a lousy student, I made pretty good progress, but it cost my employer a lot of money. E-learning is not a cost-saving panacea either: It's an expensive add-on. It doesn't work well on its own, and it can cost up to a million dollars to produce a sophisticated module.

So how are we to pay for all the active, self-directed, and lifelong learning that we all have to do? One solution is to change the question. Asking how society is to pay for all this education implies an expensive point-to-mass service delivered by one supplier (the state or the market) to people who have little or no money to pay for it (the people). A more promising approach would be to reframe education as an ecology in which time and knowledge and money flow in many different directions. Among those flows, new ways to leverage the value of what—and whom—we know are bound to emerge that nobody has thought of yet.

Esther Dyson said before the e-learning boom that we should think of published material—books, course notes, websites, and so on—not as something to sell, to make a living, but as the means to *begin* a relationship with a learner. What people really value, Dyson realized, is attention, interaction, and the opportunity thereby to discover new insights, to make new connections between ideas.[54] This is why a business model for learning based on the sale of intellectual property and copyrights will never work. Turning teachers into free agents and expecting them to earn a living as content providers, by selling copyrights and royalties, or on some kind of fee-per-use basis, won't work either. People will pay only for what is scarce, personal, customized, tangible, nonreproducible. In a learning society, that's the presence, time, and attention of wise or interesting people. If intellectual value is the presence of other people, often specific ones, interacting formally or casually or both, new business models need to be based not on the sale of content, but on personalized services—such as hosting online forums, rating others' contributions, custom programming, and consulting.

A similar problem afflicts the attractive notion of an economy of micropayments. Quite a lot of people visit my website, for example, and if they all left me a five-cent tip each time they visited, my pension would finally be taken care of. If it works in the restaurant business, why not in the writing or teaching business? A business model along these lines can be based on hits and links—people pay a higher price to look at my stuff the more people are linked to it. As a content provider I would be paid every time someone clicked on one of my texts (or "reusable information object"—RIO—in the ineffable language of Cisco). This business model for publishing, including personal publishing, has been discussed for a decade. The system architectures and software applications for such schemes are nearly in place, including the cryptolopes that will enable secure micropayments. But institutional barriers, especially the wretched banks, continue to slow things down. The fact must also be faced that revenue from micropayments is unlikely to cover the huge amounts of time that teachers need in order to teach, professionals to study, mentors to mentor. These activities are even more time- and more labor-intensive than traditional teaching. Teaching a set curriculum lends itself more to standardization and mass production than helping students assess their own progress, helping design and facilitate learning projects in the real world, building and supporting learning communities, or integrating real and virtual, synchronous and asynchronous learning processes. We don't have sustainable business models for all this yet. But as I explained in chapter 6, the raw materials for a hybrid cash and time barter economy are in place. It's just a matter of combining them in new ways.

Design Factor 9: Playtime

The film director Jean-Luc Godard regretted that growing up meant losing permission to play: "It takes a lifetime to become the child that you should be," he lamented.[55] Play informs our culture, our imaginations, our experiences. But most educational policies—and nearly all projects to wire up classrooms to the Internet—take us in the opposite direction. Rather than make space for all of us to learn in new and playful ways, most "wired classrooms" are more like cages filled with experimental rats. Only the rats are our children—or ourselves.

It is a welcome irony that budgets for school Internet projects are increasingly overshadowed by the amounts now being spent each year on computer games. The market for video, computer, online, and wireless games is growing far faster than the market for e-learning, and the games industry has overtaken Hollywood in terms of its gross revenues. Many parents worry about the shoot-and-slash storylines of computer games and fear their children's minds are being turned to mush. But experts who study these effects tend to be more sanguine. When Sonia Livingstone, a professor at the London School of Economics, studied the media habits and expectations of children and the impacts of the stroboscopic effects of fast-moving multimedia on children, her results were surprising. She discovered no measurable deterioration in terms of their powers of persuasion, retention, and recall—and observed that computer gaming often demands extraordinary feats of skill, intelligence, and motor coordination. She concluded that children were learning to learn in new ways.[56]

For the writer Douglas Rushkoff, too, "the television remote-control, the videogame joystick, and the computer mouse, have irrevocably changed young people's relationship to media...young people have adapted well to this constant barrage on their senses and have mutated into 'screenagers.'"[57] Where children have led, business now follows. Gaming theory in general, and visual simulations in particular, are a hot topic in business. When it comes to understanding how an economy, a company, or an ecosystem works, modeling and simulation—which provide a rich mixture of learning and doing—are a remarkably powerful tool for genuine understanding. Banks, oil companies, city planners, and environmental agencies are all using gaming and simulation techniques to enrich their understanding of future scenarios. Might we design these qualities into the rest of our learning and work?

According to J. C. Herz, even in their first incarnation, computer games exhibited the same qualities that we saw are key to all successful projects for learning—especially meaningfulness and collaboration. "All the knowledge and skills acquired in the process of creating Spacewar were a means to an end," writes Herz of an early game; "programming physics simulations, allocating resources, representing scale and perspective—all of these were necessary to make the game better." For Herz, the dynamics of networked learning differ fundamentally from classroom instruction, and from traditional notions of distance learning. "Where classroom instruction is one-to-many, and traditional distance learning (i.e., correspondence schools and most online 'courses') are one-to-one," she writes, "networked learning environments have their own design principles, criteria by which people and their projects are evaluated."[58] Online games are an object lesson for academia, Herz says, not because universities need to be making games, but because online games illustrate the learning potential of a network and the social ecology that unlocks that potential.

Among young people who appear demotivated in formal learning situations, learning and teaching occur in a collaborative, highly social way in a game context. Herz continues: "If a gamer doesn't understand something, there is a continuously updated, distributed knowledge base maintained by a sprawling community of players from whom he can learn. Newbies are schooled by more skilled and experienced players. Far from being every man for himself, multiplayer online games actively foster the formation of teams, clans, guilds, and other self-organizing groups."[59] The salient point here for Herz is that "players are a constituency, not just an audience. The designers, far from being *auteurs*, are more like local politicians." The very nature of the product enables distributed innovation to happen in a parallel, decentralized fashion. "Of course, not all players roll up their sleeves and write plug-ins," she concedes, "but if even one percent contribute to the innovation of the product, even if they are only making minor, incremental improvements or subtle tweaks, that's ten thousand people in research and development."[60]

All this is a bottom-up, distributed, self-organizing process. The relevance of this, for institutions of higher learning, is not that students should create their own courses. Rather, it is that online content needs to leverage the same kind of social ecology that drives networked interaction in online multiplayer games. Says Herz: "Beyond the technological infrastructure, there is a cultural infrastructure in place to leverage these interpersonal dynamics. Tools and editing modes allow players to extend the game experience. But more important than the stand-alone benefit of these assets is their value as social currency. The creator of a popular level, object, or plug-in may not receive monetary remuneration. But he garners notice, and even acclaim, from his fellow gamers."[61]

New Geographies of Learning

Technology fixes for education are an old and discredited story. The delivery of precooked content, by whatever means, is not teaching. Radio, film, television, the videocassette recorder, fax machines, the personal computer, the Internet, and now the mobile phone: It was promised of each of these, in turn, that here was a wonder cure that would transform education for the better. And yet here we are, hundreds of years after the first books were printed, and teachers are still giving lectures, and students still line up to hear them. Why? They do this because the best learning involves embodiment—live experiences and conversation between people: Most people prefer talking to one another to talking to themselves. Educational institutions change slowly and social interaction remains their core activity. This is not to deny that our learning infrastructures need to evolve. More than 70 percent of learning experiences in the modern workplace are informal or accidental, not structured or sponsored by an employer or a school.[62] This kind of learning is pervasive, continuous, and profoundly social. It happens wherever people do their work: on a shop floor, around a conference table, on site with customers, or in a laboratory.

So let's be optimistic and anticipate a near future in which tech disappears quietly into the background, just as electricity did a hundred years ago. What, then, will be the important design issues among those I have discussed here? There are three that matter. The first issue before us is time: We need far more time for learning than we allow ourselves now. The second issue is the need to redesign the job descriptions that define how learners, teachers, and everyone else relate to one another. The third issue is how best to design the support systems, platforms, and institutions we need if those first two changes are to happen.

You may object to my having highlighted those three issues at the beginning of this chapter rather than now, at its end. But I don't have the answers to the questions they raise, and I am in good company in declining to make them up. Socrates once acknowledged (in words attributed to him by Plato) "the common reproach against me, that I am always asking questions of other people, but never expressing my own views about anything." Socrates' self-defense was that he did not set out to teach people; he set out to pose interesting questions to them that would get them thinking about a topic he felt needed attention. The same applies to the design of learning: Questions are more powerful than answers in stimulating our curiosity and creativity. As Pekka Himanen writes in *The Hacker Ethic:*

The metaphor was that of the teacher as master of ceremonies—the *symposiarch*—at banquets. These took place in the evenings and, in conjunction with the dialogues of the day, they were an essential learning experience. They were powerful experiential events. The symposiarch was responsible for the success of their banquets in two ways: first, from his elevated position he made sure that the intellectual goals of dialogue were attained; second, it was also his responsibility to make sure that none of the participants remained too stiff. To this latter end, he had two means at his disposal. First, he has the right to order excessively stiff participants to drink more wine. If this did not work, the symposiarch could order the participant to remove his clothes and dance![63]

Ever since I read this text I've described myself as a symposiarch. The worlds of learning would be lighter and more playful places if we could recapture this ancient Greek approach in a world in which social, industrial, and natural systems are gently nudged and stimulated rather than steered.

8 | Literacy

A few years ago I met a woman in Bombay who was completing her Ph.D. in social anthropology. She had just returned from a field trip to Rajasthan, where she had spent time with a group of traveling storytellers. This particular group went from village to village, unannounced, and would simply start a performance in the village square. Although each story would have a familiar plot—the storytelling tradition dates back thousands of years— each event would be unique. Prompted by the storytellers, who held up pictorial symbols on sticks, villagers would interact with the story. They would be part of the performance. I commented to the woman that with that depth of knowledge about interaction and the combined use of words and images, she could get a job with Microsoft tomorrow. "What's Microsoft?" was her reply.

This episode confirmed my prejudice that when we talk about design for communication, what we actually mean and do is the design of messages. As a consequence, the world is awash in print and ads and packaging and e-mail spam, but these one-way messages do not contribute to our understanding. On the contrary, they are the output of a point-to-mass mentality that lies behind the brand intrusion and semiotic pollution that despoil our perceptual landscape. The average American is now exposed to 254 different commercial messages in a day, up nearly 25 percent since the 1970s. Advertising people call this the "clutter problem"—and solve it, of course, by adding to the clutter.[1] We're so flooded by noise that it's hard to understand what's going on. True, we have learned to filter out noise and distraction, but in so doing we have also constrained our capacity to reflect on and make sense of the bigger picture. Our perceptions of change through time and the behavior of processes are especially weak. Our way of life is probably threatened by changes to our natural and social support system taking place over years and decades—but we tend not to notice changes over a few years or decades. Cumulatively wasteful behaviors often seem trivial in themselves—leaving the light on, printing out an e-mail, eating a plate of Kenyan beans—but the accumulation of such tiny acts can weigh on the planet.

In order to do things differently, to reassert some kind of control over the evolution of events, we need to design ways to see things differently. Tomorrow's literacies therefore need to be process and systems literacies. In this chapter I explore what it might mean to design new perceptual aids to understanding the state of our natural, human, and industrial systems. I ask whether new kinds of sights, sounds, symbols, and experiences could tell us about how these systems work, what stimulates them, and how and why they change through time. And I conclude by asking which, if any, of these design actions would help us more than simply talking to one another.

We are not starting from scratch here. Many affective representations of complex phenomena have been developed in recent times. Physicists have illustrated quarks. Biologists have mapped the genome. Doctors have found ways to represent immune systems in the body. Network designers have mapped communication flows in buildings. Managers have charted the locations of expertise in their organizations. Our world is filled with representations of invisible or complex phenomena. But most of them have been made and used by specialists as objects of research. So the design challenge described in this chapter has a second aspect: how to deploy new representations in such a way that they influence wider groups of people.

Overloaded, Underframed

A word first about the perceptual context. Although information overload is frequently discussed in the media—which help cause it—our dilemma is not that we receive too much information. We don't receive anywhere near the quantity of data it takes to overload our neurons; our minds are capable of processing and analyzing many gigabits of data per second—a lot more data than any of today's supercomputers can process and act on in real time. We feel flooded because we're getting information unfiltered, unsorted, and unframed. We lack ways to select what's important. The design task is to make information digestible, not to keep it out.

In biblical times, a shepherd boy sitting under a tree would "see" more of that tree than we would today, sitting under the same tree, because he was not distracted by other inputs. William Horton, a documentation designer, has to deal with the fact that we are horribly distracted by an oversupply of prepackaged information: "The 545 miles of shelves in the Library of Congress hold over one hundred million pieces of literature, including twenty-seven million books, twelve hundred newspapers on file, one hundred thousand films, eighty thousand television and five hundred thousand radio broadcasts, and a million other sound recordings. Those shelves bulge remorselessly: Every day of the year a thousand new book titles are added."[2] Ninety-five percent of all the scientists and writers who ever lived are alive,[3] and among them they publish twenty million words of technical information each day. The filtering systems we've designed, such as peer review, are collapsing. More than fifty-five hundred papers a day are being published. As a former magazine editor myself, this last number struck me as fearsome until I read that fewer than one-third of these texts are read by the editor of the journal concerned—and that 10 percent of them have not even been read by the professor whose name appears in print as its author, thanks to sterling work by armies of graduate students.[4] A big proportion of this data explosion is the product of a global science and technology machine in which specialists of a thousand persuasions write in private languages for a tiny number of their peers. Virtually none of their output makes it easier for citizens to engage in meaningful dialogue about the environment.

Scientific publishing makes a sizable contribution to the bigger picture, but the manuals of our high-tech society, which are meant to explain how it works, are an even worse distraction. The quantity of instructions needed to understand a technological device has multiplied a thousandfold in my lifetime. The pilot of a World War II Spitfire would consult a thousand-page manual if it wouldn't start and he wanted to fix it. By the early 1950s, the manual for the Spitfire's more sophisticated jet-propelled successor had grown to ten thousand pages. This document bloated to one hundred thousand pages by the 1960s, when avionics as well as jet propulsion had to be described. Today, it takes one million pages of documentation to explain how the B-2 stealth bomber works; no one person reads it cover to cover. The mobility of high-tech navy ships was compromised by this documentation proliferation: By the 1980s, they were carrying forty tons of paper, most of it kept above deck for ready reference; this raised the ship's center of gravity so much that its speed, maneuverability, and fuel economy were adversely affected. When the time came to build the Space Station Freedom, the only way to measure the amount of documentation required was not by quantity, but by cost: a billion dollars for documentation—5 percent of its total cost.[5]

Top-heavy warships, and warplanes that could not take off while carrying their own manual, were among the main drivers of the digitization of technical documentation. But this dematerialization of technical data has accelerated its growth. We now produce between one and two billion gigabytes of original information per year—roughly 250 megabytes for every man, woman, and child on the planet. In 2002 alone, five exabytes of new information—roughly five billion gigabytes—was created: That's like half a million libraries as big as the previously mentioned print collections of the Library of Congress.[6] Over a three-year period, we create significantly more information than has been created since the beginning of time.[7]

Vital Signs

Some of the scientists who helped unleash this data explosion are well aware of the dangers and want to fix the problem. One of these, computer scientist Danny Hillis, says we need "more signal, and less noise."[8] A long-running attempt to capture the biggest picture began when NASA launched the first civilian Earth observation satellite, Landsat, in 1972. This complex project was the fruit of governments' enthusiasm to peer down on Earth to monitor its atmosphere, oceans, forests, and deserts. The trouble is that although governments are always keen to know more about areas of the planet under their control—or about the location of natural resources in areas they do not—they are not yet inclined to be interested in, let alone take responsibility for, the whole.[9]

What would it mean to monitor our planet's signs in real time? Would it be feasible to design perceptual aids to help us to understand the invisible natural systems that surround us? In Germany, a design group called Art+Com has an interface ready and waiting. This interface, called T-Vision, generates the entire face of the Earth out of topographical data and satellite images. Using a level of detail to manage scenic complexity, the work presents a model of Earth as seen from a million kilometers above its surface or at the level of an office interior in Berlin. Other media artists have achieved just as stunning results at ground level. At a recent Venice Biennale of Architecture, multimedia artist David Rokeby presented a work entitled *Seen* that visualized the flows of people passing through and hanging out in Piazza San Marco. Rokeby used a video camera and applied special algorithms to each pixel to capture the trajectory of every pigeon and pedestrian in the piazza; each track left a fading trail that defined the direction and speed of movement. "We have a highly developed visual system that outperforms computers at many tasks involving large correlated fields of data," says Rokeby; "the computer is capable of shifting invisible phenomena into the range of our perception, allowing us to use our own highly refined abilities." This is especially true, Rokeby notes, of cross-temporal phenomena that constitute flow: movement patterns that happen too quickly or too slowly for us to properly register with our eyes.[10] We might feed into a T-Vision interface data from sensors spread over the landscape. John Gage of Sun Microsystems talks about sprinkling "smart dust" over the world—millions of tiny sensors that would monitor the physical world remotely. Wireless sensors could be dispersed anywhere: Tiny thermometers, miniature microphones, electronic noses, location detectors, or motion sensors could provide information about the condition of the physical world and convert analog data about anything physical—pressure, light, gas, genes—into bits and bytes that they communicate wirelessly to a network.[11]

A lot of research into remote sensing is funded by the military. True, many of the military's applications of this technology involve sensing things in order to kill them, but it would not take much to repurpose these tools for civilian applications. The advertising for a once-classified product called GammaMaster proclaims, "Where Is Your Radiation Detector When You Really Need It?—On Your Wrist!" A precision timepiece with a built-in Geiger counter, the GammaMaster bills itself as "ideal for emergency personnel who may have to respond to accidents, incidents or terrorist attacks, which could involve radioactive material."[12] I'm also taken by the HazMat Smart Strip, a baseball-card-sized device that changes color when exposed to nerve agents, cyanide, chlorine, fluoride, arsenic—in liquid or aerosol form—and other substances that are toxic in small quantities. A change in color in any of eight categories alerts users to "get additional gear, decontaminate, or evacuate." "It's not cool to use your nose to detect chemical spills," said Lieutenant Cris Aguirre, a hazardous materials technician and a Smart Strip user from the Miami-Dade Fire Department in South Florida.[13] I can imagine repurposing such a gadget so that it yells at me when I waste a lot of energy, too.

Some inventive activists are already using environmental sensors as an extension of human senses in a real-world context. The Digital Library for Earth Systems Education (DLESE) involves teachers, students, and scientists in a project to create a library of maps, images, data sets, visualizations, assessment activities, and online courses.[14] In New York State's Black Rock Forest, a consortium of schools, colleges, and research institutions, participants in DLESE, study topics ranging from tree rings to glacial geology, in situ. The forest has been "instrumented" (their word) with environmental sensors that continuously measure and record properties of the air, soil, and water. The sensors sense the same phenomena as human senses, but do so 24 hours a day and 365 days a year. Interpretation of data is as important in the project as collecting them. "Probably the most important insight you can convey from real time data is that environmental factors vary across both time and space," says Kim Kastens at the forest's Lamont-Doherty Earth Observatory, a partner in the educational effort. "Thinking about causes leads to questions like: why is it that air temperature goes up and down on a 24 hour cycle? why is it that one site consistently has lower relative humidity than the other?" Another educational tool used in the Black Rock Forest work, Data Harvester, enables students to perceive the ways that environmental data vary through time (by generating time series graphs) and through space (by plotting the data on maps).[15]

For the Australian engineer and artist Natalie Jeremijenko, our places are so complex that robust understanding of them needs to develop from approaching phenomena from many different angles, disciplines, and points of view and trying to make sense of conflicting evidence. In her project OneTree, Jeremijenko uses trees as a kind of electronic and biological instrument, or "blogservatory." Cloned trees that have been raised in identical environmental conditions are planted in pairs throughout parks and other public sites around the San Francisco Bay Area. "In the next 50–100 years," according to Jeremijenko, "they will continue to render the environmental and social differences to which they are exposed. This is the basis for a distributed data collection project that...provides a different context for public discourse of global climate change than one that is based on passive consumption of authoritative data."[16] The goal of this project is a collective one: to enable ongoing monitoring and intelligent interpretation of data thereby gathered by many interested persons, lay and expert alike. For instance, a local perfume developer, Yosh Han, anticipates that leaves from the different sites of these genetically identical trees will have different smells; researchers interested in asthma rates in varying neighborhoods can monitor the absorption of particulate matter, or grime (which clogs the stomata in leaves and irritates the alveoli in our lungs), on the leaves of the genetically identical trees. In another project, the Map for Bikes and Birds, Jeremijenko and colleagues will facilitate the collective observation and volunteer monitoring of many other environmental interactions that create the dynamic spectacle of the San Francisco Bay Area. Anyone can upload his or her observations, speculations, and ideas onto each site's blogservatory.

Harvesting accurate data is one thing; deciding what the data mean, and what to do about them, is another. Environmental sensing—by humans, by remote sensors, or by trees—raises tricky issues of calibration. Who determines where the red line starts that indicates when the measurements of a variable have reached a level that shows it is harmful? People and cultures evaluate data in different ways. An Eskimo might judge to be too hot a room that a child from New York would find just right. Comparable differences of interpretation occur on a planetary scale. Violent arguments greeted publication of the Danish scientist Bjorn Lomborg's *The Skeptical Environmentalist* in 2001 because Lomborg questioned the way ecological data had been interpreted.[17] For me, the Lomborg debate missed the point. Without defending sloppy scientific reporting, I question whether it is necessary for ecological doomsday scenarios to be true for them to be important. Uncertainty is a persistent feature of a complex world. We cannot prove that the world will become uninhabitable for humans. Neither can we prove that it will not.[18]

Planetary Dashboards

Systems literacy is not just about measurement. The learning journey up the ladder of complexity—from quarks, to atoms, to molecules, to organisms, to ecosystems—will be made using judgment as much as instruments. Simulations about key scientific ideas and visualizations of complex knowledge can attract attention—but the best learning takes place when groups of people interact physically and perceptually with scientific knowledge, and with each other, in a critical spirit. The point of systems literacy is to enable collaborative action, to develop a shared vision of where we want to be.

Before-and-after knowledge maps are useful in this regard; they can represent the state of a system now and its state as we would wish it to be in the future. Many businesses already use spreadsheets in this way for numbers: Spreadsheets are a kind of map that enables "what if?" scenarios to be recalculated with different variables factored in. As I explained in chapter 3, spreadsheets have evolved into important tools for the control of complex systems. Gary Reiner, chief information officer of General Electric, has a long-term plan to put all the company's vital processes into an uber-spreadsheet, digitizing as much of the business as possible. As he told the journalist Ludwig Siegele, this not only means buying and selling most things online but, more important, "setting up a digital nervous system that connects anything and everything involved in the company's business." The aim is to monitor IT systems, factories, and employees, as well as suppliers, customers, and products, in real time, he told Siegele; company-wide "digital dashboards" would compare how certain measurements, such as response times or sales, perform against goals.[19] "From a distance it [Reiner's dashboard] looks like a Mondrian canvas in green, yellow and red," Siegele recounted; "a closer look reveals that the colours signal the status of software applications critical to GE's business. If one of the programs stays red or even yellow for too long, Mr. Reiner gets the system to e-mail the people in charge. He can also see when he had to intervene the last time, or how individual applications—such as programs to manage book-keeping or orders—have performed." According to Siegele, "to advocates of the concept, the real-time enterprise is a giant spreadsheet in which new information, such as an order, is automatically processed and percolates through a firm's computer systems and those of its suppliers."[20]

In the civilian domain, the Canadian designer Bruce Mau staged a large exhibition as his response to our pressing need to make visible the as yet invisible. "So much of life occurs outside the range of visible light," explained Mau at the time. "Through scientific tools and methods, we have reached far beyond this narrow slice of the electromagnetic spectrum to colonize its full range, from radio waves and infrared to x-rays, gamma radiation and cosmic rays. Now, existence in all its glorious complexity, from the dynamic division of living cells to the vastness and vibrancy of the entire known universe, has been rendered accessible to our visual capacity."[21]

Many of the components and systems required for real-time business already exist. The global spreadsheet is a matter of joining them together. Juice Software, based in New York, helps users link spreadsheet cells to data sources. KnowNow helps firms improve the visibility of critical business information. A company called Rapt provides pricing optimization software based on real-time feedback from markets. Arzoon (which changed its name from Vigilance) helps multinationals "globally manage your inventory motion." Closedloop Solutions, SeeBeyond, CrossWorlds: The list of players in this vast enterprise is as endless as is the inventiveness of their names.

The potential market is huge. Dashboards will be needed for buildings, cities, and regions—not just for corporations. Buildings, for example, consume a lot of energy—but we don't "see" heat flying out of the windows. If we could, our behavior and use of the building would probably change. A dashboard to monitor the ecological footprint of a city would also be handy. Real-time representations of energy performance can help us use buildings and places in new and more sustainable (and cheaper) ways.

A Word of Caution

Some late entries to the field are wildly exaggerating what dashboards might (or should) do. Unisys is selling something called the 3D Visible Enterprise with a bewitching promise: "Imagine any change, strategic or operational, and knowing how it will affect every layer and process of your organization. See cause-effect relationships that were hidden. See interactions from multiple perspectives. We're creating a highly predictive tool that allows you to see effects of change and make smarter choices." Bizarrely, the website of the new service features a crystal ball on its home page that shatters as the page announces, "The future isn't what it used to be. Now it's more predictable because it's more visible." An informational page then appears, from which one can link to a case study headlined "Integrated Justice Optimized with 3D Visible Enterprise," which make the implausible—if not logically impossible—promise that the "Unisys 3D Visible Enterprise methodology will help government decision-makers see the effects of changes even before they're made."[22]

Criticism of the global-dashboard idea goes back a long way. Saint Augustine, in *City of God*, attacked "scenic games" as being responsible for the death of the soul. Ivan Illich believed that things all started to go wrong in 1120, when monks stopped reading texts aloud to each other and became solitary scholars.[23] Some art historians date the birth of the spectator to the seventeenth-century invention of linear perspective. Martin Jay, a contemporary chronicler of the passive role accorded to spectators in Western thought, charges that visual information tends to be "too static . . . in comparison with other senses; vision still seems tied to the Platonic valorization of static eternal Being, over dynamic, ephemeral Becoming."[24] Another critic of pictorial information, Susan Sontag, memorably alerted us to the danger that photographs—and by implication all visualizations—have a tendency to "shrivel sympathy. An image is drained of its force by the way that it is used," she warned. "Images shown on television are, by definition, images of which one sooner or later tires. Image-glut keeps attention light, mobile, relatively indifferent to content."[25]

The other problem with dashboards is that new images, however striking, enter a world that is already filled with signs and ads and a million other competing signals. Matthew Chalmers, a psychologist at Glasgow University, warns that striking visuals can cause a loss of narrative flow if they obliterate the links and connections that constitute the trail of a story.[26] Understanding is situational, and we live in a society of spectacle wherein a thousand and one other messages vie constantly for our attention.

Visual to Sensual

Visual representations also undervalue the knowledge we have by virtue of having bodies. Sensitivity to changes in our environment through time develop best if we learn to use all our senses, not just sight. Otherwise stated, our monitoring systems need to be more visceral. In his 1945 book *The Phenomenology of Perception*, the philosopher Maurice Merleau-Ponty argued that perception is a process in which an active body enters into a "communion" with its surroundings. Perception, for Merleau-Ponty, is a continuous interaction that involves the subject's intentions, expectations, and physical actions. There is no purely active "sender" nor any purely passive "receiver," he wrote; without action, there can be no experience of anything "external" to the subject. "The body is our general medium for having a world; sight and movement are specific ways of entering into relationships with objects," he wrote.[27] For Merleau-Ponty and other critics of visuality as a privileged medium of understanding, it is meaningless to talk about perceptual processes of seeing without reference to all the senses, to the total physical environment in which the body is situated.[28] Merleau-Ponty memorably counseled us to "move beyond high altitude thinking... towards a closer engagement with the world made flesh."[29]

Designers struggling to improve the usability of computer systems have learned the hard way about the limits to disembodied visual information. "Understanding is not only embodied, it is also situated," says anthropologist Lucy Suchman, who wrote a classic text on the subject. Suchman has spent her career trying to persuade senior managers and computer scientists that "human activity is not primarily as rational, planned and controlled as we like to think. It is better described as situated, social, and in direct response to the physical and social environment." Meaning is always created in a situation, continues Suchman; "ordinary interpersonal interaction is far more complex than the constrained and choreographed interactions enabled by computers."[30] The problem for Suchman and her design colleagues is that their bosses and clients remain in thrall to technology-based notions such as "context independence" and "anytime, anywhere functionality"—a beguiling litany now augmented by the 3D Visible Enterprise I mentioned earlier in the chapter. These are catchy sales slogans, but misleading and irresponsible descriptions of how computers and people interact.

In reaction to the limited bandwidth of technology-enhanced vision, ecological thinkers emphasize that our senses—taste, smell, sight, hearing, touch—are the fundamental avenues of connection between the self and the world.[31] Luis Fernández-Galiano, in a remarkable book called *Fire and Memory*, argues that we need to shift our perceptions "from the eye to the skin—to develop not just an understanding, but a feeling of how complex urban flows and processes work."[32] When I met him at a 2002 Doors of Perception conference in Amsterdam, Fernández-Galiano elaborated that "we need sensual, not just visual, seismographs."

The Internet, especially when coupled with sensors and telerobotic devices, potentially enables us to observe and even act on distant objects. But do these techniques provide us with meaningful knowledge? This is the central question of what Ken Goldberg, a professor at the University of California at Los Angeles, calls "telepistemology"—the study of knowledge acquired at a distance. Cyberspace presents us with a dilemma, he says; we are physical beings who experience the world through our bodies. Are we being deceived? What can we know? "These questions in the philosophy are hardly new—they date back to Plato and Aristotle," Goldberg notes. "Now, however, if we are to measure and interpret the state of invisible systems around us, we have to make important judgments about the value of knowledge that is technologically mediated."[33]

We cannot wait for philosophers to resolve two-thousand-year-old differences about the status of different kinds of knowledge before looking for new ways to perceive the consequences of our actions for the health of the planet. Whether or not one set of data is or is not "true" is not the main issue. The purpose of new perceptual aids is to stimulate us to reflect more critically about the consequences of our actions for larger systems. For Terry Winograd and Fernando Flores, authors of a classic book called *Understanding Computers and Cognition*, the issue is not one of theoretical exactitude. Practical understanding, they argue, is more fundamental than detached theoretical understanding. "We cannot," they observe, "deal with 'organism' and 'environment' as two interacting, independent things."[34] The consequence of that appears to be that augmenting reality and augmenting our capacity to sense the invisible are interrelated tasks.

Teach the World to Speak

At Teyler's Museum in Haarlem, in The Netherlands, a magnificent sound synthesizer is on display that was once used for imitating vocal sounds. Eight chunky resonators, a bit like miniature brass water boilers, are attached to electronic tuning forks that are actuated by clunky copper coils. A keyboard, containing eight white keys, is mounted on an aged wooden plinth. The machine is dated 1859.

Nearly 150 years later, it's still not much fun listening to machines. Microsoft, IBM, and other companies have spent billions of dollars trying to enable us to converse with computers the way people did with HAL in the movie *2001: A Space Odyssey*. But progress is painfully slow. Computer scientist Ben Shneiderman believes the whole effort is misguided, if only because—for computers and people alike—"it's hard to speak and think at the same time."[35] Speech interfaces are difficult to design effectively at the best of times, he says; they flourish most where they employ normal human conversational techniques—but that's terribly hard to achieve. Other designers agree that natural language is so heavily dependent on shared understanding, a shared knowledge base, and shared cultural experiences that there is no evidence that computers will ever be able to understand human language in the way other humans do. "So much of our communication is based on nuance, gesture, and inflection, that although it might be a year or two before computers can recognize our words, it might be decades—if ever—before computers correctly infer our meaning," say Winograd and Flores.[36] Even then, the simplest of tasks can go wrong. I once visited the research labs of Sharp, in Japan, where our host boldly stated "Open!" (in English) to a sliding glass door. It stayed shut, however, until he went behind a curtain and flipped a switch. "Sorry," said my rueful host, "it was set to Japanese." The upshot is that while speech may help blind and disabled people interact with computers, it's unlikely to become the dominant way we connect with the planet and its vital signs.

Pssst!

Natural-language interfaces may elude us, but those based on other kinds of sound are more promising. The advent of ubiquitous computing has accelerated interest in sound as a medium of interaction with the environment—human-made or otherwise. So although computers may disappear, they are unlikely to go quietly. Research into the "sonification of hybrid objects" proceeds apace. This is the use of sound to display data, monitor systems, and provide enhanced user interfaces for computers and virtual-reality systems.[37] Behind the beeps and squawks that emanate from the technical devices that fill our lives lies a growing body of research into sonification. In one pan-European project called The Sounding Object, researchers from diverse fields, such as experimental psychology, signal processing, human-computer interaction, and acoustics, are developing a phenomenology and a psychophysics of "sound events" (which I think means noises) that are relevant for interaction with and among artifacts.[38] Researchers at Stanford University are even using synthesized human vowel sounds to help clinicians interpret data as they investigate tissue in the human colon.[39] (I have not had the opportunity to listen to what the experiment sounds like, but it boggles the mind.)

Sound is particularly good for signaling changes in system states. With sonification, applications can be designed to produce a background tone or tempo that increases in pitch or speed as data change. Sound also provides insight into patterns that may not be apparent on a purely visual interface. "If you're driving a stick shift, you change gears when the engine revs up too high, without thinking," explains David Jameson, a project manager at IBM's Computer Music Center and former member of the 1970s Irish band Time Machine. "You do it without thinking, even while talking to a passenger."[40] Much of the research on sonification focuses on determining what kinds of noises work best to indicate information flow. Thus, a tone tracking the stock market would likely be a pleasant background tone that changes pitch with the arrival of new data.[41] Rhythm and pitch can be used to give each alarm a distinct identity, to convey the appropriate sense of urgency, and to mimic the alarm's meaning. Bill Gaver, a pioneer of sound used in interaction design, says that "auditory interfaces have so far drawn relatively little on the profound possibilities of music. Rhythm, for example, offers a great deal of inherent structure that could be mapped to the structure of data or events. Gaver cites the example of increasing tempo that indicates that the speed of an aircraft is too high. If there's a drawback to the use of sonic alarms, it's that they quickly proliferate. As many as sixty alarms may have sounded during the 1979 Three Mile Island nuclear power plant accident.[42]

The idea that sound might be a better communication medium than vision in the way that it attracts and holds our attention through time is not new. In 1917 the founder of the futurist movement, F. T. Marinetti, wrote that "noise is the language of the new human-mechanical life...music is closely related to human perceptions of time and its segmentation."[43] The art historian Ernst Gombrich has explained that in listening to repeated sounds, like the ticking of a clock, the dripping of a tap, or the rumbling of a train, we subdivide and shape the flow of identical impressions by projecting alternative rhythms. In music, it is the performer who sets the accents according to the demands of the score: There is no choice but to follow the auditory patterning. "Humans are sensitive to change, but we don't like perceiving too much of it," Gombrich observed. "Our mental apparatus is set somewhat like a homeostat indicating 'no change' until a break in continuity demands and arouses attention."[44] This is why the Geiger counter is so effective. Its low-level clicking makes us aware; a crescendo of noise triggers our bodily flight responses: Get out of here!

There's a relationship, of course, between the design of sound-based information systems and making music. Good musicians know all about ways to attract, but not overload, our attention. In recent years, as human beings have become increasingly frazzled by acceleration, some artists have searched for stillness. Brian Eno's *Music for Airports* album, in 1978, offered nervous travelers a moment of calm amid the worry and confusion of perpetual motion. Recalls David Toop, "Eno's music offered a kind of glue with which briefly to cement together the fragments engendered by such a fluid, potentially stressful environment."[45]

Whereas Eno created music as a counterpoint to urban clamor, others are tackling the clamor itself. The first person to tackle noise pollution directly was a Canadian, R. Murray Schafer. Schafer established the World Soundscape Project during the late 1960s as an educational and research group. He argued at the time that to improve the soundscape, we need to increase sonological competence through an education program that attempts to imbue new generations with an appreciation of environmental sound. It is hard not to pity Schafer as a sonic King Canute; the world is surely noisier now than when he began his crusade. But three decades later, sound-sensitive design projects continue to emerge.[46] In a project called Tuning the City, interaction designer Benjamin Rubin studied the use of sound as an information medium in the New York City subway network. This huge system, with its hundreds of stations and thousands of trains, uses three designed signals: those marking turnstile transactions, train arrival, and the closing of subway car doors. The three sounds are clearly audible but bear no meaningful harmonic relationship to one another; the train arrival signal, for example, is often masked by the turnstile beeps. This is the predictable result, says Rubin, of using sounds within the same one-third-octave frequency range: "Despite its use of tonal signals, the mix that results sounds unintentional, technological, and out of tune; the New York City subway system sounds decidedly unmusical." The turnstile bank in particular, with its microtonal pitch variations, often sounds like a badly tuned instrument. Since the pitch variation is random and carries no information, we perceive it as mildly grating dissonance. Sound in the subway is viewed by riders as entirely utilitarian. Rubin has now designed a new set of sounds, based on the notion of a wind chime, to improve communication effectiveness by using a wider variety of easily distinguished signals and to improve listenability through the use of an expanded sound palette and deliberate composition. A variety of timbres, pitches, and rhythms are used to create a soundscape that is harmonic, varied, and textured.[47]

"Our cities talk to us," says the typographer Paul Elliman. They speak from the walls and ceilings of buildings, from elevator cars, supermarket checkouts, and subway trains. Objects and spaces offer directional advice, even warnings. These exchanges may not amount to a full dialog, but through a range of technology, involving recordings as well as complex language-modeling programs, our movement is guided increasingly by the voices of audio signage. These spoken forms of way finding occupy their own place in the city, which Elliman calls an "acousmatic space."[48] The term, which comes from Michel Chion's film theory, describes characters that speak but remain concealed. New York subway car announcements feature presenters from Bloomberg radio, the station owned by the mayor, Michael Bloomberg—making Bloomberg one of Chion's concealed speakers.

Airports and railway stations were the first places to adopt talking signs. Since the 1970s, "Mind the Gap!" warnings on London's underground have been a sonic landmark for anyone visiting the city. In Amsterdam, a row ensued when a soap actor's voice was used to announce stations on the city's metro. On the Madrid subway, the recorded voices of two opera singers perform a short duet just before each station. The male singer opens with "Próxima estación" and is closely followed by the female singer, who identifies the stop: "Plaza de Castilla." In Shanghai, a friendly female voice follows you from train to platform, to ticket hall, to street, pointing out safety features and directions, suggesting bars, restaurants, and department stores. Voice, once thought of as uniquely human, is "a new benchmark in our relationship with technology," says Elliman—talking and walking us though the spaces of the city.[49]

In his book *Audio-Vision*, the film theorist Michel Chion proposes that one kind of sensual perception influences another and transforms it. People have a natural urge to fuse sounds and images, in particular, as a strategy for making sense of the world. We never see the same thing when we also hear; we don't hear the same thing when we see it as well. Chion's book is about how this tendency extends to our experiences of viewing films, in which cinematic and theatrical sound influences our perception of time, including our perception of movement, speed, rhythm, and pacing. The eye is more spatially adept, the ear more temporally adept. The eye perceives more slowly because it has more to do at once: It must explore in space as well as follow along in time. People are more capable of acutely tracking the details of motion with the ear than with the eye; people who possess both sight and hearing can usually understand spoken language faster than they can read.[50]

Ouch!

Our monitoring systems might have more impact if they could touch us, literally. Some designers are working on this. Interaction that involves physical contact between a user and a computer is referred to as haptic, after the Greek word meaning touch, or contact. A surprising thesis is that rather than the most difficult of social senses to transmit, touch may well be the easiest. Back in 1993 Ken Goldberg (who edited the book on telepistemology I referred to earlier) and Richard Wallace connected two simple touch sensors and haptic actuators to create Datamitt. One of these devices was placed inside a metal tube on each coast of the United States, so that if a participant in Los Angeles placed her hand inside the Datamitt there and squeezed, a participant in New York with her hand inside the Datamitt there would feel the pressure, and vice versa. Datamitt was remarkable for its low resolution: It incorporated a one-bit sensor actuator whose modes were squeeze or no-squeeze, with nothing in between. And yet the effect was quite engaging. So while it is true that a true handshake is a highly situated, multisensory experience—complete with eye contact, sweaty palms or otherwise—a low-bandwidth version can do a pretty good job.[51]

Yuck!

What if things smelled bad when they were going wrong? Robert Levine, in *A Geography of Time*, tells us that for the Ongee of the Andaman Islands (in the Indian Ocean), the universe and everything in it is defined by smell. Their calendar is constructed on the basis of the odors of flowers that come into bloom at different times of the year. When greeting someone, the Ongee do not ask, "How are you?" but "Konyune onorange-tanka?" meaning "How is your nose?" Natives of the Adaman jungle in India have constructed a complex annual calendar built around the sequence of dominant smells of trees and shrubs in their environment. According to Levine, "When they want to check the time of year, they simply smell the odors outside their door."[52]

Smell is probably the most undervalued of the senses in modern Western cultures. According to cultural historian Kate Fox, this was not always so: The current low status of smell in the West is a result of the "revaluation of the senses" by philosophers and scientists of the eighteenth and nineteenth centuries. The intellectual elite of this period decreed sight to be the all-important, up-market, superior sense, the sense of reason and civilization, writes Fox, "while the sense of smell was deemed to be of a considerably lower order—a primitive, brutish ability associated with savagery and even madness. The emotional potency of smell was felt to threaten the impersonal, rational detachment of modern scientific thinking."[53] Although the human sense of smell is a hundred times less acute than that of a dog, it is nonetheless more acute than we sometimes realize. We can recognize thousands of different smells, and we are able to detect odors even in infinitesimal quantities. According to Fox, humans are capable of detecting certain substances in dilutions of less than one part in several billion parts of air. "We may not be able to match the olfactory feats of bloodhounds," she writes, "but we can, for example, 'track' a trail of invisible human footprints across clean blotting paper."[54]

The development of more sophisticated technology for synthesizing or "capturing" previously elusive smells appears to be keeping pace with the advances in high-tech noses to detect the smells we already have. "Headspace" technology now allows accurate analysis and synthetic reproduction of almost any smell. One new fragrance for men allegedly includes both the distinctive odor of a famous New York tobacconist shop and "essence of racing car." Another manufacturer claims to have reproduced the scent of financial newspapers. A process known as "soft extraction," which has been in use for some time in the food industry, is the latest vogue among perfume manufacturers. By passing a special form of carbon dioxide through an object such as a coffee bean, food technologists have been able to extract coffee aroma. The procedure is now being used to capture the fragrance of flowers that are resistant to more traditional scent extraction techniques.

When he was a researcher at MIT's Media Lab, Joseph "Jofish" Kaye looked at ways to use smell proactively as a medium of interaction.[55] Scent can exist quietly in the background, he observes, unnoticed by our conscious mind, but can bring itself to our attention when necessary—as in cases such as the alarming odor of burning electrical insulation. A number of companies, notably Digiscents and TriSenx, have announced plans to produce computer-controlled devices that output smell. The companies' literature proposes scented websites and "smelltracks" for DVDs or games.

Kaye believes that the optimal use of the smell emission technology is in generation of a smell icon, or "smicon": a release of scent to convey information about an event or condition. "We have evolved to use olfaction to sense information about our environment," says Kaye. "Information about burning, what's being cooked, food freshness, and disease diagnosis can all be conveyed using smell."[56] Another interaction designer, Bill Gaver, at the Royal College of Art in London, has proposed the use of scent emission to let the user know a loved one is thinking of him or her.[57] Other designers have proposed less poetic applications such as the display of stock market changes through a personal device held in the pocket that would heat up or cool down depending on the state of the market. A device known as Dollars & Scents releases scents into the air: roses if the market is going up, and lemons if it is going down.

I began this chapter with a story about traveling storytellers in India. They are an example of embodied, situated, and unmediated communication that prevailed before we invented mass media. For hundreds of years, when the majority of the population was illiterate, participatory ritual and performance were the main ways that beliefs were shared within a culture. Today's Internet, virtual-reality technology, and new media as a whole are exciting additions to the communication landscape—but they are not a substitute for direct, embodied communication. Besides, if the ozone layer had a voice and could tell us about its hole, would we listen? I doubt it. Adding more voices to an already noisy environment is more likely to make us switch off than on—especially if those voices are harbingers of bad news about the environment. The same caveat applies if we feed the data from remote environmental sensing into fancy interactive displays.

A backlash against interactive displays in museums and science centers is already evident. Armando Iannucci, a British writer, took his children to the Natural History Museum in London; he concluded that "interactivity is a superficial sham leading only to hunger and emptiness. The relentless, raucous, lapel-grabbing interactivity of the newer displays was so off-putting. The display cases invited participation in a process, only to lead you to the conclusion that the process was not worth pursuing. Interactivity implies participation—but does not deliver it."[58] Dwell time at an interactive exhibit at the average science center is forty seconds.

Don't Look, Talk

"All knowledge is dialogic," said the theologian Martin Buber.[59] Maybe we just need to talk to other human beings more—face to face. It sounds trite, but for thousands of years, talk was one of the main ways that humans tried to understand and influence the world around them. Then came media. Ivan Illich discovered that in the 1930s, nine out of ten words that a man had heard when he reached the age of twenty were words spoken to him directly—one to one, or as a member of a crowd—by somebody whom he could touch and feel and smell. By the 1970s, that proportion had been reversed: About nine out of ten words heard in a day were spoken through a loudspeaker. "Computers are doing to communication what fences did to pastures and cars did to streets," Illich said in 1982.[60] For Illich, there was a huge difference between a colloquial tongue—what people say to each other in a context, with meaning—and a language uttered by people into microphones.

Theodor Zeldin, who has written a book about conversation, believes that conversation can penetrate the intellectual barriers that are often associated with specialized professions. "The really big scientific revolutions have been the invention not of some new machine, but of new ways of talking about things," argues Zeldin, adding, "what we need now is stimulation, not information."[61] Thirty-five years after Illich's comments about conversation, Zeldin's book has clearly struck a chord; one reviewer said

Zeldin's book signified "the end of rational planning and the turn to conversational communities."[62]

Zeldin's ideas on conversation are not just talk. He has set up a organization called The Oxford Muse to help people and organizations converse to good effect. At one conversation dinner, held at the World Economic Forum in Davos, participants sat at tables laid for two, each with a partner they had never met before. A "Muse Conversation Menu" listed twenty-four topics through which they could discover what sort of person they were meeting and his or her ideas on many different aspects of life (such as ambition, curiosity, fear, friendship, and the relations of the sexes and of civilizations). One eminent participant said he would never again give a dinner party without this menu, because he hated superficial chat. Another said he had in just two hours made a friend who was closer than many he had known much longer. A third said he had never revealed so much about himself to anybody except his wife.

When someone we trust tells us to our face that a thing is important, we pay attention. Conversation is a more powerful medium of understanding than messages projected at us by media. But tomorrow's literacies need not exclude artifice and creativity. Someone has to orchestrate the dinners and cook the food. The context where we eat and talk can be enhanced by artful means. Music, the visual arts, and especially time-based or performance art can powerfully enhance our capacity to understand processes and systems. When added to the designer's powerful representations, the artist's critical intuition—especially when used to trigger our own insight—can shift our focus away from the material world and its visual artifacts toward a deeper understanding of natural processes and social relationships.

Joining In

For nearly a hundred years now, the artistic avant garde has fought to bridge the schism in Western thought that separates the creator from the spectator. Three generations of nonconformists have bitterly opposed art and literature whose sole purpose is entertainment. Throughout the twentieth century, avant-garde artists' groups such as the Russian Constructivists, the Dada artists, Surrealists, COBRA, Lettrists, and Fluxus fought against the idea that art was about the creation of beautiful, static forms.

Fluxus—a movement of artists influenced by John Cage—considered trace-less art forms (dance, music, song, and storytelling) to be an opportunity to modify the evolution of culture. Their approach was to make unexpected social contact with people. These artists remind their audiences: "there is no artifice here: this is happening now, in real time."[63] These groups and ideas all confronted the movement, energy, dynamism, and sheer process-ness that modern man encounters in the modern places we have made. They treated the deadness and catatonia of the technology-swamped public domain as both a rebuke and a challenge. Robert Irwin, who constantly pushes at the barriers that keep art from dealing with the universal experience of change, concludes that art should be "knowing in action" and "delegate a major share of the creative act to the observer."[64]

In recent times media art and so-called telepresence art have repurposed the Internet and wireless communication to trigger new kinds of experience. In the Australian artist Jeffrey Shaw's *Legible City*, participants bicycle down a virtual street where, instead of buildings, they pass words. Shaw worked with a writer to create the project, and together they produced a template for the words based on the grid—and actual buildings—of Manhattan. If the participant turns a corner, she moves from one narrative—or sentence—into another one. Another artistic use of technology that moved me tremendously was installed in the Netherlands Design Institute in 1994 by an English artist, Paul Sermon. Two identical blue sofas were placed in different locations. Each sofa faced a very large video monitor. On top of each monitor sat a video camera, pointing at you, the participant, as you sat on "your" sofa. Whenever someone sat down on the sofa at the other location, the two video camera images merged into one on the screen. The technology was simple, but the experience was sublime.

Keiici Irie, one of the most media-savvy of Japanese architects, used sound to animate and delineate space in a work called *Movable Realities*. Wearing headphones and walking round a space, participants passed through "cones" of sound, each a different sound or sequence. In a show called T-Zone, which Riiche Miyake and I did together in London and Glasgow, Irie created ten-meter-high slabs of glass behind which were video cameras that captured one's picture as one walked past and replayed it, with a delay, on small monitors. In Scotland we had to turn the thing off because the frequencies were interfering with air traffic control at Glasgow Airport. Another Japanese artist, Masaki Fujihata, has also achieved magical results with simple technology. In a piece called *Light on the Net*, visitors encountered a large monitor displaying the entrance hall to a building somewhere else, plus a seven-by-seven matrix of light bulbs in one corner of the screen. By clicking on any of them, participants from anywhere in the world were able to switch on one of the real bulbs in the distant building. The concept and its implementation were simple and beautiful. Even with something so simple as spelling out "Hi" from a distance, the effect was extraordinary.

The idea that time delay and distance contribute positively to reflection is not a new one. Aesthetic theories since the eighteenth century have seen spatial distance and temporal delay as preconditions for critical musing. Twentieth-century thinkers worried that space and time for reflection would be undermined by the culture of simultaneity ushered in by the telegraph. Decades later, Susan Sontag restated the same dilemma: How much do we really know about the trash heaps, slums, and wars depicted by today's imaging technologies? These technologies are supposed to give us a clearer image—but by sanitizing the subject, they prevent us from knowing reality itself.[65]

"In the Bay Area we are more likely to look to our palm pilots for information, than to look to the tree we are standing under," says Natalie Jeremijenko (who lives in San Francisco). "We are more familiar with distributed computation than the distributed human intelligence."[66] Today's media artists work with the ambiguity and tension between "here" and "there" that is an inherent property of communication technologies. They play games with mediation so that the participant is both the observer and the observed. In so doing, they sensitize us to the need to use media critically. Jeremijenko (discussed earlier as the originator of the OneTree project) created feral robotic dogs that would "sniff out" radioactive contamination and thereby locate radioactive hot spots.

Tomorrow's Literacies

If tomorrow's literacies are to be system and process literacies, then the tools and sensibility of media and network art have two crucial roles to play. First, in terms of content, media art can draw our attention to phenomena in our world that exist but are not seen—the hidden forces that shape the places and situations we live in. Second, media art can also teach us new processes of collaborative inquiry. Increasing numbers of artists work in a collaborative mode using telecommunications. Employing computers, video, modems, and other devices, these artists use visual outputs within a much larger interactive, bidirectional communication context. Images and graphics are created not simply to be transmitted by an artist from one point to another, but to spark a multidirectional visual dialogue with other artists and participants in remote locations. "Once an event is over," explains the critic Eduardo Kac, "images and graphics stand not as the result, but as documentation of the process of visual dialogue promoted by the participants."[67] This new art is collaborative and interactive. It uses text, sound, image, and virtual touch to provoke a critical response to the dominant linear model of communication that privileges the artist as the codifier of messages. The new shape of communications is more like a place than a production line.

9 | Smartness

Imagine, for a moment, that you are a penguin. You hang around on ice floes, in extreme cold, for weeks on end. Standing there, in bare feet, you are able to sustain a temperature differential between your own body and the outside environment of eighty degrees Celsius. Every now and again, when you're feeling hungry, you jump into the icy water, catch a fish, and then clamber back onto a sunny beach. You do this without ever over- or underheating. The secret behind this impressive thermal performance lies in your dense feathers: When a nasty wind gets up, they reduce airflow around your body so that it slows down and warms up, like the water inside a wetsuit. Your feet are also remarkable: They open like a fan to get rid of excess heat when you land from a flight—then, back on the ice, they act like radiators and heat up the ground where you're standing.[1]

I often wish I were a penguin when contemplating the Honeywell Chromotherm III central heating controller that sits on the wall of my home in Amsterdam. This little box is covered with arrows and buttons and words and—of course—a digital display. It was designed to look technical and smart, and I don't doubt that somewhere inside its little head thoughts, of a kind, are clattering around. But the Chromo's interface is, to me at least, incomprehensible, and the fifty-page instruction manual long ago disappeared. So it leads a life of its own. And a profligate life it is: The central heating system it "controls" is ruinously inefficient. My house is heated uniformly from top to bottom throughout the days and evenings—whether or not I am at home or even in the country. A thermal-engineering acquaintance reckons that my domestic energy performance is *ten thousand times* less efficient than the penguin's.

How smart is that? I'm the most advanced mammal on the planet, and my Chromotherm is supposed to be a smart product—but the penguin is just a dumb bird. It doesn't add up. And if it doesn't add up now, how much worse will things get when my Chromotherm's children and grandchildren, swarms of smart devices and pervasive computing and "ambient intelligence," turn up?

Ubiquitous computing spreads the appearance of intelligence and connectivity to more or less everything. Whether all these chips will make for a better product—let alone a better life—is a moot point. Not long ago, I rented a car in which was installed a high-end Pioneer car radio. I want to share with you a summary of the specifications that appear in the owner's manual (see box 9.1). I felt as if I had an "auto-flap motorized face" myself by the time I'd struggled through this list, only to find that one piece of high-tech wizardry was missing: an on-off switch! As a result, I did the entire journey without music.

They call this phenomenon "feature drift" in consumer electronics—the engineering equivalent of playing with your food. And it's beginning to hurt a lot of companies, because a gap is opening up between the functionality of technology, on the one hand, and the perceived value of that

Box 9.1
Feature drift: Car radios

Supertuner III TM with RDS (Radio Data System); 24-Station, 6-Button (18FM/ 6AM) Presets; BSM (Best Stations Memory); AGC (Automatic Gain Control); Optimum CD Tracking Performance; Playback Compatible with Digital Audio CD-R; IP (Interactive Pioneer) Bus System Control; Multi-CD Player; Component Single CD or MD Players; Voice Commander (CD-VC50 & CD-VC60); TV Tuner (GEX-P7000TV); Disc Title Memory; 10-Character Display for Disc Title; Memory, CD Text (SCD & MCD) & NMD Title (With Scroll); Disc List; MOSFET45 (45W × 4-Channel High Power); HiVolt RCA PreOuts (×3 Pair); Two-Way Crossover (HPF and LPF); Front/Rear HPF; Sub-Out LBF; Sub-Out Level and Phase Control; EEQ Performance Chip; 3-Band Performance Equalizer; Easy EQ (EEQ) Switches; I-User EQ Presets (SuperBass, Powerful, Natural, Vocal, Flat, Custom); Source Custom EQ Memory; Selectable Loudness Control (Low, Mid, High, Off); Selectable FIE (Front Image Enhancer); Rear LPF; Auto-Flap Motorized Face; Detachable Face Security; DFS Alarm; Wireless Full-Function Smart Remote Control with Mounting Base; Cellular/Navigation Mute; Multi-Color Organic EL Display; Full-Motion Animated 3D Graphics; High Resolution Display (256 × 52 Pixels); High Resolution Display; Super Bright (60 Candela) with Wide Viewing Angle (170 Degrees); Level Indicator technology to the people who are supposed to buy it, on the other. I have enshrined this tendency in two design laws, the first of which I have taken the liberty of naming after myself. Thackara's law states:

If you put smart technology into a pointless product, the result will be a stupid product.

Thackara's law has a daughter, the law of diminishing amazement (LODA). LODA states that the more fancy tech you pack into a product, the harder it becomes to impress people with its benefits. I invented LODA after someone drove me across Germany in a brand-new top-of-the-line Mercedes. This mobile temple to technology had everything: remote keyless entry, full power train control, aircraft-like instrument clusters, adaptive suspension, theft-deterrent systems, crash sensors, diagnostics, traction control, seat memory (in five directions), satellite-based navigation, vehicle radar, intelligent cruise control. It was fun, I have to admit, being driven down an autobahn in the big Benz at 150 miles an hour—but the litany of gadgets recited by the proud owner left me cold. I felt: "So?" My nonamazement must have been a disappointment to my host, who had paid two hundred thousand dollars for the car—never mind to the brilliant engineers at Benz who sweated blood getting all this stuff to work.

When not hurtling down autobahnen, we also hear a lot in Europe about wired domestic appliances. But I can't say the prospect fills me with joy. Ericsson and Electrolux (among others) are developing a refrigerator that will sense when it is low on milk and order more direct from the supplier. Direct from the cow for all I know. I can just see it. I'll be driving home from work, and the phone will ring. "Your refrigerator is on the line," the car will say; "it wants you to pick up some milk on your way home." To which my response will be: "Tell the refrigerator I'm in a meeting."

Biomimicry

Why can't we all live as lightly as penguins? Nature offers us countless examples of designs that could help us meet our basic needs in more elegant and efficient ways than our man-made ones: how to keep warm, find shelter from the rain, get food. "Nature," says Janine Benyus, "crafts materials of a complexity and functionality that we can only envy." Benyus, author of a definitive book on biomimicry, points out that the inner shell of an abalone is twice as tough as our high-tech ceramics. Spider silk, ounce for ounce, is five times stronger than steel. Mussel adhesive works underwater and sticks to anything—without a primer. Bone, wood, tusks, heart muscle, antlers, skin, blood vessels, tendons—they are a "bounty of resilience," says Benyus, "miracle materials all."[2]

We do, on occasion, learn from nature—but we are clumsy students. The design of Kevlar, for example, was inspired by the properties of silk. Kevlar is indeed extremely tough: It can stop bullets. But compare, as Benyus has done, a quietly spinning spider to the violent and expensive process we need to manufacture Kevlar: "We pour petroleum-derived molecules into a pressurized vat of concentrated sulfuric acid and boil the noxious brew at several hundred degrees Celsius into a liquid crystal form. We subject this crunchy mush to extremely high pressures, in order to force the fibers into alignment as we draw them out. The energy input in this process is extreme, and the by-products are toxic. The spider, by comparison, makes her equally strong (and much tougher) fiber at body temperature—and without the need for high-pressure vats, heat, or corrosive acids. "She also produces locally," concludes Benyus, "with no need to drill holes in the middle of stormy oceans in order to obtain her raw materials."[3]

Perhaps we would learn more quickly from penguins and spiders if we were not surrounded by swarms of our own technologies. Stranded on an ice floe, with nothing but penguins for company, we'd probably study them more closely. But we live in a world filled with materials and devices invented by ourselves. I touched on today's flood of technical information in chapter 8. A comprehensive technical directory, in the improbable event that one could be produced, would contain four and a half million terms today—and would be growing at a fast-accelerating pace.

"I have a hammer, but I need a nail," say Swedish materials scientists. New opportunities presented by our global technology machine come faster than we can find uses for them. We've never before had to deal with such an uncontrolled increase in technical performance and forms. For the first million years or so after his appearance, man used essentially five materials to make all his tools and objects and structures: wood, rock, bone, horn, and leather—a small number, but themselves the product of millions of years of evolution. Today, in contrast, most big companies own research factories that churn out technical knowledge in impressive quantities. But they often don't know what to do with it. Sometimes they are unaware that particularly valuable inventions—which they have paid for—even exist. A few years ago, I organized the visit of twenty postgraduate design students to the six-hundred-person research labs of one of the world's leading glass manufacturers. For the students, it was like visiting Aladdin's cave. Everywhere they turned, they encountered technical innovations that triggered their imaginations: exotic surface treatments, lasers being used to project images on glass, experimental ways to suffuse light. In just two days, they came up with a series of scenarios for applying these technical marvels in daily-life contexts: "smart" shop windows, house windows that changed color, tabletops as monitors, even spectacles as personal digital assistants. The glass company's boffins (who you in the United States refer to as "experts") and management were astounded. It turned out that the company's economic lifeblood was the sale, in gigantic quantities, of plate glass—which preoccupied their marketing people—while the labs were busy mainly with well-paid but narrowly focused defense-related work on such applications as cockpits for military jump jets.

The great majority of the world's research facilities are just as narrowly focused, and the career model of scientific research amplifies the tendency for knowledge to pile up in vertically specialized "silos." Your career goes well if you specialize, and you become a star among stars if you invent a new discipline that nobody else understands. As a result we confront an innovation dilemma. We've constructed ourselves an industrial system that is brilliant on means, but pretty hopeless when it comes to ends. We can deliver amazing performance, but we are increasingly at a loss to understand what to make and why.

Materials of Invention

This is where design comes in. A conscious effort is needed—a design effort—to connect the properties of the myriad materials and processes available—whether natural or man-made—to the needs we have as people in our daily lives. This takes us into unknown territory. Designers and manufacturers are faced with an enormous and expanding field of possibilities—in the selection of materials and of industrial processes to transform them. Known and trusted physical limits, which used to be embedded in the skills and cultures of craftsmen and production engineers, are disappearing. As well as choosing among myriad alternatives to meet existing needs, designers also confront the problem: What should a product look like? What form should it take? New materials have no absolute form. Neither do they have "natural properties" to determine a product's shape. We are confronted, for the first time, by what the Museum of Modern Art's design curator Paola Antonelli has nicknamed "mutant materials."[4] Or as Ezio Manzini put it in his modern classic, *The Material of Invention*, "materials are no longer 'found.' Rather, we can now engineer materials to achieve a specific, desired performance."[5]

But what performance? The problem for companies and designers is that inventors and laboratories tend to categorize their materials according to what they are—rather than what they do or what they are for. Grouping materials by type makes sense in an archive and (to itself at least) in a company's sales catalogue—but such classification systems are of little help to the product designer or structural engineer. Confronted as she is by directories and databases bulging with thousands of plastics, ceramics, fiber, composites, rubbers and foams, glass, wood, and metals, it's hardly surprising that the busy designer so often reverts to tried and tested materials she has used in the past. What's needed are information systems—and multidisciplinary professional communities of knowledge exchange—that direct designers first to *properties*, and thence to the different materials or systems that possess them.

The most important property quality required of tomorrow's materials is lightness. The structures and systems we design have to act light, as well as be light—light to make, light to assemble, light in operation, light to recover, and light to recycle. For a natural organism, Benyus tells us in *Biomimicry*, shape is cheap, material is expensive. All the material it uses, it uses in an effective way. This is because a lot of metabolic energy is needed not just to assemble material, but also to disassemble it: According to the eminent British engineer Julian Vincent, who is one of the fathers of biomimetics, there are good reasons, based on evolutionary selection pressure, why biological organisms usually represent minimum-energy solutions to particular problems. "Biological organisms compete with each other for the use of available energy which comes from sunlight, or it is stored, as biomass, from previous eons of sunlight," explains Vincent. "If an organism uses more energy than its neighbor, it usually does not reproduce so well, leaves fewer offspring, so eventually dies out. The most successful organisms therefore take the minimum amount of energy and optimize the distribution of the energy between all its different functions."[6]

We're in a transition from an industrial system organized on the basis of the idea that material is cheap and that shape—the forming processes—is expensive. "To make a structure that stands up, we have tended to slap on layers of heavy reinforcement, which we call redundancy, not to design it more cunningly," says Vincent. Nature has completely internalized the chemistry of materials and the need to recycle. "We would not be here," says Vincent, "had not our ancestors rotted. All organisms are designed with the intention of being recycled. Learning from nature, this means we have to be careful about bond energies in materials and see that they can be broken down easily."[7]

Light structures need not only to use less matter, but also to use their matter more effectively. According to scientists at Xerox's Palo Alto Research Center (PARC), materials with these properties could be used in the future to build skyscrapers with "smart" structural columns that can change their physical properties. These columns could stiffen the building to resist high wind loads but could also soften it to help it ride out shock waves from an earthquake.[8] The problem with a technology-based smart structure—with its sensors, actuators, structural members, and control hardware—is that it's complex. Many elements have to work in harmony together to produce a system that works. So-called active systems of this kind require fast, real-time, stable, and failure-free computing. Scaling them up so that the system includes the deployment of the millions of sensors you'd need in a large building poses a tremendous complexity challenge in the design of software control architectures.

Could smartness be simpler? Researchers at Smart Architecture, in Holland, in their search for light structural solutions, have looked at the foundations that houses, factories, and other structures rest on.[9] The Earth itself is easily strong enough to support houses, towers, and offices. But builders have become accustomed to the tradition of hammering or pushing heavy concrete piles, weighing thousands of tons, deep into the ground. In Amsterdam, where I live, concrete piles sixty feet long are being hammered by gigantic machines into the Earth, one meter apart, as I (try to) write. Smart architecture proposes, as an alternative, to build structures on a light "floating" raft made out of polystyrene foam. This can only be part of the solution, since the density of the ground and the mud under a building tend to vary through time. Therefore, the raft needs to be put on some kind of smart stabilizing base that would be able to compensate for these changes. A structure with these properties could, say the researchers at PARC, be designed like a cuttlefish skeleton—which is extremely rigid despite the fact that its volume is only 7 percent solid.[10] Inside a cuttlefish are channels that alternate with layers of plates. Inside these narrow channels is a gas: By changing its pressure, the fish can go up and down. A cuttlefish-style trim layer under a building could work in a similar way.

But back to my penguin story. Buildings consume some 50 percent of the world's energy.[11] By some estimates, at least half that could be saved if heating and cooling systems were more sensitive to the minute-by-minute needs of users.[12] At present, even the most advanced buildings—never mind my wasteful home in Amsterdam—consume vast amounts of energy to sustain average temperatures even when rooms or buildings are empty. Traditional buildings perform little better: In the classic sealed-skin solution, a layer of bricks or cladding on the outside is backed by a layer of insulating foam: The system excludes the cold to a degree—but the gap has to be filled by energy-guzzling heating systems.

To act light, and not just be light, our buildings need the ability to sense and respond to changes in their environment—just like our own skin or a penguin's fur. Energy, materials, and space are consumed at prodigious rates when buildings are put up, but over the life of most buildings, cumulative energy costs usually exceed even these initial construction costs. Computer-driven actuators can adjust sunshades and enable the local control of openings, surfaces, and heating and cooling systems. A good example is the "liquid architecture" projects of NOX in The Netherlands.[13] Biomimics are impressed—but so far also baffled—by the penguin. So some designers are attempting to transform the skins of our buildings by learning from the polar bear.[14] Like the penguin, the polar bear maintains a steady body heat in extreme cold. The bear's skin, which is black, is covered in a thick layer of translucent white hairs; these combine with trapped air to form an insulating layer that absorbs heat brilliantly. The hairs themselves guide infrared light toward the skin. Each individual hair is able to convey any external heat back to the skin, which absorbs it. Transferring this kind of functionality to a building, say researchers, would mean a black facade: Panels would consist of two transparent layers with capillary-like tubes mimicking the hairs between them.

The potential is fantastic, but we have work to do persuading architects and building designers of our case. A growing number of building designers have recently begun to tackle the profligate and unsustainable energy performance of buildings, but many others have been more interested in the *appearance* of transparency, demassification, and lightness in buildings—with the result that their buildings' environmental footprint has in some cases increased in size.[15] Lightweight glazing systems, translucent floor and wall panels, and light-reflective finishes that look transparent, almost ethereal, can be horrendously heat inefficient when the total life costs are added up. Other "smart" and hard materials, such as modern ceramics and advanced composites, can be nearly as hard as diamonds and are equally resistant to heat and corrosion: They are being made into turbines, dental braces, prosthetic body implants, even bullet-proof face masks. But they require enormous amounts of energy to manufacture.

Other new materials are so light and ethereal that we have not yet worked out how to exploit them: Silica aerogel, for example, is an ultralight material, comprising 99.9 percent air, developed at the Livermore National Laboratories in California. For one design critic the substance had "the translucency of clouds and the eerie, phantasmagoric look of a hologram."[16] Aerogel is used as an insulating material and as a filter—but has not yet been exploited by product design.

Flying by Light

An aircraft or a building with a smart skin can do without a good bit of heavy-engineering redundancy. Such a skin might incorporate different kinds of sensors and strain gauges—myriad little bits of fine wire, or piezo-ceramics, that generate an electric charge when strained. The "nerves" in such smart structures are optical fibers that distribute signals about changes to processors so that distant environments, such as a wingtip, may be monitored remotely.

In a smart system, sensors give us information. But a great deal of processing power is needed to analyze and make useful sense out of the mass of information generated and transmitted by arrays of sensors. And once the information system has decided what needs to be done, it must relay instructions back to the structure and cause it to respond in an appropriate way—avoiding something, repairing itself, or activating a control surface.

Julian Vincent sees carbon fiber structures as a more elegant solution. Carbon fiber is conductive: If it is damaged, the whole potential field across the structure changes—and that can be sensed. Rather than discrete sensors' being attached on discrete points, the whole structure becomes an integrated sensing element.[17] Vincent also sees more actuator potential in collagen, a load-bearing material that the Achilles tendon is made of, as are many other membranes that hold the body together. Collagen can under some circumstances be made into an actuator by changing its cross-linking properties.[18] One group of animals—sea urchins, brittle stars, starfish, sea cucumbers, and sea lilies—performs a trick with collagen. By changing the amount of calcium, these creatures have made themselves a skeleton, or skeletal appendages, that can be modified and redesigned. Vincent's team has been looking at the sea cucumber and trying to understand—and then model—the mechanism whereby it changes its stiffness and shape.[19] Another potential actuator, elastin, is a rubbery substance found in arteries. By changing its chemistry, elastin expands and contracts over different temperature ranges. Researchers are looking at leaves that can open and close as potential internal pressure actuators. A possible application: tents that can be unfolded in a very short time.[20]

Aircraft designers, who usually have access to the most advanced technology around, are looking at birds for ideas. Martin Kemp, a technical expert on smart sensing who works in the aviation industry, marvels at the way a bird's wing adapts during flight and changes its shape during landing, whereas an aircraft is kept in the air by a great slab of aluminum wobbling up and down with hydraulic cylinders and a flap at the back end. "It is incredibly crude engineering, compared to nature," he says. "If we could change the aircraft's whole shape during flight, we'd have a very elegant, lightweight structure. The way a bird's wing changes shape is so natural and obvious. If you were in an aircraft and the wing just sort of gracefully twisted, as you came in to land, you'd think: Beautiful!"[21]

Before one air show, when his company's marketing department requested a smart-technology demonstrator, Kemp realized that most of his applied research was actually invisible—embedded or inside something else:

We had all the technology on the shelf. We knew that piezo-ceramics change shape when voltage is applied to them. We knew that shape memory alloy wires change shape when you heat them up. But when we tried to make [a model dragonfly to demonstrate their performance in practice], we found lots and lots of little problems. Like: How do we connect the wires to the composites? Run things down the body, down this branch? Then there was the whole control side: we had a complete 486 PC underneath the thing, controlling it. The Duck Syndrome: very calm and sedate on top—but underneath, paddling like mad! We had about three kilos of power supplies, with computers of all sorts controlling it. It brought home the whole issue that lab technology is very nice, that in theory you can do anything, but the actual realisation can completely defeat you.[22]

Man-made smartness tends to be overly complicated. Every step, every intermediary process, in a smart-technology-based system, takes time and reduces efficiency. There are three thousand lines of code in my electric toothbrush.[23] The mouth of a polar bear, so far as I am aware, contains none—but benefits from many thousands of years of evolutionary design. Natural lightness, which has evolved over eons, tends to be simple. Engineers, realizing this, now try to minimize complex and therefore failure-prone assemblies of subcomponents. The most sought-after material innovations behave like mechanical devices but are simpler—for example, the substitution of membrane keyboards for mechanical ones, or of electro-luminescent surfaces for light bulbs. The ambition of today's engineers is to keep the "nuts and bolts" in absolutely the most simple state possible, because that's where they expect most problems to occur. As one eminent engineer told me, "if you have twenty micro-chips and one soldered joint, chances are, the latter will fail."

Clearly, my mechanical friend had never used MSWord! A lot of today's modern software is buggier than a pile of dung. Communications systems are always at risk of failure because the million lines of software they comprise are impossible to check. Software architects are trying to reconfigure large technical systems so that they are built up from self-contained modules of verifiable code. Their hope is that software systems composed of many small blocks will be more stable than those made up of a large mass of undifferentiated code. This kind of modularity and hierarchy, an elegant solution in nature, can render man-made systems more stable. Vincent explains: "Cells are all only about ten microns across, and anything large tends to be made up in layers. You can pull out bits at different levels and replace them without bringing down the whole structure, which is more efficient on the repair side."[24]

Structural self-repair is another area in which we are learning from nature. An Australian researcher, Robyn Overall, cut into some pea roots to see what would happen. She used an immune system to investigate the orientation of microfilaments in the cell membrane in order to find out about the orientation of cellulose in the cells. Cells in the wounded root responded to stresses around them, she found. These cells are under a high internal pressure, anything up to ten atmospheres; when their internal pressure changes, the cell elongates. This enables the cells to grow into the wound area and to repair it.[25] Vincent is convinced that damage control in man-made systems can benefit from this approach: local, isolated effectors.[26]

We tend to think of products as lumps of dead matter: inert, passive, dumb. But products are becoming lively, active, and intelligent. Objects that are sensitive to their environment, act with some intelligence, and talk to each other are changing the basic phenomenology of products—the way they exist in the world. The result is to undermine long-standing design principles. "Form follows function" made sense when products were designed for a specific task—but not when responsive materials that modify a product's behavior are available. Another nostrum, "truth to materials," was a moral imperative of the modern movement in design; it made sense when products were made of "found" or natural materials whose properties were predetermined. But "truth" is less helpful as a design principle when the performance and behavior of materials can be specified in advance.

Learning, Not Copying

To what questions will all this stuff be an answer? After 3.8 billion years of evolution, nature has a pretty good idea of what works, what is appropriate, and what lasts. "Nature solves problems; engineers seek answers; what better marriage could you ask for?" asks Vincent.[27] Learning from the principles of nature can save a lot of time and cost. We can learn about the ways in which natural systems have achieved minimum-energy solutions, run on sunlight, use only the energy they need, and so on. We can learn how natural systems optimize, rather than maximize, their use of materials. We can learn, like nature, how to create artifacts that sense and respond to their local situation, recycle everything, and do not foul their nests. But any attempt simply to copy the results of nature misses a crucial point: Nature never stands still. So neither should we. Rather than try to replicate a natural mechanism on a one-to-one basis, we would be better off understanding both the principles of its operation and the specificities of its context and design from there. Vincent uses the example of wood to explain this approach. Wood is one of the most efficient of all materials in terms of toughness and stiffness per unit weight. As a result of the angle of the fibers in the wood cell, it has a very high energy of fracture. But in terms of lightness, natural materials are not always the best choice. A Dutch consulting firm, PRé, cautions that although manufacturing a product using one kilogram of wood causes fewer emissions than the production of one kilogram of plastic, we also need to think about the paint to preserve the wood, the energy needed to dry it, and the amount of materials wasted during sawing. "In some products you would need about ten times as much wood than plastic. Plastics can often be recycled, wood cannot," says PRé.[28] Mindful of these factors, biomics like Vincent say that once you understand *why* natural materials behave as they do, one can start to incorporate their qualities into other materials. Vincent's team at Reading University in England is developing a glass fiber composite material that mimics the fracture properties of wood. (A partner in the project is Britain's Ministry of Defence, which needs an impact-resistant material for bullet-proof vests with a much lighter weight than current versions.)[29]

Intelligent?

Biomimics want us to consider the properties not just of individual things, but of whole systems, and the ways a system adapts to its context. Man-made smartness can be awfully dumb. A while back I stopped off at an airport washroom to freshen up. Before moving to a stand-up cubicle, I placed my bag on one of the sinks. A few moments later, when I picked the bag up again, it was full of water. The tap had opened automatically. For cost-saving and no doubt good environmental reasons, the tap had been fitted with a chip and a sensor and told: "Only release water when someone is standing in front of you." In nature, a tap that mistook a bag for a person would soon be extinct. I suppose a smarter successor will be developed for the man-made world too—but at what cost in the meantime? Trial and error works when millions of years are available, but we humans are flooding the world with error-prone gadgets all at once.

Trillions of smart tags, sensors, smart materials, connected appliances, wearable computing, and body implants are now being unleashed upon the world all at once. It's by no means clear to what question they are an answer—or who is going to look after them, and how. According to one industry expert, "80 percent of embedded systems are delivered late, are hopelessly bug-ridden, and share the same problems of lousy quality, buggy tool chains, (and) poorly thought-out product specifications."[30]

You might think that the social consequences that could follow when every object around us becomes smart and connected would be widely discussed—but they're not. The slogan of the main Web portal for embedded systems developers is "thinking inside the box."[31] Most of us think about technology in much the same way that a frog thinks about boiling water. The story goes that if you drop a frog into a pan when the water is boiling, it will leap out; but if you put the frog into a pan of cold water, and then heat it steadily toward the boiling point, the frog—unaware that any dramatic change is taking place—will just sit there and slowly cook. So, is technology cooking us? Many hard objects around us are certainly beginning to "soften." In New York, Tokyo, or London, right now, we encounter an embedded system on average 150 times a day.[32] The world is already filled with hundreds of microprocessors for every man, woman, and child on the planet. Think of all those ATMs, ticket-vending machines, traffic lights, billboards, cellular phones, pagers, and cash registers. A new car from General Motors contains $675 worth of steel and $2,500 worth of electronics. Ted Lewis, a professor at the U.S. Navy's graduate school, says that as global sales of PCs reach one hundred million, embedded systems are set to expand to at least a thousand times as many units. Concludes Lewis, "the business of 'sense-and-communicate' is already many times larger than the business of 'compute-and-store.'"[33] More and more of the objects around us do not function alone, but as part of a service enabled by networks. This is why people in the airline industry describe a Boeing 747 as "equipment"—as in, "The equipment is late incoming from Detroit." One of the largest and most complicated objects made by man is more or less useless unless connected. Along with objects so small we can barely see them, the 747 has joined the "internet of things."[34]

Increasingly, many of the chips around us will sense their environment in rudimentary but effective ways. The sensory and motoric capacities of networks will continue to grow. Companies are already building so-called hard, real-time systems in which the maximum response time will be one microsecond. These systems are based on billions of microprocessors—man-made synapses, processing away silently all around us.[35] More than half of all devices sold with computing in them nowadays include a thirty-two-bit chip—the threshold needed to make them truly networked and interactive. As writer Bruce Sterling so memorably put it, the way things are going, "you will go into the garden to look at the flowers—and the flowers will look at you."[36]

A world in which products and appliances talk to one another sounds fantastic, but it's not so long since the advent of electricity was greeted with similar amazement. Then, objects that once had to be worked by hand began to power themselves. When electricity was first introduced into the home, there was a tendency in industry to portray its aims, its technological prowess, and its dynamic power in mythological terms. Germany's AEG, for example, used the goddess of light as its trademark. But once electricity's magical novelty wore off and a majority of everyday products began to be "electrified," designers had to find new ways to make electric irons, kettles, lightbulbs, and cookers interesting to consumers. Reasoning that "even an electric motor must look like a birthday present," artist-designers like AEG's Peter Behrens turned themselves into industrial designers to accomplish just that. In 1903 Behrens's boss, Paul Westheim, observed of design at the dawn of the electrical age that "in order to make a lucid, logical and clearly articulated entity out of an arc lamp, a complete transformation of our aesthetic notions was necessary."[37] Does the same apply today to embedded computing? If the rapid electrification of everyday life just three generations ago is any guide, embedded computing will not prove controversial for people. Electric motors, too, soon disappeared from view, where they remain, in vast numbers, humming away inside a swarm of everyday household products. With pervasive computing another new presence has come into our lives, and it, too, lacks visible form or expression.

Embedded—but Not Asleep

The disappearance of computing is a bad reason to stop thinking about it. If citizens do not set the agenda for its use, others will. The most energetic developers of new applications for pervasive computing right now are logistics industries, as we saw in chapter 3, and security and police interests. When the computing industry started pushing pervasive computing hard in the late 1990s, it often used "House of the Future" mock-ups to showcase potential applications and attract the attention of potential funders. These mock-ups usually featured (and still do) lots of voice-controlled and touch screens. Microsoft's Easy Living project focused on the software technologies needed to create a smart home environment, such as software agents, computer vision, and machine learning.[38]

But in the aftermath of September 11, attention switched en masse from home to homeland security (HS). Reliable figures for the total public and private expenditures on HS technologies are hard to find, but estimates are that total HS outlays—by federal, state, local, and private entities in the United States—grew from $5 billion in 2000 to $85 billion in 2004, with a forecast that they will grow to $130 billion—and possibly as high as $210 billion—by 2010.[39]

Are disappearing computers a menace? Think about that frog again. How does his behavior compare with our own relationship to technology? I'd say that like the frog, we have a vague sensation that "things seem to be getting warmer around here"—but for most of us, the condition of "getting warmer and less comfortable" has been a constant throughout our lives. We're used to it. It's not so much that technology is changing quickly; change is one of the constants we have become used to. And it's not that technology is penetrating every aspect of our lives; that, too, has been happening to all of us since we were born. The shocking thing to me, at least, is the *rate of acceleration* of change—right now. As I described in chapter 2, the accelerometer has disappeared off the right-hand side of the dial.

And critical reflection on this new wave of technology is in short supply. And yet, in the domain of policing and law enforcement, a whole new industry has emerged called digital ID. It already has its own conference and trade show, Digital ID World, which specializes in "the identity management space."[40] The world's largest smart-card rollout has already started in China; all Chinese over the age of sixteen are being issued a smart card as an identification document. The rollout of these chip-bearing cards to 1.3 billion citizens is expected to be completed by the year 2008, according to the official news agency Xinhua.[41] Surveillance is permeating our environments. As the writer Mike Davis puts it, "Tall buildings are becoming increasingly sentient and packed with firepower. The sensory system of the average office tower already includes panoptic vision, smell, sensitivity to temperature and humidity, motion detection, and, in some cases, hearing. Some architects predict the day when the building's own AI security computer will be able automatically to screen and identify its human population and even, perhaps, respond to their emotional states (fear, panic, etc.)."[42]

Bodies in the Network

We seem equally unperturbed by—or are simply unaware of—the new machines and systems that scan, probe, penetrate, and enhance our bodies. As often happens, artists and writers have seen the big picture more clearly. Donna Haraway, in her celebrated "Cyborg Manifesto," wrote back in 1991 that "late twentieth century machines have made thoroughly ambiguous the difference between natural and artificial, mind and body, self-developing and externally designed. Our machines are disturbingly lively, and we are frighteningly inert."[43] The ethical issues raised by these developments are profound but remain low to invisible on the radar of public awareness.

In chapter 6 I described this passive acceptance of technology into our bodies as "Borg drift." It's what happens when knowledge from many branches of science and design—a million small, specialized acts—converge without our really noticing. Bio-mechatronics and medical telematics are spreading at tremendous speed, not because there's a Dr. Frankenstein out there, but because thousands of creative and well-meaning people go to work every day to fix or improve a tiny bit of our bodies. Oticon, in Denmark, for example, is developing hundred-channel amplifiers for the inner ear.[44] Scientists are cloning artificial livers and hearts and kidneys and blood and knees and fingers and toes—smart prostheses of every kind.[45] Progress on excellent artificial skin is excellent.[46] Tongues are a tough challenge, but they'll crack that one, too, in due course. As one prosthetic manufacturer somewhat creepily puts it, "Artificial limbs are taking on new life thanks to advances in embedded-chip technology."[47] According to writer Thomas Grose, "Because of embedded chip technology, artificial limbs permanently attached to amputees and controlled by their brains could be available some time within the next decade or two. And while it's unlikely that such prostheses could ever improve upon a real arm or leg, bioengineering nevertheless offers America's 1.3 million amputees the real possibility of mechanical limbs that closely mimic nature's. 'It is a matter of when, and not if, such technology will be ultimately realized,' says Joel W. Burdick, deputy director of the California Institute of Technology's Center for Neuromorphic Systems Engineering."[48] Our bodies are not just being synthesized bit by bit; they're also being connected to the Net. Soon we'll all be always on, thanks to fast-spreading connectivity between monitoring devices on (or in) our bodies, on the one hand—and health care practitioners, their institutions, and their knowledge systems, on the other. Heart disease is a big driver of the trend. You give every heart patient a wearable or implanted monitor; it talks wirelessly to computers, which are trained to keep an eye open for abnormalities: Bingo! Your body is very securely plugged into the network. That's pervasive computing, too. Health and medical telematics are expanding and connecting to each other in the same unobtrusive—and unplanned—manner that characterizes the way our body parts are being changed. In one project, a vast database containing information about tens of millions of experiments and drug tests is being centralized.[49] In dozens of different experiments, patient records are being digitized and coded—which means they can be accessed online from anywhere.[50] Medical journals are migrating at high speed to online publishing environments, thereby shrinking the time lag between discovery and dissemination of new discoveries.[51] The drug industry is putting performance data about thousands of drugs online.[52] And bioengineers have devised a multitude of noninvasive, digital patient-monitoring systems that measure, record, and evaluate our vital functions—continuously.[53]

The result of this is a vast, distributed, and—for the wired-up patient—*immersive* medical knowledge system in which the boundaries between "me" and "the system" are dissolving. This is why artists talk about "wetware" and "the recombinant body." The body itself will become a communication device if some engineers have their way. IBM's Thomas Zimmerman is a specialist in "intrabody communications"; he says our own bodies will be used before too long as the wiring of a very small but very useful "personal area network" (PAN). "Wearable" electronic devices will exchange data by passing low-voltage currents through the body and into hand-held appliances, head-mounted displays, shoes, watches, credit cards, and the like. The hardware necessary to build such a novel interface is inexpensive and could be implemented with cheap microcontroller chips costing a few dollars. Once this technology is perfected and standardized, all kinds of devices monitoring bodily functions can be given networking capability. Adds Zimmerman, "the usefulness of each will be multiplied by the exchange of information with any other device we carry with us, and completely new devices will be invented to take advantage of this networking frenzy."[54] PAN medical sensors, for example, could provide any kind of biological monitoring, transfer the data to your cellular phone, and relay everything to a nearby hospital. Arthur Kroker, an iconoclastic writer who has observed the convergence of technology and the body with glee, is enthusiastic. Writing with Michael Weinstein, he says: "Why be nostalgic? The old body type was always OK, but the wired body is infinitely better— a wired nervous system embedded in living flesh."[55]

One of those medical sensors could well be monitoring your brain. A Finnish company, Neuromag, offers a spectacular example of the speed with which brain-scanning technology has advanced in recent years. Wilhelm Konrad Roentgen's discovery of X rays was one of the wonders of the twentiety century; brain imaging is as impressive now. It's completely noninvasive, too: With magnetoencephalography (MEG), cortical activity all over the head can be followed from outside.[56]

Neuromag's system has the potential to identify neurological and psychiatric disorders invisible to existing diagnostics. It is able simultaneously to measure 370 discrete channels. Neuromag's system is a large device, but soon brain scanning will be done remotely. A team from the Centre for Physical Electronics at the University of Sussex has developed a technique that, instead of measuring electric current flow through a fixed-on electrode, takes advantage of the latest developments in sensor technology to measure electric fields from the brain without actually having to make direct contact with the head. "We deal with patients who have Alzheimer's disease and schizophrenia who often have delusions about electrodes in their head," Professor Yonmoy Sharma told the BBC.[57]

AmI?

The mission for ambient intelligence (AmI), as expressed by the European Commission's Information Society Technologies Advisory Group (ISTAG), sounds innocuous enough: "See how information technology can be diffused into everyday objects and settings, leading to new ways of supporting and enhancing people's lives." In the ambient intelligent environment (which in the United States tends to be called "ubiquitous computing" or "pervasive computing") envisaged by its promoters, human beings will be surrounded by computing and networking technology embedded in everyday objects. Furniture, clothes, vehicles, roads, and smart materials—even particles of decorative substances, like paint—will merge, as ISTAG puts it, in a "seamless environment of computing, advanced networking technology and specific interfaces." Technology will be embedded, personalized, adaptive, and anticipatory.

All of which sounds fine and dandy, except that all these promises are based on wildly implausible assumptions. No technology delivered by competing private companies will ever be "seamlessly" integrated. No foreseeable software will be able to "respond intelligently to spoken or gestured indications of desire," as ISTAG asserts.[58]

A visit to Greece in the summer of 2003, for the "Tales of the Disappearing Computer" conference, amplified my feelings of unease. It's not so much that bad men in black hats are plotting dastardly deeds—more that enthusiastic researchers are failing to think at all about possible downsides to their inventions. One paper presented at the conference, held in Santorini, looked forward to "anthropocentric interfaces" that, enabled by "cognition technologies," will "enhance or substitute for our senses."[59] Context-aware and proactive systems will "hide overall system complexity, and preserve human attention, by delivering to us only information which is rich with meanings and contexts." Faced with a "tera-world" filled with "open, unbound, dynamic and intelligent systems," we will soon need to "provide them with learning, and gracefully evolving capabilities, as well as self-diagnosis, self-adaptation, and self-organization capabilities." Now maybe I am missing something, but to me this translates as: Build systems that are too complicated to understand and then, after they are deployed, find ways to master their complexity. Hmmm.

Greger Linden, a Finnish expert in "psychosocial computing," antici-pated, in another conference presentation, that when direct brain-computer interfaces are implemented, "people will be the problem. Rather than concentrate on one thing at a time, which suits the software, people tend to think about other things. This messes up the results."[60] Linden, who leads a large Franco-Finnish "proactive computing" consortium, ap-peared undeterred by twenty thousand years of human subtlety: He plans to develop models for "disambiguating" users' vague commands and anticipating their actions. Alas, poor Yorick.

Other researchers are developing machine vision systems that will scan us for "psycho-physiological signals" and "sense and understand human actions."[61] Eye gaze, pupil dilation and contraction, gaze direction through time, blinking, facial tics, breathing, and heart rates—all will be monitored remotely by systems designed to "understand our cognitive and emotional state of mind."[62] Serious dangers are often created by individuals who try to carry out critical activity when they are "not in a fit state to," said one scientist at the conference. Agents will monitor these users and decide on behalf of them for their welfare. He mentioned driving cars while under the influence and drowsing at the wheel of a bus—but it was not evident that the system could not be recalibrated to detect other impure thoughts.

Civilian companies are also taking liberties with our liberty. Several firms are pushing the concept of "proactive" computing. This kind of comput-ing, according to Intel, is "perceptive of our needs." Intel, which is also pushing the "proactive computing paradigm," makes the airy promise that "autonomic computing...will make us...more productive...and leave human beings free to concentrate on higher level functions." Intel-enabled "robotic hypothesis generation software...produces answers be-fore they are required."[63]

Many of the policymakers, engineers, designers, and companies now promoting pervasive computing speak as if the natural world and its inhabitants—you and I—simply did not exist. The inaugural issue of *Perva-sive Computing* is not untypical: "Our world is like the American West...a rich, open space where the rules have yet to be written and the borders to be drawn."[64] Think about the last part of that statement. In the brave new world of pervasive computing, people everywhere are reduced to the status of Native American Indians—and we know what happened to them.

Pervasive computing technologies promise to transform the ways we experience and live in the world. But did anyone ask our permission to "produce answers before they are required"? Have we debated the consequences of proactive computing? No, we have not. In its *Scenarios for Ambient Intelligence in 2010*, the European Union is not much more thoughtful. This key document outlines a vision of "convergence" as a point at which "the human is surrounded by computing and advanced networking technology which is aware of his presence, his personality, his needs—and is capable of responding intelligently to spoken or gestured indications of desire, and even in engaging in intelligent dialogue." The AmI landscape, as it's known in Euro-speak, is *embedded*, *personalized*, *adaptive*, and *anticipatory*. It provides "an evolutionary path from current modes of human behaviour to new behaviours that benefit from AmI enhancement." The dominant mode of communication is laid-back, rather than lean-forward, concludes the document, with great confidence.[65]

The problem with these visions is that they are based on one implausible assumption and one plain wrong assumption. The implausible assumption is that all people, and all systems, will perform optimally at all times. No technology has ever done that, and none ever will. Even if 99.9 percent of the smart tags, sensors, smart materials, connected appliances, wearable computing, and (soon) implants that are now being unleashed upon the world work as instructed—what about the millions that, inevitably, will fail, or run amok? As my water-filled bag testifies, when human beings issue instructions to devices, the results are not always benign.

The plain-wrong assumption is that we know what the consequences of these new technologies will be. We know, for a fact, that technology always has unexpected as well as expected consequences.

People Will Always Be Smarter

The worst-case scenario is the most likely: that smart technology will be used in dumb ways, for the wrong reasons, with irritating if not disastrous results. I recently purchased a train ticket from Amsterdam to Switzerland—a ten-hour, four-train journey. A pleasant and expert woman at the ticket desk, in Amsterdam Central Station, helped me select the best route. It was a complicated transaction, but she was an expert intermediary between me and the various databases and websites that needed to be consulted. The twenty-minute transaction, as a result, was not unpleasant, and I made the trip without trouble. Imagine my horror, then, when the train company, NS International, announced its intention to close all its international ticket desks. Anyone traveling to Belgium, Germany, France, or Switzerland would have to buy their ticket from "self-service" websites or—and here it boggles the mind—via text messages on their mobile phones.

The director of NS International at the time (February 2004), Frits Marckmann, told me that "we are adopting modern methods of distribution." Now, technically speaking, it may well be more "modern" to sell tickets by SMS than via a human being. But as an example of service design—not to mention plain common sense—the NS action would be laughable if it were not also irresponsible. If it takes an expert human being, with years of experience, twenty minutes to sell me one ticket to Switzerland, how many hours would the same transaction take me using SMS? Ten? If I am elderly, if I do not speak English or Dutch, if I do not have Internet access, or if I simply refuse to spend hours of my life in clunky NS websites—in these cases, I will be denied access to the service altogether. By the time we reach that point, it will be too late to turn back. Up to three hundred jobs are being designed out of the NS system. Assuming an average of ten years' experience per person, that's *three thousand years of human experience* that will be have been removed from the system. How smart is that?

The defining feature of services in this self-service economy is that they take place with little or no human contact. The customer does work once carried out by an employee but is not paid for so doing. On the contrary: Netonomy, a firm that provides self-service software to telecom operators, reckons online self-service can cut the costs of a transaction to as little as ten cents, compared with around seven dollars to handle the same transaction at a call center. A self-service kiosk in a supermarket can handle the work of two and a half employees at a fraction of the cost. In 2001, Amtrak introduced an interactive voice recognition (IVR) system called Julie. The service handles a third of the rail system's bookings, and *The Economist* reported at the time that 80 percent of callers surveyed were happy with the service.[66] That doesn't sound so bad until you remember that Amtrak carries an average of 22 million passengers a year—which means that nearly 4.5 million passengers had a bad experience buying their ticket online. When Forrester Research surveyed 110 large companies, it found that only 18 percent of customer needs were met by IVR systems.[67]

Zeroing Out

When an IVR/speech system does not meet a customer's expectations, the customer becomes frustrated and hang ups or "zeroes out" to a live agent. According to the Forrester research cited previously, customer satisfaction levels with IVR systems fall in the 10 percent range, compared with a satisfaction rate of approximately 80 percent for face-to-face interactions. This confronts service providers with a financial dilemma. Tal Cohen, a data-modeling expert, asks service providers to consider this recognizable scenario. Suppose a company receives fifty thousand customer calls each day, and its automated system is not meeting their needs. The result is that 20 percent of these callers "zero out" to live agents who cost the company ten dollars per call handled. The service-providing company spends one hundred thousand dollars each day to have live agents complete customer transactions. Companies such as NS International look at those numbers and think, "get rid of the human agents." But automated systems cannot—and never will—take their place.[68]

The transition to a light and sustainable economy means moving from an economy of transactions—selling and buying things—to an economy in which the quality of services, not the acquisition of goods, becomes our measure of well-being. In previous chapters, we saw examples of what it means in practice to take one aspect of daily life and make it better using information technology as one of the tools. The problem with NS International, and a thousand near-blind companies like it, is that they believe their own propaganda about the capacity of technology to do things for us as well as people can.

Even the most tireless boosters of technology have become aware that describing a wish, attached to a memorable name, as something that already exists can rebound against them. Ambient intelligence is a bewitching vision of the future—but it may be further away than we think. James Woudhuysen, a former manager of long-term market research for Philips, thinks many of the more fanciful scenarios described in industry forecasts are suspect: "The consumer of digital media (and appliances) meets 'convergence' only in the same way that, in a blizzard, the snow seems to 'converge' upon you. We all may hope that everything will one day be controlled by a single, submissive black box below the stairs—but in new technology, systems are more prone to being incompatible than to matching up with each other."[69] Our world is already filled with complex technical systems whose integration—although a huge industry—is also a migraine-inducing one. "A world full of interacting artifacts could easily confuse people," mentions (with sublime understatement) the same ISTAG report I quoted from earlier in the chapter.[70]

One of the other big unanswered questions about ambient intelligence concerns who will look after it. In Europe alone, it is estimated that there are currently between 1.5 and 2 million unfilled vacancies in the information technology sector.[71] AmI technologies are neither stable nor 100 percent reliable. We all know, from our daily experience using PCs, how bug-ridden and frustrating the software programs we use every day can be. That frustration can quickly escalate when we seek help. According to Dataquest, users made some two hundred million calls to PC technical support hotlines in 1995. The ideal solution would be a SysOp in every home, but that option is available only to the likes of Bill Gates.

Four grand pianos, their lids removed, are placed nose to nose, like the leaves of a flower, under sharp spotlights in the concourse of a railway station. Each of the four musicians plays from a double-width score that is half as wide as the piano itself. Every now and again, one of the players signals the transition to a new section by nodding his head backward. Every hour or so, a new team of pianists takes over, in a kind of relay: The old shift keeps playing but in sequence, one stands up, and a pianist from the new shift takes her place. This happens four times until the new team is in place. *Canto Ostinato*, as the piece is called, has no prescribed end; it can go on for hours. Simeon ten Holt, its composer, describes it as a perpetual work in progress. "My own life has been largely determined by chance," he says, "and as composer, I decline to indicate intensity, phrasing and so on, on the score. Too-rigid instructions are in conflict with the dynamics of the overall sound balance, and they frustrate the performers in formulating a staging of their own."[1] The score of *Canto Ostinato* is laid out as a route for the performers to take, says ten Holt; they use so-called drift parts at will, but its total length, and the number of repetitions of the various sections on which the composition is built, are undetermined.

Canto Ostinato is a metaphor for a new approach to design. Its composer, his incomplete score, the pianists, the railway station, the people present on the night of the performance—all these elements interact in subtle and complex ways. These interactions are difficult to describe to someone not present—and they would be impossible to orchestrate remotely. Neither the pianists nor the audience know exactly what will happen next, so no complete score or blueprint is possible. But they do not fly blind. They understand the principles of the system and work with it. They follow the score, to a point. They interact with one another. And they interact with the situation. In a sense the situation is itself designed: The composer places an idea, a score, and people on the stage, but he does not furnish a finished script.

Designing in the Space of Flows

The Spanish economist Manuel Castells describes the modern world as a "space of flows"—flows of people, capital, information, technology, images, sounds, and symbols. "Flows are not just one element of social organization," says Castells, "they are the expression of the processes dominating our economic, social and symbolic life."[2]

Flows sound soft, and smooth, and benign—but flows also wash things away, sometimes unexpectedly. We have been taken aback by events, such as climate change, that we seem to have caused, but that were not our intention. Other flows have brought changes that were the opposite of what we hoped and intended: These are the so-called rebound effects, such as the increased traffic that the Internet has stimulated or the additional use of paper it has generated, rather than replaced.

One reason we feel helpless in the face of this type of change is that experts tell us we are. Economists describe as "exogenous"—arising from outside society—the seismic forces, such as technology, that are changing our world. They are wrong. Technology has not come from "outside society"—we made it. Technology is a product of human decisions and actions. These actions may have been misguided or based on assumptions that we are now beginning to question—but they were not an accident.

A redesign of this space of flows is a tall order, because the precise behavior of complex systems—including human ones—is not predictable. But we are now beginning to understand the principles by which complex systems evolve. Redesigning the space of flows needs to be continuous, rather than episodic. It needs to focus on how things work, rather than (just) on what they look like. And it entails a fundamental change in the relationship between the people who make things and the people who use them.

In this concluding chapter I summarize the lessons I have learned about designing in a complex world. Rather like ten Holt with *Canto Ostinato*, I will suggest frameworks for action rather than lay down hard-and-fast rules. This is partly because I don't know what fixed rules there ought to be. As the eminent American designer John Carroll says of design in today's complex world, "its ultimate objective and approach have to be discovered, not specified."[3] Theodor Zeldin, the storyteller and good listener, echoes Carroll the system designer: Our age, he observes, is one in which "deliberation replaces specification."[4] For your deliberation, therefore, I conclude with observations on seven design frameworks:

- From blueprint and plan to sense and respond
- From high concept to deep context
- From top-down design to seeding edge effects
- From blank sheets of paper to smart recombination
- From science fiction to social fiction
- From designing for people to designing with us
- From design as project to design as service

From Blueprint and Plan to Sense and Respond

Traditional design thinking focuses on form and structure. Problems are "decomposed" into smaller steps, and these are prioritized in lists. Actions and inputs are described in a blueprint or plan—and other people produce or implement it. This is a top-down, outside-in approach. It doesn't work well now because complex systems, especially human-centered ones, won't sit still while we redesign them. A sense-and-respond kind of design seems to work better: Desired outcomes are described, but not the detailed means of getting to those outcomes.

Sense and respond means being responsive to events in a context—such as a city or a marketplace—and being able to respond quickly and appropriately when reality changes. This approach implies that we develop an understanding and sensitivity to the morphology of systems, their dynamics, their "intelligence"—how they work and what stimulates them. This is a challenge to what Brian Arthur, of the Santa Fe Institute, calls "the cognitive abilities of people and organizations"[5]—their ability to interpret, to see things differently, and to focus on principles of relationship, connection, communication, and interaction.

To complicate matters, desired outcomes in service and flow contexts will themselves not be static. Viewing systems through "the lens of complexity"[6] (to borrow a phrase from Canadian educator Alain Findeli) enables us to reframe the design tasks that confront us. By understanding why a system is in one state, we can explore the kind of interventions that would nudge it into another more desirable one. This means designing as steering more than designing as shaping. From thinking of ourselves as the authors of a finished work, we had better evolve toward thinking of ourselves as facilitators whose job is to help people act more intelligently, in a more design-minded way, in the systems we all live in.

This shift in emphasis from what things look like to how they behave—from designing *on* the world to designing *in* the world—is a big one for design. Peter Bøgh Andersen, who designs maritime instrumentation, compares interacting with today's dynamic environments to navigating a ship. "When I started teaching human-computer interaction in the 1980s," he recalls, "the ideal was that the user should be in control of the system. The system should not act unless the user asked it to do so. In process control, however, the situation is quite different. Here, physical processes are running independently of the user, whose task is partially to control them. The art of navigation is similar: it is to pit the controllable forces—rudder, propeller—against the uncontrollable ones—the sea and the wind—to achieve one's purpose." The computer game world is analogous, he says. Process control and computer games share important features: In both cases there is a dramatic conflict between a protagonist (on a ship, it's the captain) and bad guys (which for the captain, are the wind and the sea) who are active, unpredictable, and only indirectly controllable.[7]

The systems themselves can also change our activities in ways that we do not need or want. "Design changes the world within which people act and experience, and this changes the requirements for further designs," says Carroll.[8] Design in such a framework becomes a process of continuous observation, measurement, and feedback. In Japan, designers describe this kind of reactive, incremental innovation as "the patter of tiny feet." Kyoshi Sakashita, when he was design director of Sharp, told me that teams designing complex systems proceed not by great leaps forward, but by "thousands of tiny steps": partial solutions, continually produced. In the development phase, the rapid-prototyping approach involves the use of computer simulations and physical mock-ups—but it need never, in principle, stop.[9]

From High Concept to Deep Context

Hippocrates said twenty-five hudred years ago, in *Ancient Medicine: Airs, Waters, Places*, that in order to understand the disorders in any subject, we must study its environment. "The greater part of the soul lies outside the body," said the sage; "treatment of the inner requires treatment of the outer."[10] Peter Drucker, a modern business sage, teaches businesspeople a similar lesson: "Innovation is a system's adjustment to its surroundings— and sometimes this is best accomplished by adjusting the surroundings."[11] Now what Drucker describes innocuously as an "adjustment," others might judge to be cultural imperialism, global domination, or ecological devastation—but the basic point is clear enough: When one is designing in the space of flows, context is key.

As I explained when discussing situations in chapter 5, life in systems-rich environments is understudied—but insights into a variety of contexts are beginning to emerge. What we have now come to appreciate is that the more diverse an ecological system is—be it a swamp or a city—the richer it is. Sprawling monocultural suburbs, multilane highways, golf courses, airports, and the like are impoverished contexts. Our speed culture fosters particularly barren contexts. Very large grids, very big global hubs, and the massive flows of people and matter in between them are functional but not nourishing. The close, the complex, and the slow can be much richer.[12]

I have mentioned throughout this book the importance of thinking about consequences as we contemplate design actions. Context matters, says Malcolm Gladwell, because specific and relatively small changes in the environment can serve as tipping points that transform the bigger picture.[13] Small changes to interconnecting subsystems can make things better, but they can also make things worse. This is why the application of "high-concept" design to contexts we barely understand is irresponsible and probably counterproductive. A good example of high-altitude but low-quality thinking is evident, as I write, in a clutch of advertisements for information technology firms. IBM, British Telecom, and Hewlett-Packard have released television commercials and print ads that feature besuited young professionals floating, gravity free, in abstract urban spaces that look just like scenes in computer games.

A more sensitive approach to people, contexts, and networks leads to a way of approaching the world that is, as Tom Bentley puts it, "purposeful and ambitious, but also careful and humble, seeking to maintain and develop systems of increasing complexity so that they support people's needs and interests in appropriate, sophisticated ways."[14] Networks and systems in nature generally start out small and develop during a process of gradual growth. That's also how we should design man-made ones: Act lightly, sense the feedback, act again.

From Top-Down Design to Seeding Edge Effects

Biologists describe as "the edge effect" the tendency for a greater variety and density of organisms to cluster in the boundaries between communities. In complexity theory, too, there is an "edge of chaos" paradigm that posits that in a system containing perfect internal order, such as a crystal, there can be no further change. At the opposite extreme, in a chaotic system such as boiling liquid, there is very little order to change. The system that will evolve most rapidly, explains Edward O. Wilson, "must fall between, and more precisely on the edge, of chaos—possessing order, but with the parts connected loosely enough to be easily altered either singly or in small groups."[15]

As in nature, so too in a networked economy: Variety, density, and interaction are success factors. But the way we organize things now, the potential benefits of edge effects are designed out, not in. Most of us live and work in sealed-off boxes: a company, a university, a profession. We work *within* communities, not between them. Stuck inside organizations that perpetuate divisions between domains and that isolate knowledge from the contexts in which it is to be used, we become less competent at tackling complex and multidimensional social questions. If our connections to the edge are inadequate, we find it hard to figure out what people really need— and end up pushing products that they don't.

The idea of edge effects is not new. Ever since Aristotle, people have criticized the division between disciplines and professional communities. But the problem has now become acute. Specialization may well have helped build industrial society—but it's like grit in the wheels of the network society we're building now. What to do about the edge effect is a design issue. To find out what's happening on the edge, we first need good *peripheral vision*. We need to spot opportunities at the juncture between industries, to imagine relationships and connections where none existed before. Above all, we need to look in new places for inspiration, because most solutions will involve new alliances and new connections. We need to cultivate the habit of looking for the people, places, organizations, projects, and ideas that do not appear on the radar screens used by our captains up there on the bridge.

Edge cities, and the boundary zones between them, are always good places to look. So, too, are places that specialize in exchange—hubs, entrepôts, ports like Hong Kong, Singapore, Hanseatic cities, Venice and Genoa, and Amsterdam. Places whose lifeblood flows through a rich web of connections are a better bet than places that think of themselves as centers. This applies to countries and regions, too. The first major industry, textiles, owed a great deal to the transfer of knowledge from India. A great deal of potential innovation comes from the study of plants. Of the roughly 265,000 plant species that we know exist, probably 40,000 have medicinal or nutritional applications for humans—yet only 1,100 have been thoroughly studied. In catching up, we would be wise to learn from other cultures, which are often better informed about their potential than we are. Ethnoecology, the study of indigenous ways of using local resources, can help us here. Forest-dwelling peoples classify and use 99 percent of the rich biological diversity.[16]

Susantha Goonatilake describes as "civilizational knowledge" such cultural constructs as metaphors, which he describes as "the pregnant mother to scientific innovation." Theories in science often originate in metaphors, says Goonatilake; "a vast soup of metaphors and theoretical constructs exists in the Asian world. These vary from sophisticated debates on the nature of ontology and epistemology to discussions in psychology, the nature of mind, mathematics, and medicine. Such an infusion would help enlarge our scientific horizons."[17] The potential is huge. During the last hundred years, probably two thousand catalogues of known South Asian manuscripts have been compiled. Each catalogue encompasses about two hundred manuscripts, so the resource adds up to four hundred thousand manuscripts. Others have estimated that South Asian manuscripts amount to some five hundred million. "The Renaissance, the Scientific Revolution, the Enlightenment and the great discoveries in the 19th and 20th centuries were the result of recombining, not just discovering, ideas," says Goonatilake. "The rediscovery of Asian thought is a second renaissance in the cultural history of the West, with the potential to be equally important as the rediscovery of Greek thought in the European renaissance."[18] We need to become hunter-gatherers of ideas and tools: How have other societies lived in the past? How do societies live in other parts of the world today? Has this question been answered somewhere else already?

From Blank Sheets of Paper to Smart Recombination

Designers are needlessly constrained by the myth that everything they do has to be a unique and creative act. Rather than expect to design everything from scratch, we should search far and wide for tried-and-tested solutions that others have already created. Kevin Gavaghan, who set up Britain's first Internet bank, FirstDirect, says that wherever possible, we need to reuse and recombine actors, ideas, and organizations.[19] The capacity to think across boundaries, to spot opportunities at the juncture of two or more industries, and to draw relevant analogies from seemingly unrelated industries is as valuable as deep experience of a single sector.

When edge people, edge ideas, and edge organizations are brought together, something interesting and valuable usually happens. What management consultants refer to as "strategy creation" (and I call design) involves the creation of new combinations of knowledge, resources, and capabilities—many or most of which may already exist. It means connecting with actors from different economic and knowledge domains. We need to recombine relationships—among people, ideas, and organizations—and exploit scientific, natural, and cultural knowledge that is usually ignored, whether it be mimicking biology or learning from storytellers in India. Putting old knowledge into a new context creates new knowledge. We need to become hunter-gatherers of models, processes, and ways of living.

The challenge is to innovate by learning *from* the world. For Yves Doz, a business professor at Insead in France, competitive advantage in the future will come from discovering, accessing, mobilizing, and leveraging knowledge from many locations around the world. "Most multinationals fail to harvest the most precious resources—ideas and innovation—from the far-flung regions in which they operate," says Doz.[20] In an economic world dealing in knowledge, the secret of success is the combination of different types of expertise in a productive manner. For Nobel laureate Murray Gell-Mann, innovation is an "emergent phenomenon" that occurs when a person or organization fosters interaction among different kinds of people and disparate forms of knowledge. When edge people, edge ideas, and edge organizations are connected, something interesting and valuable usually happens. In my work as a conference organizer and advisor, this approach certainly seems to work. Recombining relationships—among people, ideas, and organizations—does seem to foster innovation.

From Science Fiction to Social Fiction

I have tried in this book to describe an approach to innovation that, rather than foist technology onto a world that does not need it, looks for ways to enhance the kinds of daily life that we experience here and now. Of course it's true that new technologies give rise to new ways of living and organizing that would not exist without them—and some of those changes are benign. But they should be the result of human actions informed by intelligent reflection on alternatives. Innovation is not a neutral activity. Many innovation agendas are driven by technological determinism; they often disguise creepy social agendas, too. "From *The Matrix* to *Enemy of the State*, successful descriptions of the future have an ability to draw us towards them, to command us to make them flesh," complains the English writer Harry Kunzru; "the effect of futurist fictions, projections and predictions is to fuel our desire for a technology boom."[21]

Overblown research agendas, such as Europe's Information Societies Technology (IST) program, hog too much public money for technology projects—but at least they are subject to discussion. Hollywood's hymns of praise to the machine do more damage because they paint reactionary social futures as inevitable and dress them up as progress. "The worst culprits are those apologists of the new economy," writes Kunzru; "wearing liberal and countercultural hats, [they] eulogize decentralization, nonlinear causality, and the impossibility of control—but fail to explain why these trends are so wonderful when centralized power, extreme social inequality, and ecological devastation are increasing in the world."[22]

A better innovation approach is to switch attention from science-dominated futures to social fictions in which imagined new contexts enrich an otherwise familiar world. Design scenarios are powerful innovation tools because they make a possible future familiar and enable the participation of potential users in conceiving and shaping what they want.

The important point when envisioning scenarios of human activity is to distinguish explicitly between what Ezio Manzini calls *disabling* and *enabling* solutions.[23] Many of the frustrating and stress-inducing encounters we have with service providers have been given an anodyne name in recent times: the "self-service economy."[24] The hallmark of such services is that they take place with little or no human contact; the customer does the work once done by an employee. This arrangement saves the service supplier a ton of money but simply loads work onto—and steals time from—the user. Nine out of ten people would rather talk to a person when searching for advice or service on the Internet—so we need to demand of providers that they put a person at the other end of the line.

What service designers refer to as sweet spots—instances in which real value is created—occur at the intersection of latent social needs, open systems, smart consumers, and smart companies. New services constantly evolve. This is one reason why Lavrans Løvlie, a service designer with Live|Work in London, prefers what he calls "topological" social scenarios that enable people to become participants rather than audiences for a scenario and imagine their own ways of engaging with services and products. Løvlie and his colleagues use a technique called "evidencing" to create the impression an imagined service might make—but without generating a working prototype at an early stage. In a project on time banking for the telecommunications operator Orange, for example, Live|Work mocked up computer screens, paper invoices, magazine advertisements, reviews in newspapers, and a range of other "touch points" that gave people an impression of a service that did not yet exist.[25]

Too many design methods can indeed limit innovation. Someone also has to provide aesthetic stimulus—to throw wild ideas into the ring—to provoke fresh thinking. Social critics and artists are good candidates for this role. Avant-garde media artists, in particular, intervene on issues of networks, the body, identity, and collaboration. Many of their ideas are exciting and insightful in a way that methods-driven solutions are not. Design can be a useful mediator in breaking down the isolation from one another of artists, computer scientists, and users and in promoting the fruitful interaction among them that may just yield the new concepts and applications that are needed to fulfill the promise of the new technologies.

From Designing For to Designing With

We have learned by now that information technology changes the world continuously. So do people when they use it. Anyone using a system—responding to it, interacting with it, feeding back into it—changes it. Technology has penetrated every aspect of our lives. Human, natural, and industrial systems are irrevocably interpenetrated.

So where does this leave our relationship with complex systems—as designers or as citizens? The story of the Netherlands and its water control system is one example of where our relationships with technology may be headed. The creation of new land out of water is a several-centuries-old tradition in the Netherlands. The famous Delta Works, the biggest Dutch public project ever, created giant pumping stations, dikes, and modern tidal protection systems to protect the land from the sea and the rivers. Behind these impressive achievements were a select cadre of engineers and planners,[26] the true "makers" of Holland—people whom writer A. den Doolaard called the "water wizards."[27] A sense of civic duty and solidarity motivated the Dutch citizenry to take care of the dikes collectively—with the *dike warden* as a key figure to this day. The dike warden can order people to work in the dikes for the greater good of shared protection from the water. The tradition of the dike warden and his approach to managing the water lies behind the Dutch "polder model" of shared responsibility, consensus, and a degree of skill at living together in a small space.[28] The relationship of the Dutch to dikes demonstrates that looking after technology is as much a matter of social organization as it is of engineering. People are too often described and thought of by designers as users or consumers when we really need to think of them as *actors*.

A sense of responsibility comparable to that demonstrated in the water systems of Holland is evident in the open-source movement, in which a new collaborative approach, uniquely adapted to the Internet, has enabled the development of high-quality infrastructures. The collaborative approach of open source is now spreading to other domains. Biologists have embraced open-source methods in genomics and informatics, building massive databases to genetically sequence *E. coli* (yeast). NASA has adopted open-source principles as part of its Mars mission, calling on volunteer "clickworkers" to identify millions of craters and help draw a map of the Red Planet. Astronomy, too, has been transformed by the growth of collaborative networks. Hilary Cottam and Charles Leadbeater, who are studying the implications of open systems for the design of services, report that ten thousand professional astronomers in the world—as well as hundreds of thousands of dedicated amateurs—now collaborate across the Internet. In the last twenty years, they say, "the earth has acquired thousands of new eyes to look into deep space—and the Internet has provided the optic nerves to connect them up. Increasingly astronomy is a science in which a small body of professionals will work in alliance with a vast body of dedicated amateurs." The basic principles of this new landscape, say the authors, can be described as "share the goal; share the work; share the results." They quote as a more down-to-earth example the BBC's Neighbourhood Gardener scheme, which aims to create thousands of local user experts whom people can call on for help and advice. The scheme is being orchestrated around the BBC's well-known gardening programs and aims to create local peer-to-peer communities of learning and support.[29]

Unlike the point-to-mass paradigm of the manufacturing era, a collaborative or open model implies mass participation in creation of a service or situation. A new kind of immersive innovation emerges as the functional divisions between users and producers of a service become blurred. More than seventy-five thousand collaborative software projects are listed at Sourceforge.net, a website for the open-source community with eight hundred thousand registered users. Sourceforge is part of the Open Source Development Network, whose websites deliver more than 160 million page views and reach 9 million unique visitors per month. Projects listed on Sourceforge range from communications (10,327 projects) and games/entertainment (9,648 projects) to sociology (262 projects) and religion (194 projects).[30]

Canadian writers Felix Stalder and Jesse Hirsh call this collaborative gathering and analysis of information "open-source intelligence." Its principles include peer review, reputation, the free sharing of products, and flexible levels of involvement and responsibility.[31] For Thomas Goetz in *Wired*, "open source is doing for mass innovation what the assembly line did for mass production." Goetz tells the story of how an intravenous (IV) saline drip was redesigned by a group called Design That Matters to make it cheaper to use in cholera outbreaks. (These most often occur in less-developed countries, where the high costs of products designed in the North are hard or impossible to sustain.) The team needed to draw on more medical expertise than it had available, so it turned to ThinkCycle, a Web-based industrial-design project that brings together engineers, designers, academics, and professionals from a variety of disciplines. Physicians and engineers pitched in—vetting designs and recommending new paths. Suggestions that emerged from ThinkCycle's collaborative approach led to an ingenious new IV system that costs about $1.25 to manufacture, against the $2,000 of previous solutions. "Open source harnesses the distributive powers of the Internet, parcels the work out to thousands, and uses their piecework to build a better whole," reported Goetz; "it works like an ant colony, where the collective intelligence of the network supersedes any single contributor."[32]

Our world is fast being suffused with software as well as devices, and the open-source approach is a revolution in the way software is designed. "The free sharing of information has nothing to do with altruism or a specific anti-authoritarian social vision," say Stalder and Hirsh. "It is motivated by the fact that in a complex collaborative process, new creations are built on previous creations and provide inspiration for future ones. The ability to freely use and refine those previous creations increases the possibilities for future creativity."[33] Lawrence Lessig calls this an "innovation commons" and cites its existence as one of the major reasons why the Internet as a whole developed so rapidly and innovatively. In the open-source environment, the hurdle to participating in a project is extremely low. Valuable contributions can be as small as a single, one-time effort—a bug report, a penetrating comment in a discussion.[34]

Yochai Benkler, a law professor at New York University, calls this new mode of production in the digitally networked environment "commons-based peer production." Its central characteristic is that groups of individuals successfully collaborate on large-scale projects following a diverse cluster of motivational drives and social signals—rather than market prices or managerial commands. Collaborative design means finding ways to share a vision of a system among all its actors and stakeholders as the system evolves.

Open, networked collaboration works best in the real world and face to face. The most advanced software designers, who call themselves "extreme programmers," have come to value individuals and interactions among them over abstract processes and tools. These principles are the basis of a new paradigm in software that is embodied in the Agile Alliance, which I mentioned in chapter 5. As its website explains, the alliance wants to "restore a balance. We embrace modeling, but not in order to file some diagram in a dusty corporate repository. We embrace documentation, but not hundreds of pages of never-maintained and rarely used tomes. We plan, but recognize the limits of planning in a turbulent environment."[35] The alliance's "Manifesto for Agile Software Development" describes better ways of developing software by doing it and helping others do it. "Through this work," says the manifesto, "we have come to value individuals and interactions over processes and tools, working software over comprehensive documentation, customer collaboration over contract negotiation, [and] responding to change over following a plan."[36]

From Design as Project to Design as Service

Our business models in design have to change if collaborative, open, and continuous design is to flourish. In the past, design was about the form and function of things. These features, which were limited in space and time, could be delivered in a fixed form, such as a blueprint. In today's ultranetworked world, it makes more sense to think of design as a process that continuously defines a system's rules rather than its outcomes. Stand-alone products—refrigerators, cars, cookers, televisions, and wide-bodied jets—are needed within product-service systems, but the real action will take place among the organizations developing new services and infrastructures.

In logistics and manufacturing, the elements of a light economy are already being prepared—although their designers are not always aware of it. A growing number of companies that once sold only products now think of themselves as service providers. Their number includes Xerox (formerly photocopiers, now document services), Interface (formerly carpets, now floor-covering services), Electrolux (formerly vacuum cleaners, now industrial cleaning), IBM (formerly computers, now a whole range of business transformation services), and Wilkhahn (formerly a desk maker, now in service support for "working, conferencing and relaxing"). Few of these companies have made ethical decisions to go green, but a product-service system approach allows a firm to move away from the commodification of the product and the reduced profit margins that typically entails.[37] Demand-responsive services and dynamic resource allocation are transforming the ways matter, energy, money, and people are flowing through the system.

Against this backdrop of situations in which systems don't stop changing, the idea of a self-contained design project—of "signing off" on a design when it is finished—makes no sense. A project-based business model in design is like a water company that delivers a bucket of water to your door and pronounces its mission accomplished. Interaction designer Alan Cooper is scornful of this flawed development model. "It's harder than you think to squander millions of dollars, but a flawed software development process is a tool well-suited to the task," he quips. "Most software products don't have a description; all they have is a shopping list of features. [But] a shopping bag filled with flour, eggs, milk and sugar is not the same thing as a cake."[38] Designing *with*, rather than *for*, people raises further questions about current business models. Who pays whom, and for what, when "consumers" add value to a system by being part of its development?

As a wide range of organizations transforms itself into service providers, design too is better thought of as a service than as a manufacturing activity. "System design is a complex process, period," says Carroll. "The novelty and complexity of technical issues is compounded by interactions among these issues, and with the particular skills and backgrounds of team members. Managing such processes is not just a matter of control and coordination: management means finding ways to share a vision of the system among all the team members as it evolves."[39]

I don't know how service as a utility should be paid for, or by whom. But because demand for it is clear enough, new business models will surely emerge. I can foresee a design economy that is based on rolling service contracts—but then again, perhaps a totally different business model will emerge. I hope so.

The Dance of the Big and the Small

"What do I see when I think of History? I see the dance of the Big and the Small." Eugenio Barba, who runs the Odin Theatre in Denmark, describes our situation beautifully. There are moments during this dance when we are swept along by events, he says, and others when we ourselves influence the course of time. Says Barba: "Children who build a small dam on the margins of the current of a great river, who make a tiny pool in which to bathe and splash around, do not play in the rushing current, yet neither are they separated from the water flowing in the centre of the river. They create, along its banks, small inlets and unexpected habitats, thus passing to the future the marks of their difference."[40]

We've allowed too long the idea that the world is "out of control"—be it our cities, the economy, or technology. We've filled the world with complex systems and technologies that are indeed hard to understand, let alone shape or redirect. But we're people, not ants. We have a culture, and language, and the ability to understand and share knowledge about abstract phenomena. Ants don't have that. Neither do they have a tool, design, with which to shape them. We do.

The dance of the big and the small entails a new kind of design. It involves a new relationship between subject and object and a commitment to think about the consequences of design actions before we take them, in a state of mind—design mindfulness—that values place, time, and cultural difference.

This book will have done its job if it provokes you to think about one or two small design steps you might take on Monday morning. Design a way to monitor the natural and industrial systems around you and make them knowable to you and your colleagues. Design a way to close loops in the flows of matter and energy in your immediate surroundings. Design things to be closer together, in webs rather than in drawn-out chains, in daily-life situations. Design connections between you and new people, knowledge, and disciplines. Design a new way to collaborate and do projects. Whatever you choose to do, don't try to do it alone. We are all designers now.

Notes

Introduction

1. Statistic quoted in Design Council, *Annual Review 2002* (London: Design Council, 2002), 19.

2. Herbert Simon, *The Sciences of the Artificial* (Cambridge, Mass.: MIT Press, 1996), chap. 1.

3. Victor Papanek, *Design for the Real World: Human Ecology and Social Change* (New York: Random House, 1972), 23.

4. In 1970 Herman Kahn, the first modern "futurist" (and allegedly the role model for Dr. Strangelove in Stanley Kubrick's film), anticipated that Japan's unique cultural values would enable its economy to reach and surpass that of the United States in per capita GDP. Herman Kahn, *The Emerging Japanese Superstate: Challenge and Response* (Englewood Cliffs, N.J.: Prentice Hall, 1970).

5. The European Commission, which is responsible for 5 percent of the continent's research spending, is looking for ways to manage technology research as a self-organizing complex network. Peter Johnston, who helps run the Commision's Information Society Technologies program, says that the value of EU support to research cooperation in the EU lies as much in the social capital and cohesion it generates as in the knowledge capital it produces: "The effectiveness of research now depends critically on the strength of networking between research institutes and between research disciplines." Peter Johnston, "Introduction," in *Complexity Tools in Evaluation of Policy Options for a Networked Knowledge Society*, ed. Peter Johnston (Brussels: European Commission Directorate General, Information Society Technologies, 2003), 3.

6. Daniel Cohen, *Our Modern Times: The New Nature of Capitalism in the Information Age* (Cambridge, Mass.: MIT Press, 2003).

7. During the early years of the twentieth century, several thousand people were developing applications of the internal-combustion engine, often unique ones. Most of the endeavors went under, and a decade later only a handful survived. But one of these applications, the automobile, became an icon of modernity and a driver of

transformation in our cities and lives. Along the way the car has enabled sprawl, disrupted communities, polluted the air, and killed a lot of people—and it continues to do so. But its inventors could not have known this would happen.

8. For Thacker, the main actors in biotech imagineering are science research institutions, pharmaceutical companies, public policy negotiations, science education, medicine, and popular science culture. "Its primary aim," he says, "is to forge intimate links, if not outright linear histories, between future promises and current research." Eugene Thacker, "The Science Fictioning of Biotechnology," *032c*, no. 4 (Winter 2002–2003), 106, available through the publisher's website (www.032c.com).

9. The "vested interests" Thacker refers to are those mentioned in note 8. Thacker, "The Science Fictioning of Biotechnology," 109.

10. "Conversation is our next instrument providing the inspiration for achieving ambitions which have hitherto seemed impossible," says Zeldin. "Big changes are superficial unless they are the sum of a lot of little changes in the way we understand and treat one another." To faciliate such conversations, Zeldin set up The Oxford Muse in 2001. "The First Outline of the Aims of The Oxford Muse 2001," available on The Oxford Muse website at http://www.oxfordmuse.com/museideas/museaims.htm.

11. Statistics taken from the South African website CellularOnline (http://www .mobileoffice.co.za/stats/stats-main.htm).

12. François Jégou and Ezio Manzini, *Sustainable Everyday: A Catalogue of Promising Solutions* (Milan: Edizione Ambiente, 2004). Manzini ran design scenario workshops in several countries as preparation for the exhibition "Sustainable Everyday: Scenarios for Urban Life," which was held at the Milan Triennale in 2003.

13. The English writer Charles Leadbeater has written extensively about innovation as platform building. See, for example, Charles Leadbeater, *Personalisation through Participation* (London: Demos, 2004).

14. Papanek, *Design for the Real World*, 14.

15. Alain Findeli, "Rethinking Design Education for the 21st Century: Theoretical, Methodological, and Ethical Discussion," *Design Issues* 17, no. 1, 5–7.

16. *BoloBolo* is a visionary booklet that addresses the question "How would I really like to live?" The book's author, styled only as "P.M.," discusses the constituent elements of a human-scale utopia. P.M., *BoloBolo* (New York: Autonomedia, 1995), 58.

1 Lightness

1. According to the U.S. National Academy of Sciences, the Earth's surface temperature has risen by about one degree Fahrenheit in the past century, with accelerated

warming during the past two decades. The UN Intergovernmental Panel on Climate Change says that if we carry on burning fossil fuels at present rates, the concentration of greenhouse gases in the atmosphere will increase by 50 percent within fifteen years—risking catastrophic climate shifts.

2. A team of international climatologists, led by Paul Grutzen, whose work on the ozone hole won him the 1995 Nobel Prize for Science, identified the cloud. At the time of my visit, the monsoon in many parts of India and Southeast Asia either had not arrived or had been particularly severe. This terrifying story only made page 2 of the local media and disappeared completely after a couple of days. Hong Kong shrugged and went about its business.

3. Sarah Graham, "Making Microchips Takes Mountain of Materials," *Scientific American*, November 6, 2002, available at http://www.sciam.com/article.cfm?chanID=sa003&articleID=0000E57E-E47B-1DC6-AF71809EC588EEDF.

4. Producing a single chip—the tiny wafer used for memory in personal computers—requires at least 3.7 pounds of fossil fuel and chemical inputs. Each chip requires 3.5 pounds of fossil fuels, 0.16 pounds of chemicals, 70.5 pounds of water, and 1.5 pounds of elemental gases (mainly nitrogen). These estimates were reported in *Environmental Science and Technology*, a peer-reviewed journal of the American Chemical Society, the world's largest scientific society. Eric Williams, Robert U. Ayres, and Miriam Heller, "The 1.7 Kg Microchip: Energy and Material Use in the Production of Semiconductor Devices," *Environmental Science and Technology* 36, no. 24 (December 15, 2002), 5504–5510.

5. IDC, a research firm based in Washington, D.C., publishes regular forecasts about future microprocessor production. An overview of the topics, including microprocessors, on which the firm has conducted research is available on its website at http://www.idc.com/research/.

In September 2003, a network to connect many of the millions of radio frequency identification tags that are already in the world (and the billions more on their way) was launched. Their aim was to replace the global barcode with a universal system that can provide a unique number for every object in the world. Sean Dodson, "The Internet of Things," *Guardian* (U.K.), October 9, 2003, available at http://www.guardian.co.uk/online/story/0,3605,1058506,00.html.

6. Paul Hawken, Amory Lovins, and Hunter Lovins, *Natural Capitalism* (London: Earthscan, 1999).

7. "Accelerated Life, Computers, and the Environment," *NETFUTURE: Technology and Human Responsibility*, no. 54 (July 30, 1997), available at www.praxagora.com/stevet/netfuture/1997/Jul3097_54.html. See also Wolfgang Sachs, "Post-Fossil Development Patterns in the North" (paper presented at the IPCC Expert Meeting on Development, Equity and Sustainability, Colombo, Sri Lanka, April 27–29, 1999).

8. Lennart Forseback, *Case Studies of the Information Society and Sustainable Development* (Brussels: European Commission Information Society Directorate General, 2000), available at www.forseback.se/pdf/case_infosoc.pdf.

9. Each year in Europe around seven million metric tons of electronic waste are generated. When electronic devices are disposed of, some materials can be put back through various cycles to be recouped. But for this to be possible, the recouping needs to be designed in at the start. Since 1994, a system has been in place in Switzerland for take back and disposal of office electronics, computers, equipment from the graphics industry, telephone end devices such as answering machines, mobile telephones, and equipment from entertainment electronics. The system is financed by means of a recycling fee that is included in the contract. Following Switzerland, the European Union has now specified binding recycling targets, and other countries are developing similar initiatives. Manufacturers of equipment, of components, and of the materials contained in them are considering how best to react to the European Union's new directive. Swiss Association for Information, Communication and Organisational Technology (SWICO), *Activity Report 2001: The Environment* (Zurich: SWICO, 2002); and Association of Plastics Manufacturers in Europe (APME), *Eco-efficiency of Plastic from Electronic and Electric Equipment* (Brussels: APME, 2002).

10. Franz A. Hartmann and Lorenz M. Hilty, "Integration von Material- und Informationsflussanalysen" (Information of Material and Information Flows Analysis), in *Proceedings of the Workshop "Operations Research im Umweltschutz" of the German Society for Operations Research, Karlsruhe, 2001*, ed. Franz A. Hartmann and Lorenz M. Hilty, available at http://www.empa.ch/plugin/template/empa/*/7132/---/l=3.

11. George Gilder, *Telecosm: How Infinite Bandwidth Will Revolutionize Our World* (New York: Free Press, 2000), 5.

12. Rachel Konrad, "Server Farms on Hot Seat amid Power Woes," CNET News.com, May 14, 2001, available at http://news.com.com/2100-1017-257567.html?legacy=cnet.

13. Hawken, Lovins, and Lovins, *Natural Capitalism*, 81.

14. Ibid., 51.

15. Ibid., 52. A lot of the million-pounds weight in an ecological rucksack consists of building materials. Mass balance, and other modeling tools, are used to assess impacts associated with various construction processes, and thus to develop a more sustainable system for their management. A British initiative coming to grips with these material flows is called "Rocks to Rubble," available at http://www.biffa.co.uk/pdfs/massbalance/Rocks2RubbleNW.pdf.

16. The complex interaction between a product and the environment is dealt with in a life cycle assessment (LCA). The basis of an LCA is an inventory of all the inputs

and outputs of industrial processes that occur during the life cycle of a product: the production, distribution, use, and final disposal of the product. A Dutch company, PRé Consultants, has developed a variety of methods and software tools that help organizations with materials flow analysis, environmental impact measurement, environmental accounting, and life cycle costing, as well as complex system modeling. PRé Consultants, "What Is LCA?" available at http://www.pre.nl/life_cycle _assessment/life_cycle_assessment.htm.

17. Mathis Wackernagel leads the Indicators Program at Redefining Progress in San Francisco, a project to publish ecological footprints country by country. The subtitle of the project's report asks, "How Much Nature Do They Use?—How Much Nature Do They Have?" Wackernagel's group estimates that by 2020, humans will consume between 180 and 220 percent of Earth's biological capacity. Mathis Wackernagel, Larry Onisto, Alejandro Callejas Linares, Ina Susana López Falfán, Jesus Mén dez García, Ana Isabel Suárez Guerrero, and M. Guadalupe Suárez Guerrero, *Ecological Footprints of Nations: How Much Nature Do They Use? How Much Nature Do They Have?* available on the Earth Council website at http://www.ecouncil.ac.cr/rio/focus/report/ english/footprint/.

18. DALYs rate different disability levels caused by various forms of damage: respiratory and carcinogenic effects and the effects of climate change, ozone layer depletion, and ionizing radiation. Ecotoxicity is expressed as the percentage of all species present in the environment living under toxic stress—the potentially affected fraction (PAF).

19. If a manufacturer of a product is asked to take extended producer responsibility, data need to be made available on all stages of the product life cycle, from production to disposal. ELIMA is a project to design and test information systems and life cycle models. "ELIMA Project," available on the website of the School of Engineering at Sheffield Hallam University at http://www.shu.ac.uk/schools/eng/industry/ELIMA .html.

20. PRé Consultants, "What Is LCA?"

21. The first Eternally Yours conference, in 1997, led to the publication of an award-winning book called *Visions on Product Endurance*. The book is now out of print, but the text is available as a .pdf file in the archives of the Eternally Yours website at http://www.eternally-yours.org/. The organization published another book, *Time in Design—Product Value Sustenance* (Rotterdam: 010 Publishers, 2004), available at http://www.010publishers.nl/.

22. Arnold Tukker, Erick Haag, and Peter Eder, *Eco-Design: European State of the Art, Part I: Comparative Analysis and Conclusions* (report prepared by the European Science and Technology Observatory [ESTO] for the European Commission's Joint Research Centre, Institute for Prospective Technological Studies, Seville, Spain, 2000).

23. Han Brezet, Philip Vergragt, and Tom van der Horst, eds., *Vision on Sustainable Product Innovation* (Amsterdam: BIS Publishers, 2001); see also the Kathalys website (http://www.kathalys.com).

24. Hawken, Lovins, and Lovins, *Natural Capitalism*, 9.

25. Ibid., 73.

26. "*Natural capital*," according to the forum, "is any stock or flow of energy and material that produces goods and services. It includes:

Resources   renewable and non-renewable materials

Sinks   that absorb, neutralise or recycle wastes

Processes   climate regulation

Natural capital is the basis not only of production but of life itself! *Human capital* consists of people's health, knowledge, skills and motivation. All these things are needed for productive work. Enhancing human capital through education and training is central to a flourishing economy. *Social capital* concerns the institutions that help us maintain and develop human capital in partnership with others; e.g., families, communities, businesses, trade unions, schools, and voluntary organisations. *Manufactured capital* comprises material goods or fixed assets which contribute to the production process rather than being the output itself—e.g., tools, machines and buildings. *Financial capital* plays an important role in our economy, enabling the other types of Capital to be owned and traded. But unlike the other types, it has no real value itself but is representative of natural, human, social or manufactured capital; e.g., shares, bonds or banknotes. Sustainable development is the best way to manage these capital assets in the long-term. It is a dynamic process through which organisations can begin to achieve a balance between their environmental, social and economic activities." Forum for the Future's extensive website includes explanations of four different models of sustainable development: Triple-Bottom Line, Five Capitals Model, Twelve Features of a Sustainable Society, and The Natural Step Framework. The text quoted here is from "The Five Capitals Model," available at http://www.forumforthefuture.org.uk/aboutus/fivecapitalsmodel_page814.aspx.

27. Hartmann and Hilty, "Integration von Material- und Informationsflussanalysen"; Ernst von Weizsäcker, Amory Lovins, and L. Hunter Lovins, *Factor Four: Doubling Wealth, Halving Resource Use* (London: Earthscan, 1997); E. Heiskanen and M. Jalas, *Dematerialization through Services—A Review and Evaluation of the Debate* (Helsinki: Ministry of the Environment, 2000); E. Heiskanen, M. Halme, M. Jalas, A. Kärnä, and R. Lovio, *Dematerialisation: The Potential of ICT and Services* (Helsinki: Ministry of the Environment, 2001); H. Herring, "The Rebound Effect, Sustainable Consumption and Electronic Appliances," in "Sustainability in the Information Society," special issue, *Environmental Impact Assessment Review* 22, no. 5 (2002); Lorenz M. Hilty, T. F. Ruddy, and D. Schulthess, "Resource Intensity and Dematerialization Potential of Information Society Technologies" (discussion paper no. 2000-01, Sus-

tainable Europe Research Institute [SERI], Solothurn University of Applied Sciences, Olten, Switzerland, 2000, available at http://www.seri.at/globalisation/).

28. The three hundred watts of electricity consumed by a computer server may not sound like a lot, but one thousand such servers in a building require enormous amounts of electricity (see Konrad, "Server Farms on Hot Seat Amid Power Woes"). Most of the time personal computers, too, are powered on even when not in use. One study found that 74 percent of PCs are on during the day but used only about 12 percent of the time. G. Newsham and D. Tiller, "The Energy Consumption of Desktop Computers: Measurement and Savings Potential," *IEEE Transactions on Industry Applications* 30, no. 4 (July/August 1994).

29. Ian Swingland, *Capturing Carbon and Conserving Biodiversity: The Market Approach* (London: Earthscan/The Royal Society, 2003).

30. Major companies such as British Airports Authority, British Petroleum, DuPont, Ford, Novartis, British Telecom, Co-operative Bank, Shell, and Unilever have already acknowledged formally the need to address the "triple bottom line" of sustainable development. Shell is developing internal management systems, in its case the Sustainable Development Management Framework, to take things to the next level. A consulting firm called SustainAbility helps businesses from a variety of industries and world regions understand and respond strategically to the evolving challenges of sustainable development. SustainAbility's website (http://www.sustainability.com) includes a well-selected range of links, case studies, and publications.

31. Statistic quoted in Design Council, *Annual Review 2002* (London: Design Council, 2002), 19.

32. Hawken, Lovins, and Lovins, *Natural Capitalism*, 73.

33. For examples of this trend, see Per Sorup and Tom Gameson, *Natural Resources and the Environment Panel Report* (Futures Report Series 05, Institute for Prospective Technological Studies, Seville, Spain, June 1999), 59. A comprehensive archive of European policy and research publications on environmental issues is available at http://europa.eu.int/comm/sustainable/pages/links_en.htm.

34. Ezio Manzini and Carlo Vezzoli, *Product-Service Systems and Sustainability: Opportunities for Sustainable Solutions* (Paris: United Nations Environment Programme, 2002).

35. François Jégou and Ezio Manzini, *Sustainable Everyday: A Catalogue of Promising Solutions* (Milan: Edizione Ambiente, 2004).

36. Ibid.

37. In Amsterdam, where my wife and I lived, it is illegal to throw away electrical appliances, or even batteries—but the city runs a collection service for these items, and once a month, a truck came to our area. It took me several trips to throw the

defunct answering machines and other electrical junk of just one household into the back of the truck.

38. Forsebäck, *Case Studies of the Information Society and Sustainable Development*, 61.

39. Ibid., 27.

40. Chris Pacione, "Bodymedia Case Study" (keynote address at Doors of Perception 6: Lightness, Amsterdam, November 11–13, 2000, available on the Doors of Perception website at http://museum.doorsofperception.com/doors/revamped_ frameset.php?doorid).

41. Ibid.

42. Paul Brown, "Life on the Planet under Threat: Influential Body Says Last Chances Must Be Seized," *Guardian* (U.K.), January 9, 2003, p. 13.

43. Theodore Roszak, Mary E. Gomes, and Allen D. Kanner, eds., *Ecopsychology* (San Francisco: Sierra Club Books, 1995).

44. Ezio Manzini, "Space and Pace of Flows" (presentation at Doors of Perception 7: Flow, Amsterdam, November 14–16, 2000, available on the Doors of Perception website at http://flow.doorsofperception.com/content/manzini_trans.html).

45. Hawkens, Lovins, and Lovins, *Natural Capitalism*, 176.

46. Clive Hamilton, *Growth Fetish* (London: Pluto, 2004), 14.

47. Antoine Saint-Exupéry, *Flight to Anas* (1942), trans. Lewis Galantiere (New York: Harvest, 1969).

48. William McDonough and Partners, "The Hannover Principles: Design for Sustainability" (report prepared for EXPO 2000, Hannover, Germany, William McDonough Architects, Charlottesville, Va., 1992, available at http://www .mcdonough.com/principles.pdf).

49. William Uricchio, "Technologies of Time," in *Visions of Modernity*, ed. J. Olsson (Berkeley and Los Angeles: University of California Press).

50. Ibid., 42.

51. William McDonough and Michael Baumgart, in introduction to *Cradle to Cradle: Remake the Way We Make Things* (New York: North Point, 2002).

52. Theodore Roszak, "Where Psyche Meets Gaia," in Theodore Roszak, Mary E. Gomes, and Allen D. Kanner, eds., *Ecopsychology* (San Francisco: Sierra Club Books, 1995), 12.

53. Italo Calvino, "Lightness," in *Six Memos for a New Millennium* (London: Vintage, 1996), 7.

2 Speed

1. Bruce Chatwin, *The Songlines* (London: Vintage, 1987), 228.

2. Michael Dell, quoted in Joan Magretta, "Managing Velocity: The Power of Virtual Integration" (interview with Michael Dell), *Harvard Business Review* (March–April 1998).

3. The slogan was attributed to the head of Hitachi's portable computer division during the 1990s in M. Ryan, *The Power of Patience* (Manchester, Vt.: Northshire, 2003).

4. World Bank, *Globalization, Growth and Poverty: Building an Inclusive World Economy* (Washington, D.C.: International Bank for Settlements and the World Bank, 2002), available at http://econ.worldbank.org/prr/globalization/text-2857/.

5. Edward O. Wilson, *Consilience: The Unity of Knowledge* (London: Little Brown, 1998), 146–147.

6. Dee W. Hoch, quoted in Uffe Elbek, ed., *KaosPilot A–Z* (Aarhus, Denmark: Kaos-Pilots, 2004), 100.

7. Jim Clark, quoted in Michael Lewis, *The New New Thing: A Silicon Valley Story* (New York: Norton, 1999).

8. Wolfgang Sachs, "Why Speed Matters" (presentation at Doors of Perception 4: Speed, Amsterdam, November 7–8, 1996, available on the Doors of Perception website at http://museum.doorsofperception.com/doors/revamped_frameset.php?doorid =sachs).

9. Ibid.

10. Susan George, "When I Was Growing Up" (presentation at Doors of Perception 5: Speed, Amsterdam, November 7–8, 1996, available on the Doors of Perception website at http://museum.doorsofperception.com/doors/revamped_frameset .php?doorid=george).

11. T. S. Ray, "A Network-Wide Biodiversity Reserve for Digital Organisms," in *Proceedings of Imagina 96* (Bry-sur-Marne, France: Institut National De L'audiovisuel, 1996), 15–26.

12. Sachs, "Why Speed Matters."

13. Lewis Mumford, *Technics and Civilization* (1934), quoted in Robert Levine, *A Geography of Time: The Temporal Misadventures of a Social Psychologist* (New York: Basic Books, 1997), 63.

14. Levine, *A Geography of Time*, 57.

15. Ibid., 164.

16. Interaction designer Michael Kieslinger develops this analysis further in his project Fluid Time, which is also discussed on page 47. See the project description on the website of the Interaction Design Institute Ivrea (http://projects.interaction-ivrea.it/endofyear/it/research/fluidtime.asp) for further information.

17. Writing, in 1846, about his time in the woods, Thoreau noted, "here is an incessant flow of novelty into the world, and yet we tolerate incredible dullness." Henry David Thoreau, *Thoughts from Walden Pond* (Petaluma, Calif.: Pomegranate Communications, 1998).

18. Marshall Sahlins, *Stone Age Economics* (New York: Aldine de Gruyter, 1972).

19. P.M. (pseudonym), *Bolo Bolo* (New York: Autonomedia, 1995), 39.

20. Ibid., 41.

21. Levine, *A Geography of Time*.

22. Ibid.

23. For a popular account of the trend, see Michael Smolensky, *The Body Clock Guide to Better Health* (New York: Holt, 2000).

24. David Winnicott, *Psychoanalytic Explorations* (Cambridge, Mass.: Harvard University Press, 1989).

25. Levine, *A Geography of Time*, 27.

26. Pierre Bourdieu, quoted in Ibid., 19.

27. Levine, *A Geography of Time*, 164.

28. Tristram Hunt, *Building Jerusalem: The Rise and Fall of the Victorian City* (London: Weidenfeld and Nicolson, 2004), 4.

29. "Civilization alone does not cause nervousness. The Greeks were certainly civilized, but they were not nervous," writes Beard. "Edison's electric light is now sufficiently advanced in an experimental direction to give us the best possible illustration of the effects of modern civilization on the nervous system." George Miller Beard, *American Nervousness, With Its Causes and Consequences* (1881), available at http://condor.depaul.edu/~history/webresources/usprimary/Beard.htm.

30. Wolfgang Schivelbusch, *The Railway Journey: The Industrialization of Time and Space in the Nineteenth Century* (Berkeley and Los Angeles: University of California Press, 1987).

31. Don Tapscott, *The Digital Economy: Promise and Peril in the Age of Networked Intelligence* (New York: McGraw-Hill, 1997), 71.

32. Ludwig Siegele, "How about Now?" (survey), *The Economist*, February 2, 2002, p. 3.

33. Vivek Ranadive, *The Power of Now: How Winning Companies Sense and Respond to Change Using Real-Time Technology* (New York: McGraw-Hill, 1999).

34. Vivek Ranadive, quoted in Siegele, "How about Now?," 5.

35. Danielle Gobert, "Designing Wearable Performance Support: Insights from the Early Literature," *Technical Communication* 49, no. 4 (November 2000), 444–448, available at http://www.gloriagery.com/articles/Gobert.pdf. Another source of information on wearables and "connected clothing" is the Smart Textiles Network. Its website (http://www.smartextiles.co.uk) describes applications that include health care and telemedicine; military, police, and emergency service equipment; entertainment, sports and leisure; and fashion wear.

36. For an insightful discussion of professional knowledge in the information age, see Francis Duffy, *Architectural Knowledge* (London: Spon, 1998).

37. Henri Bergson, *Duration and Simultaneity* (Manchester, England: Clinamen Press, 1999), xiv.

38. J. Robinson, "Your Money or Your Time," *American Demographics* (November 1991), 22–25.

39. Ilya Prigogine, quoted in Robert B. Tucker, "Ilya Prigogine: Wizard of Time," *Omni* (May 1983).

40. Sustainable tourism attempts to make a low impact on the environment and local culture, while helping to generate income, employment, and the conservation of local ecosystems. It is responsible tourism that is both ecologically and culturally sensitive. "Sustainable Tourism," available on the website of the Global Development Research Center at http://www.gdrc.org/uem/eco-tour/eco-tour.html.

41. The term "eco-tourism" is used loosely in a variety of ways, but reliable definitions and data are provided by *Planeta: Global Journal of Practical Ecotourism* on its website (http://www.planeta.com).

42. Michael Douglas, "Tramjatra" (presentation at Doors of Perception 6: Lightness, Amsterdam, November 11–13, 2000, available on the Doors of Perception website at http://museum.doorsofperception.com/doors/revamped_frameset.php?doorid=4).

43. John Whitelegg, editorial, *Journal of World Transport Policy and Practice* 7, no. 1 (2001), available at http://www.ecoplan.org/wtpp/general/vol7-1.htm#editorial.

44. See the Slow Food website (http://www.slowfood.com/eng). Slow food would be spreading more quickly were it not for dysfunctional supply webs. One in three British consumers would pay more for locally produced food, for example, but six million of them are unable to buy the organic milk they want through lack of availability on the street. The result is that 50 percent of the organic milk produced is sold at a loss to the nonorganic market. Organic Milk Suppliers Cooperative (OMSCo),

"Six Million Britons Crying Over Lack of Organic Milk," August 30, 2002, available at http://www.omsco.co.uk/frameset.cfm.

45. "Dabbawallas—Epitome of Management Skills," *Times of India*, January 18, 2004, available at http://www1.timesofindia.indiatimes.com/articleshow/430392.cms.

46. The examples presented here have been extracted from François Jégou and Ezio Manzini, *Sustainable Everyday: A Catalogue of Promising Solutions* (Milan: Edizione Ambiente, 2004), available at http://www.edizioniambiente.it.

47. See the Slow Cities website at http://www.matogmer.no/slow_cities__citta_slow .htm.

48. Ezio Manzini, "Space and Pace of Flows" (presentation at Doors of Perception 7: Flow, Amsterdam, November 14–16, 2000, available on the Doors of Perception website at http://flow.doorsofperception.com/content/manzini_trans.html).

49. Juliet B. Schor, *The Overspent American: Upscaling, Downshifting, and the New Consumer* (New York: Basic Books, 1998).

50. Lee Gomes, "Can Business-to-Business Survive? Hunt Family Finds Fax and Telephone Beat Out Internet," *Wall Street Journal*, March 19, 2001, pp. 23–24.

51. For an excellent account of the nemawashi factor, see Kayoko Ota, "Tokyo," in *Workspheres: Design and Contemporary Work Styles*, ed. Paola Antonelli (New York: Museum of Modern Art, 2001). The website for the Workspheres exhibition is at http://www.moma.org/exhibitions/2001/workspheres/.

52. Esther Dyson, *Release 2.0: A Design for Living in the Digital Age* (New York: Bantam Dell, 1997).

53. Jeremy Rifkin, *Time Wars: The Primacy Conflict in Human History* (New York: Henry Holt, 1987).

54. Ivan Illich, "Speed and the Quick" (presentation at Doors of Perception 4: Speed, Amsterdam, November 7–8, 1996, available on the Doors of Perception website at http://www.doorsofperception.com/speed).

55. For further information about Project F, see the Whirlpool website (http://www.project-f.whirlpool.co.uk/).

56. As the Project F handbook explains, "Purification of 'grey' water is accomplished using phitodepuration. Loads of various sizes can be accommodated an a series of pods. Washing can take place as the need arises because an individual pod can be removed, loaded, and replaced at any time. The cycle begins in a holding tank reserved for fresh and refreshed water. The water moves to the wash pods, where it is used to clean and rinse laundry. From there, it passes to a plant-filled container for purification. Once refreshed, the water returns to the holding tank for storage until

needed again. The elimination of pollutants occurs through physical processes (filtration), chemical processes (absorption of pollutants by the plants), and biological processes (bacterial degradation and antibiosis)."

57. See the Fluid Time website (http://www.fluidtime.net).

58. National Health Service (United Kingdom), "NHS Primary Care Trust Survey" (2004), available on the NHS website at http://www.nhssurveys.org/categories.asp?parent=117.

59. Levine, *A Geography of Time*.

60. Stewart Brand, *The Clock of the Long Now: Time and Responsibility* (London: Weidenfeld and Nicolson, 1999), 2.

61. Charles Leadbeater, *Living on Thin Air* (London: Viking, 1999).

62. Matthias Rieger, "Some Remarks about Speed" (presentation at Doors of Perception 4: Speed, Amsterdam, November 7–8, 1996, available on the Doors of Perception website at http://museum.doorsofperception.com/?doorid=4).

63. Ibid.

3 Mobility

1. OECD and EC documents quoted in Per Sorup and Tom Gameson, eds., *Natural Resources and the Environment* (panel report, Institute for Prospective Technological Studies, Joint Research Centre, European Commission, Seville, Spain, available on the Joint Research Centre website [http://www.jrc.es]). Other costs of mobility are indirect but no less devastating. The average tourist uses as much water in 24 hours as a villager in a developing country uses in 100 days. In 1950, there were about 25 million international tourist visits; by 2020, 1.6 billion of us will travel overseas on holiday. If the resulting carbon emissions and water consumption were charged against the tourist industry, it would not be perceived to be the cash cow it is today. Details are available at http://www.responsible-travel.com and at http://www.planeta.com.

2. Jeffrey Kenworthy and Felix Lauba, *An International Sourcebook of Automobile Dependence in Cities, 1960–1990* (Boulder: University of Colorado Press, 2000).

3. According to the website of consultants Casella Stanger, "In July 2000, BAA Gatwick launched its Sustainable Development Strategy and signed a unique legal agreement designed to protect local communities from the impact of future airport growth.... The Strategy includes action to tackle some of the issues of most concern to stakeholders, such as aircraft noise, transport, energy, waste, air quality, and community over the next 10 years. Casella Stanger was commissioned to conduct an independent audit of progress towards these.... The results of the process are an external verification statement that becomes publicly available in October of each

year." For more information, see "Casella Stanger Clients: BAA," available at http://www.stanger.co.uk/Clients/Detail.asp?id=121.

4. Estimates for the costs of the carbon dioxide, nitrogen, sulfur dioxide, hydrocarbons, water vapor, and other gunk spewed out by airplanes ranges from one to six billion pounds a year. When five thousand participants from over two hundred countries attended the World Summit of the Information Society in Geneva in 2003, their participation at that one event generated about ten thousand tons of the carbon dioxide emissions that contribute to global warming. CLiPP is a Swiss center of competence in the area of climate protection and carbon dioxide compensation. CLiPP's climate ticket compensates for the carbon dioxide emission of travels by air. For every hour in flight, says the organization, fifty liters of kerosene are used per passenger and 125 kilograms of carbon dioxide are emitted. With the climate ticket, entire companies, business travelers, or individuals can help ecologically to absorb their travels by air. "Climate Ticket," available on the CLiPP website at http://www.clipp.org/en/angebot/klimaticket.php.

5. European Organisation for the Safety of Air Navigation, ed., *Forecast of Annual Number of IFR Flights (2004–2010)* (February 2004), available at http://www.eurocontrol.int/statfor/forecasts/.

6. Ibid.

7. European Organisation for the Safety of Air Navigation, ed., *Challenges to Growth* (December 2004), available at http://www.eurocontrol.int.

8. NASA's reasoning is that more than 98 percent of the American population lives within a thirty-minute drive of one of the country's five thousand public-use landing facilities. With suitable safety investment, enhanced air traffic control systems, and the development of small, light aircraft, far more people could fly direct point to point than are able to do so today.

9. Christian Rozycki, Heinz Koeser, and Henning Schwarz, "Ecology Profile of the German High-Speed Rail Passenger Transport System, ICE," in *Environmental Guidelines for the Procurement of New Rolling Stock* (Berlin: International Union of Railways [IUC], July 2003), available at www.railway-procurement.org/docs/Prosper/PROSPER_environmental_guideline_en.pdf (password protected).

10. A wide variety of transport and mobility statistics is published by the International Airline Transport Association (IATA) in its *World Air Transport Statistics*, from which this statistic is taken. Information about the publication is available on the IATA website at http://www.iata.org/ps/publications/9011.htm.

11. John Whitelegg, "Time Pollution," *Ecologist* 23, no. 4 (July/August 1993), available at http://www.eco-logica.co.uk/TimePollution.pdf. A list of books by Whitelegg is available at http://www.eco-logica.co.uk/books.html. Whitelegg is also involved

in the online discussion forum World Transport (http://groups.yahoo.com/group/WorldTransport/messages/).

12. Mayer Hillman, "More Public Transport Will Make Things Worse," *Independent*, July 22, 2000, p. 4.

13. Whitelegg, "Time Pollution."

14. Car sharing is another way to reduce shopping mobility. According to Lennart Forsebäck, a combination of the two approaches among Stockholm's 1.4 million inhabitants could remove two hundred million kilometers in car journeys per year. Lennart Forsebäck, *Case Studies of the Information Society and Sustainable Development* (Brussels: European Commission Information Society Directorate General, 2000), available at www.forseback.se/pdf/case_infosoc.pdf.

15. The weight of goods transported by road between Spain and Portugal and the rest of Europe grew in the 1990s from thirty to ninety-four million tons a year. "D'un réseau ferroviaire asphyxié aux autoroutes de la mer (Asphyxiated by a River of Steel on Motorways to the Sea)," *L'Humanité*, June 9, 2004, available at http://www.humanite.presse.fr/journal/2004-06-09/2004-06-09-395145.

16. 244 million containers times 40 feet (13 meters) container length divided by 5,280 feet per mile equals 1,875,000 miles, divided by 240,000 miles to the moon and back equals (approximately) 8 round trips.

17. Since 1980, according to Bob Delaney of Cass Information, a logistics company based in Bridgeton, Missouri, the ratio of inventory to GDP in the United States has declined from 25 percent to 15 percent. Bob Delaney, quoted in "Container Trade: When Trade and Security Clash," *The Economist*, April 4, 2002, p. 65.

18. Jack Short, "Road Freight Transport in Europe: Some Policy Concerns and Challenges" (paper presented at "European Road Freight Transport in the Third Millennium," Verona, Italy, March 6, 1999, 3, available at http://www1.oecd.org/cem/online/speeches/JSver99.pdf).

19. Ibid.

20. "Taking Stock," *The Economist*, September 22, 2001, p. 63.

21. Rosalyn Wilson and Robert V. Delaney, "Managing Logistics in the Perfect Storm" (Twelfth Annual Cass Information Systems/ProLogis State of Logistics Report, presented at National Press Club, Washington, D.C., June 4, 2001, available at http://www.mi-clm.org/downloads/12th%20Annual%20State%20of%20the%20Logistics.pdf).

22. An excellent source of information on the logistics industry is the website of Armstrong & Associates (http://www.3plogistics.com/), a consulting company that specializes in supply chain management and market research.

23. Hau Lee, quoted in Sarah D. Scalet, "SCM Guru Hau Lee on Demand Forecasting," *CIO*, July 15, 2001, available at http://www.cio.com/archive/071501/guru. html.

24. The just-in-time emphasis on speed adds to the burden. ProLogis, a leading global provider of integrated distribution facilities and services, operates 1,673 distribution facilities in ninety-eight markets. These occupy two hundred million square feet of space throughout North America and Europe. The company also has a large-equipment division that leases and maintains fleets of fork trucks, racks, and conveyors.

25. For a detailed discussion of the subject, see Paul Mees, *A Very Public Solution: Transport in the Dispersed City* (Melbourne: Melbourne University Press, 2000). A focal point of progressive thinking on mobility policy is available on the website and discussion lists of the Paris-based New Mobility/World Transport Agenda at http://www.ecoplan.org/wtpp/wt_index.htm and http://groups.yahoo.com/group/WorldTransport/). A Canadian site, Moving the Economy (http://stratus.city .toronto.on.ca/inter/mte/mte.nsf/Links?OpenView&Start=1&Count=300&Collapse =1#1), which is linked to a conference, also contains excellent resources. Research projects having to do with alternative rural transport scenarios are documented on the website of ARTS (Actions on the integration of Rural Transport Services), a project within the European Union, available at http://www.rural-transport.net/ demo.phtml?site=demo. Best-practice guidelines on urban freight solutions are documented in Glenn Miller, Daniela Kiguel, and Sue Zielinski, eds., *Goods in the City: Moving Goods in the New Economy: A Primer for Urban Decision Makers* (York, U.K.: Urban Source, 2002), available at http://www. detourpublications.com.

26. Three systems were used to measure and analyze the routes and evaluate impacts: GPS was used to record distribution routes, locations, and movements. A special system called LogiX was used to simulate shipments and routes and to estimate savings made in distances and journey times. And a dynamic simulation model, Modtrans, was used to describe the flow of materials and calculate vehicle emissions.

27. European Commission, Directorate General for Information Society Technologies (IST), ed., *Information Society Technologies for Transport and Mobility: Projects from the Fifth Framework Programme* (Brussels: European Commission, 2003).

28. Forsebäck, *Case Studies of the Information Society and Sustainable Development*.

29. Ibid.

30. The report was produced by twelve global automotive and energy companies that worked together under the sponsorship of the World Business Council for Sustainable Development. They set out to assess the sustainability of their products and to envision the future of mobility, with special focus on road transport. The report defines sustainable mobility as "the ability to meet the needs of society to move

freely, gain access, communicate, trade and establish relationships without sacrific-
ing other essential human or ecological values today or in the future." World Business Council for Sustainable Development (WBCSD), ed., *Mobility 2030: Meeting the
Challenges to Sustainability* (Geneva: WBCSD, 2004).

31. Two research scientists in Austria have compiled statistics for all four of the principal motorized modes of transportation through time: trains, buses, automobiles
and high-speed transport (aircraft and high-speed trains). Andrea Schaefer and David
G. Victor, *The Past and Future of Global Mobility* (Laxenburg, Austria: International Institute for Applied Systems Analysis, 1997).

32. Ibid.

33. Ibid.

34. Tor Norretranders, *The User Illusion: Cutting Consciousness Down to Size* (New
York: Viking, 1998), 143.

35. John Gray, *Straw Dogs: Thoughts on Humans and Animals* (London: Granta, 2002),
144.

36. Hubert Dreyfus, "Telepistemology: Descartes's Last Stand," in *The Robot in the
Garden: Telerobotics and Telepistemology in the Age of the Internet*, ed. Ken Goldberg
(Cambridge, Mass.: MIT Press, 2000), 48–63.

37. Further information about the Faraway project and its applications is available at
http://www.ifonly.org.

38. See the eRENA website (http://www.nada.kth.se/erena/) for additional information about the project.

39. One of the pioneers in this field is Rebecca Allen, a senior research scientist who
directs the Liminal Devices group at Media Lab Europe (see her biography at http://
www.medialabeurope.org/people/bio.php?id=7). Allen's work crosses the boundaries
of art, design, and science, and she has collaborated with artists such as Kraftwerk,
Devo, Peter Gabriel, Twyla Tharp, and La Fura dels Baus.

40. Cyrano Sciences (http://cyranosciences.com/) describes itself as "the nose-chip
company" and promises, "we digitize smell."

41. A website called Presence-Research.org (http://www.presence-research.org/) contains up-to-date and relevant information and resources on (tele-)presence, which it
defines as "the subjective experience of 'being there' in mediated environments such
as virtual reality, simulators, cinema, television, etc."

42. Judith Donath, "Being Real: Questions of Tele-identity," in *The Robot in the
Garden: Telerobotics and Telepresence in the Age of the Internet*, ed. Ken Goldberg (Cambridge, Mass.: MIT Press, 2000), 296–311.

43. Craft beer, often referred to as "microbrews," celebrated its thirty-fourth year of consecutive growth in 2003, when the craft beer industry produced the equivalent of over three million cases of new craft beer sales. See the Association of Brewers (AOB) website (http://www.beertown.org).

44. George Gilder, *Telecosm: How Infinite Bandwidth Will Revolutionize Our World* (New York: Free Press, 2000), 31–41.

45. Ibid., 137–139.

46. More information about colo sites and telegeography is available on the Tele-Geography website (http://www.telegeography.com).

47. Anthony M. Townsend, "Mobile Communications in the 21st Century City," in *The Wireless World: Social and Interactional Aspects of the Mobile Age*, ed. Barry Brown (Berlin: Springer-Verlag, 2001). The best place to find out about Townsend's current work is his blog (http://urban.blogs.com/); this site includes chapters from his forthcoming book, *Mobile Communications in the 21st Century City*.

48. Gilder, *Telecosm*.

49. Townsend, "Mobile Communications in the 21st Century City."

50. Jason Krause, "Has the Net Stopped Growing? Nortel CEO John Roth Predicts Decline in Internet Traffic," *Industry Standard*, July 2, 2001. The principle of locality guides the design and construction of network services using redundant resources that are geographically distributed across the Internet. A class of new algorithms carefully balances load, locality, and proximity. For further background, see the website of USENIX, the Advanced Computing Systems Association, at http://www.usenix .org/events/osdi02/tech/full_papers/wang/wang_html/.

51. Ibid. Since I first read in the press about the "3 percent" estimate, industry insiders have told me that the new number is closer to ... 4 percent!

52. Kevin Werbach, who runs a conference on the subject of decentralization, published these numbers in a piece for the technology news website C-Net. Kevin Werbach, "Perspective: Tech's Big Challenge: Decentralization," October 24, 2002, available at http://news.com.com/2010-1071-963113.html.

53. Edward O. Wilson, *Consilience: The Unity of Knowledge* (London: Little Brown, 1998), 106.

54. Ibid., 113–136.

55. "When cities spread out, so do waistlines and rear ends. For proof visit Charleston, West Virginia, or Fort Wayne, Indiana: These cities have North America's highest obesity rates and lowest population density—both less than three thousand people per square mile. Cities where people drive everywhere contribute significantly to obesity." Dan Ackman, "Sprawling Cities, Higher Scales," *Forbes*, August

29, 2003, available at http://www.forbes.com/2003/08/29/cx_da_0829topnews_print
.html; Ackman is reporting information he spotted in the *American Journal of Public
Health* and the *American Journal of Health Promotion*.

56. Janine Benyus, *Biomimicry: Innovation Inspired by Nature* (New York: Morrow,
1997).

4 Locality

1. Janine Benyus, *Biomimicry: Innovation Inspired by Nature* (New York: Morrow,
1997), 294.

2. Malcolm Gladwell, *The Tipping Point* (New York: Little Brown, 2000). For an
excellent discussion of the relationship between knowledge and locality, see also
John Seely Brown and Paul Duguid, *The Social Life of Information* (Cambridge, Mass.:
Harvard Business School Press, 2000).

3. A lot of business activity in the United States is already moving to smaller cities
with names like Omaha, Des Moines, Fargo, and Columbus. The retail sector—for
whom "location, location, location" is a mantra—is leaving New York en masse.
Today, none of America's top-twenty retail firms are headquartered there, and the
number of Fortune 500 firms headquartered there is down to 39 from 140 in 1955.
Helping companies decide where to go is a business in itself. *Forbes* even offers its
readers, via its website (http://infosite.promosis.com/iedc/#), access to a "corporate
relocation calculator": "a faster, smarter way to make expansion and relocation decisions" that "offers instant access to relocation hotspots." The location-finding service
lists "relocation hotspots" that are described in relation to population, income, labor, and quality-of-life statistics.

4. Stephen Graham and Simon Marvin, *Splintering Urbanism: Networked Infrastructures, Technological Mobilities, and the Urban Condition* (London: Routledge, 2001).
Graham also leads a research group called GURU (Global Urban Research Unit,
http://www.ncl.ac.uk/guru/home.htm) at the University of Newcastle upon Tyne
(England).

5. Philip Kotler, *Marketing Places: Attracting Investment, Industry and Tourism to Cities,
States and Nations* (New York: Free Press, 1993). For a European perspective on place
marketing, see Seppo K. Rainisto, "Success Factors of Place Marketing: A Study of
Place Marketing Practices in Northern Europe and the United States" (D.Sci. diss.,
Helsinki University of Technology, Espoo, Finland, 2003, available at http://lib.hut
.fi/Diss/2003/isbn9512266849/).

6. Landry and coauthor Marc Pachter refer in their analysis of place marketing to a
"cultural turn." Economically, they argue, value derives increasingly from symbolic
and cultural knowledge. Any good or service is less based on its physical presence

and more on the symbolic value inserted—whether by the quality of its design or its cultural associations (such as a fashion icon, a personality, a genre, or an artistic or subcultural movement). Marc Pachter and Charles Landry, *Culture at the Crossroads* (London: Comedia, 2001).

7. Ibid.

8. The original text comes from Ivan Illich, *Tools for Conviviality* (London: Calder and Boyars, 1973). For a lively and well-linked review of Illich's ideas, see also "Ivan Illich," *Wikipedia: The Online Encyclopedia*, available at http://en.wikipedia.org/wiki/ Ivan_Illich.

9. Christopher Everard, quoted in "Luxury Goods: When Profits Go Out of Fashion," *The Economist*, July 3, 2003.

10. Guy Debord's text *The Society of the Spectacle* remains today one of the great theoretical works on modern-day capitalism, cultural imperialism, and the role of mediation in social relationships. The text is available on the Situationist International website (http://www.nothingness.org/SI/debord.html), along with a wide range of other situationist texts.

11. Paul Kaihla, "Boom Towns," *Business 2.0*, February 19, 2004, available at http:// www.business2.com/b2/web/articles/1,17863,591952,00.html.

12. Exp appears no longer to be running. A more reflective community of practice of experience design is AIGA, the professional association for communication design (http://www.aiga.org/content.cfm/experiencedesign). The original impetus for the notion of an "experience economy" was given in B. Joseph Pine II and James H. Gilmore, *The Experience Economy* (Cambridge, Mass.: Harvard Business School Press, 1999).

13. Le Moniteur, ed., *Paris Olympiques: Twelve Architecture and Urban Planning Projects for the 2008 Games* (Paris: Editions du Moniteur, 2001), 23.

14. Says Graham: "300–400 people is the maximum size at which you can be both epic and intimate, and we simply could not find a space that would allow us to accommodate those in the way we need to do." A 1,500-person audience creates a different sense of what theater is about. Prosaic issues to do with access play an important role: where do coaches park, how far is it to the tube, and so on. Graham's brief to Theatre Projects, which led the design of his new theater, was to "put an end to the picture book model of theater, the illusion of looking into a room."

15. Peter Brook, in an address at the National Theatre London, November 5, 1993, available on the National Theatre website at http://www.nationaltheatre.org.uk/ ?lid=2632. For a more extensive review of Brook's ideas on theatre design, see Andrew Todd, *The Open Circle: Peter Brook's Theatre Environments* (London: Palgrave MacMillan, 2003).

16. Local Futures (http://www.localfutures.com) runs a research program, European Regions in the Knowledge Economy, that examines how cities and regions of Europe are planning for the knowledge economy and tackling its many policy issues.

17. "The ideal city needs to contain a rich mixture of craft-based workshops, consultants, law firms, accountants, distribution and logistics companies, advertising agencies, universities, research labs, database publishers, and local or regional government offices. Unique skills, clusters of specialized suppliers, local roots, and a variety of human skills that are unique to a region—all these are a powerful advantage for local cities and regions on today's economic stage." Will Hutton, *The State We're In* (New York: Vintage, 1996).

18. The emergence of modern urban and regional networks can be traced back to the formation of the International Union of Cities in 1913. Jennifer Mills, "The Hanseatic League in the Eastern Baltic" (SCAND 344, May 1998, part of the *Encyclopedia of Baltic History*, available on the website of the Baltic Studies Program of the University of Washington, Seattle [http://depts.washington.edu/baltic/papers/hansa.html]); "The Baltic Lands and the Hanseatic League in the XIV, XV, and XVI Centuries" (map), available on the website of the International History Sourcebooks Project, ed. Paul Halsall (http://www.fordham.edu/halsall/maps/hanse.jpg).

19. For a bibliography and numerous papers by Christopher Alexander, see the Project for Public Spaces website at http://www.pps.org/info/placemakingtools/placemakers/calexander.

20. For an explanation of how the notion of territorial capital has been applied in a European context and the lessons learned, see Mikel Landabaso, Bénédicte Mouton, and Michal Miedzinski, "Regional Innovation Strategies: A Tool to Improve Social Capital and Institutional Efficiency? Lessons from the European Regional Development Fund Innovative Actions" (paper presented at the Regional Studies Association conference "Reinventing Regions in a Global Economy," Pisa, Italy, April 12–15, 2003, available at http://www.ebms.it/SS/documents/Landabaso%20et%20al_2003_Regional%20Innovation%20Strategies_a%20tool%20to%20improve%20social%20capital%20and%20institutional%20efficiency.pdf. For a more general account, see Robert Putnam, "Social Capital, Measurement and Consequences," *ISUMA: The Canadian Journal of Policy Research* 2, no. 1 (Spring 2001), 41–51, available at http://isuma.net/v02n01/index_e.shtml.

21. The Open Planning Project website is at http://www.openplans.org/.

22. The Regionmaker decomposes a city's environment into functional units (housing, services, commercial, industry) and then runs through millions of combinations and suggests the optimal combination according to a given input of desires. The "access optimizer" function, for example, determines the physical structure of the city based on such parameters as preferred time expenditure, transportation means used, level of sustainability, economic efficiency, and ecological control.

23. Winy Maas, quoted in John M. Thackara, "A Machine to Make Cities," *Domus* (July 2003), 33.

24. MVRDV, ed., *The Regionmaker: RhineRuhrCity—The Hidden Metropolis* (Dusseldorf: Hatje Cantz, 2002).

25. Winy Maas, *Five Minute City: Architecture and (Im)mobility* (Rotterdam: Episode, 2003). The book offers a discussion of cities, time, and destiny.

26. P. V. Indiresan, "Emulating Silicon Valley," *The Hindu Business Line*, May 3, 2004, available at http://www.thehindubusinessline.com/2004/05/03/stories/2004050300300800.htm.

27. The changing impacts of technology on the ways we design and inhabit buildings are examined in Malcolm McCullough, *Digital Ground: Architecture, Pervasive Computing, and Environmental Knowing* (Cambridge, Mass.: MIT Press, 2004).

28. For an analysis of recent developments in northwestern Europe, see SPECTRE, ed., *Vision on the Relationship between Information and Communication Technologies and Space* (Haarlem, The Netherlands: Provincie Noord-Holland, 2002), 50.

29. Giulio Ceppi, Analia Cervini, and Juan Keyser, eds., *Mobile Embodiments: New Convergences in Mobile Telephony* (Ivrea, Italy: Interaction Design Institute Ivrea, 2004).

30. Amsterdam Real Time is described in detail on the Waag website at http://connected.waag.org/projects.html.

31. Jim Spohrer, "What Comes after the WWW?" (research paper, Apple Computers, 1997, available at http://www.worldboard.org/pub/spohrer/wbconcept/default.html).

32. Anthony M. Townsend, "Mobile Communications in the 21st Century City," in *The Wireless World: Social and Interactional Aspects of the Mobile Age*, ed. Barry Brown (Berlin: Springer-Verlag, 2001).

33. The projects as a whole were grouped in a major European Commission program called Intelligent Information Interfaces; background documents on the projects are available on the website of Esprit, the EU information technologies program, at http://www.cordis.lu/esprit/src/eyehome.htm.

34. Roger Coleman, quoted in transcription of part 4 of the June 25, 1999, "Presence" conference, available at http://www.presenceweb.i3net.org/papers/right.php3.

35. Louis Kahn, "Architecture," in *Louis I. Kahn: Writings, Lectures, Interviews*, ed. Alessandra Latour (New York: Rizzoli, 1991), 270–285.

36. Marko Ahtisaari, "Finally We Are No One" (presentation at Doors of Perception 7: Flow, Amsterdam, November 14–16, 2002, available on the Doors of Perception website at http://flow.doorsofperception.com/content/ahtisaari_trans.html).

37. Townsend has since started a blog, Urban Blogs (http://urban.blogs.com/).

38. Jim Baller, quoted in Karl Bode, "Jim Baller: Municipal Broadband Attorney," Broadband Reports interview, available at http://www.dslreports.com/shownews/28553.

39. Ibid.

40. "The Wireless Commons Manifesto," available at http://amsterdam.nettime.org/Lists-Archives/nettime-l-0212/msg00136.html.

41. Ibid.

42. Lars Lerup, quoted in Brandon Hookway, *Pandemonium* (New York: Princeton Architectural Press, 1999), 7.

43. Jo Reid, speech to the E-Culture Fair, Amsterdam, October 24, 2003.

44. According to Matt Adams of Blast Theory, in a keynote address at Amsterdam New Media Institute Summer School, Amsterdam, August 27, 2004.

45. See the group's website at http://www.bristolwireless.net/.

46. DAWN is a project undertaken by the Networks and Telecommunications Research Group (NTRG) of Trinity College Dublin. "The aim is to build a production ad-hoc network operational in the entire city of Dublin," the project's website (http://ntrg.cs.tcd.ie/dawn.php) explains; "DAWN aims not only to be a testbed for the research undertaken at the NTRG, but also to serve as a prototype 4th Generation Mobile Network."

47. Project archive of Doors East conference, Bangalore, India, December 2003, available on the Doors East website at http://www.doorseast.com/projectexamples.html.

48. See the Soya Choupal website at http://www.soyachoupal.com/.

49. Project archive of Doors East conference, Bangalore, India, December 2003, available on the Doors East website at http://www.doorseast.com/projectexamples.html.

50. "nLogue Communications Case Study," available on the Digital Partners website at http://www.digitalpartners.org/nlogue.html. See also the project archive of the Doors East conference, Bangalore, India, December 2003, available on the Doors East website at http://www.doorseast.com/projectexamples.html.

51. Pitroda told me about the PCO project during his participation in Doors of Perception 4: Speed in Amsterdam in November 1995. For a more recent article celebrating the ways that Pitroda "helped in connecting the remotest corners of India to the world, and paved the path for propagating IT to the masses," see "Sam Pitroda: Lifetime Achievement Award 2002," *Dataquest*, December 27, 2002, available at http://www.dqindia.com/content/top_stories/102122703.asp.

52. John Thackara, "In the Bubble," based on a presentation at Doors East 1, Ahmedabad, India, March 2000, available on the Doors East website at http://www.doorseast.com/2000doorseast/india_in_bubble.html.

53. Ed van Hinte, Narc Neelan, Jacques Vink, and Piet Vollard, *Smart Architecture* (Rotterdam: 010 Publishers, 2003); Stephen Graham and Simon Marvin, *Splintering Urbanism: Networked Infrastructures, Technological Mobilities, and the Urban Condition* (London: Routledge, 2001).

54. The seminar was sponsored by the Economics and Social Science Research Council and organized jointly by the Universities of Salford and Newcastle in the United Kingdom. Seminar presentations are available on the website of the Centre for Sustainable Urban and Regional Futures at http://www.surf.salford.ac.uk/Events/UrbanVulnerabilityAbstracts.htm#MatthewGandy.

55. Spark! was a project of Cumulus, Europe's association of design and art universities, together with Doors of Perception. The Spark! conference, hosted by the University of Oslo School of Architecture, was held May 5–6, 2004, in Oslo. See the conference website at http://www2.uiah.fi/virtu/spark/conference.html.

56. Ana Dzokic, Milica Topalovic, Marc Neelen and Ivan Kucina (The Stealth Group), "The Wild City: Genetics of Uncontrolled Urban Processes" (lecture/presentation as part of the haus.0 project, April 12, 2002, available on the haus.0 website at http://www.haussite.net/haus.0/PROGRAM/02/stealth/stealth_E.html).

57. Ibid.

58. Ibid.

5 Situation

1. The conversation took place in September 2001 at the New York opening of Workspheres. The Workspheres website is available at http://www.moma.org/exhibitions/2001/workspheres/.

2. Bill Mayon-White, *Managing Change* (London: Chapman, 1993).

3. Manuel Castells, *Rise of the Network Society* (London: Blackwell, 1996).

4. For a useful reading list on emergent phenomena (including works by Murray Gell-Mann), see http://emergent.brynmawr.edu/eprg/?page=EmergenceReadingList.

5. Los Angeles International generates more than 150,000 vehicle trips a day in and out of the central terminal area alone. That number excludes traffic in long-term parking, warehouses, nearby hotels, and their suppliers.

6. Richard Sennett, *The Fall of Public Man* (New York: Norton, 1992). Sennett argues that the public domain has been replaced by private introspection and narcissism, to the detriment of both individual and society.

7. Henry Plummer, "The Poetics of Light," *Architecture + Urbanism (A+U)* (December 1987 suppl.), 7.

8. An excellent bibliography and useful links for Bergson's ideas are available in the entry on Bergson in *Wikipedia: The Free Encyclopedia*, at http://en.wikipedia.org/wiki/ Henri_Bergson. For the best explanation of Cassirer's theory that man has created his own universe of symbolic meaning that structures and shapes his perception of reality, see Ernst Cassirer, *An Essay on Man: An Introduction to a Philosophy of Human Culture* (New Haven: Yale University Press, 1944).

9. David Winnicott, review of *The Nonhuman Environment in Normal Development and in Schizophrenia*, *International Journal of Psychoanalysis* 44 (1983), 237–238.

10. "Business Computing: Delete the Workers," *The Economist*, September 21, 2004, p. 68.

11. According to *The Economist*, days lost to stress, depression, and anxiety increased from 6.5 million in 1995 to 13.4 million in 2001–2002. "Stress: Never a Dull Moment," *The Economist*, August 28, 2004, p. 29.

12. Philip Inman, "Flying High in the Face of Logic," *Guardian* (U.K.), August 28, 2004, p. 17.

13. Lucy Suchman, *Plans and Situated Actions: The Problem of Human-Machine Communication* (Cambridge: Cambridge University Press, 1987).

14. As the architecture critic Deyan Sudjic so eloquently wrote in *100 Mile City*, the TWA terminal was obsolete before it even opened. "It was designed for fleets of propeller-driven Lockheed Constellations, but by the time it opened, the first jets, the Comets and Boeing 707s, were in use, and the building had to be encrusted with jet-blast deflectors." Deyan Sudjic, *100 Mile City* (London: Harper Collins, 1993).

15. Bernard Tschumi, "Introduction," in *The State of Architecture at the Beginning of the 21st Century*, ed. Bernard Tschumi (New York: Monacelli, 2004). Tschumi's book provides a useful review of how today's leading architects and theorists perceive the challenges of this period.

16. Schön made a remarkable contribution to our understanding of professional knowledge and its application. The best review of his work can be found in Mark K. Smith, "Donald Schön: Learning, Reflection and Change," *The Encyclopedia of Informal Education* (2001, last updated 2004), available at www.infed.org/thinkers/ et-schon.htm.

17. Rem Koolhaas, in Rem Koolhaas, Sanford Kwinter, and Sze Tsung Leong, *Rem Koolhaas: Conversations with Students* (New York: Princeton Architectural Press, 1996).

18. Information about prices of models was obtained from the Howard Models website (http://www.howardmodels.com/supplies/onlineorderform.htm).

19. Paul Mijksenaar, designer of Schiphol's signage system, describes his work as way-finding design, not sign design. As Schiphol's space bloats and the flows of people swell, Mijksenaar is keen to increase the number of human guides in the airport.

20. A research center at the University of Utrecht studies the behavior of visitors to urban nodes and network cities from a time-spatial perspective and uses state-of-the-art geomatic data sources and other research tools in the search for ways to improve accessibility and place quality.

21. Ben van Berkel, quoted in John Thackara, "Deep Planning: Ben van Berkle and Caroline Bos talk to John Thackara," *Domus* (October 2002).

22. Ibid. For its project to develop a pier in Genoa, Italy, UN Studio transformed a twenty-three-thousand-square-mile harbor pier into a three-dimensional piazza. The design uses time-based planning represented diagrammatically as a circle of experience. Programs in the piazza are organized clockwise around activities clustered on the basis of views, time of day, and time of year. Coffee can be consumed in the morning sun with a view toward the sea; midday shopping offers shadow; evenings are spent watching the sunset.

23. Malcolm McCullough, *Digital Ground: Architecture, Pervasive Computing, and Environmental Knowing* (Cambridge, Mass.: MIT Press, 2004).

24. In his best-seller *The Work of Nations*, Robert Reich predicted that we would all become "symbolic analysts." The concept was so successful that Reich ended up as Bill Clinton's first secretary of labor. Robert Reich, *The Work of Nations: Preparing Ourselves for 21st Century Capitalism* (London: Addison-Wesley, 1991).

25. "Manifesto for Agile Software Development," available on the manifesto's website (http://www.agilemanifesto.org).

6 Conviviality

1. Tom Healy and Sylvain Cote, *The Well-Being of Nations: The Role of Human and Social Capital* (Paris: Center for Educational Research and Development, Organization for Economic Cooperation and Development, 2001), 41.

2. Health care spending percentages cited here are from Centers for Medicare & Medicaid Services (CMS), Office of the Actuary, "2003 Expected to Mark First Slowdown in Health Care Cost Growth in Six Years" (press release, February 11, 2004, available at http://www.cms.hhs.gov/media/press/release.asp?Counter=961).

3. The World Health Organization published the first comparative analysis of the world's health systems in 2000. Using five performance indicators to measure health

systems in 191 member states, it found that France provides the best overall health care, followed among major countries by Italy, Spain, Oman, Austria, and Japan. The U.S. health system spends a higher portion of its GDP than any other country, but ranks 37th out of 191 countries according to its performance, the report found. "World Health Organization Assesses the World's Health Systems" (press release WHO/44, June 21, 2000, available at http://www.photius.com/rankings/who_world _health_ranks.html).

4. About one in five Americans has some form of CVD; more than twenty-six hundred Americans die of the condition each day. Apart from the human suffering involved, the costs are enormous. One estimate in 2002 put the direct and indirect costs of CVD at $253 billion a year. This number includes direct costs, such as hospital and nursing home care, physicians and other professional services, drugs and other medical durables, and home health care; it also factors in indirect costs such as lost productivity because of morbidity and mortality.

5. One major study of patients with advanced coronary heart disease found that 82 percent of those with extensive support networks survived at least five years, as opposed to only 50 percent of those who were socially isolated. S. E. Taylor, *Health Psychology*, 2nd ed. (New York: McGraw-Hill, 1991); R. Williams, "Prognostic Importance of Social and Economic Resources among Medically Treated Patients with Angiographically Documented Coronary Heart Disease," *Journal of the American Medical Association* 2676 (1992), 520–524. Other studies have confirmed that social ties predict survival after acute myocardial infarction: In these studies, patients who lacked social support, lived alone, or had not been married had an increased mortality risk following myocardial infarction.

6. Board on Neuroscience and Behavioral Health, ed., *Health and Behavior: The Interplay of Biological, Behavioral, and Societal Influences* (Washington, D.C.: Institute of Medicine, 2001), available at http://www.nap.edu/books/0309070309/html/. Health and disease are determined by dynamic interactions among biological, psychological, behavioral, and social factors. These interactions occur over time and throughout development. Cooperation and interaction of multiple disciplines are necessary for understanding and influencing health and behavior.

7. Durkheim's work is discussed in Healy and Cote, *The Well-Being of Nations*, 52.

8. Taylor, *Health Psychology*, 17.

9. TedMed (http://www.tedmed.com/) is a conference, sponsored by the *Wall Street Journal*, that focuses on the business and communication of medical technology research and health care in the twenty-first century.

10. For an overview of the quantity of currently available prosthetic devices, see the website of AbleData (http://www.abledata.com/), which provides access to a database that contains over twenty thousand items.

11. Luciano Beolchi, ed., *Telemedicine Glossary* (Brussels: European Commission, 2003).

12. U.S. Army, "Interactive Textiles for Warrior Systems Applications" and "Functional Electrical Muscle Stimulation with Smart Textile Electrodes," presented at "New Generation of Wearable Systems for Health: Towards a Revolution of Citizens' Health and Life Style Management?," December 12–14, 2003, Pisa, Italy; conference program available at http://www.piaggio.ccii.unipi.it/~ehealthw/program.htm.

13. Donna Haraway, "A Cyborg Manifesto: Science, Technology, and Socialist-Feminism in the Late Twentieth Century," in *Simians, Cyborgs and Women: The Reinvention of Nature* (New York: Routledge, 1991), 149–181, available at http://www.stanford.edu/dept/HPS/Haraway/CyborgManifesto.html.

14. A comparison of five industrialized countries published in 2004 in the journal *Health Affairs* confirmed that greater health care spending does not necessarily lead to better outcomes. America spends more on medicine than Australia, Canada, and New Zealand, for example, yet it has worse survival rates for colorectal cancer and kidney transplants, the study found. Peter S. Hussey, Gerard F. Anderson, Robin Osborn, Colin Feek, Vivienne McLaughlin, John Millar, and Arnold Epstein, "How Does the Quality of Care Compare in Five Countries?" *Health Affairs* 23, no. 3 (2004): 89–99, available at http://content.healthaffairs.org/cgi/content/abstract/23/3/89.

15. Ivan Illich, *Limits to Medicine. Medical Nemesis: The Expropriation of Health* (London: Boyars, 1976). "Beyond certain thresholds of development," Illich wrote, "institutions become an obstacle to the objectives they are meant to serve. Schools foster stupidity. Transportation immobilises. Medicine undermines health, by rendering us less and less capable of caring for ourselves." Ibid.

16. Ibid.

17. In a review of Illich's book by the editor of the journal; *British Medical Journal*, no. 324, 923, available at http://www.vaccinationnews.com/DailyNews/April2002/LimitsMedMedicalNemesis.htm.

18. Ibid.

19. Jean-Pierre Dupuy, "Medicine and Power: A Tribute to Ivan Illich," *ComPlexUs: Modelling and Understanding Functional Interactions in Life Sciences and Systems Biology* 1, no. 4 (2003), available at www.nd.edu/~networks/PDF/ComPlexUs.pdf.

20. Hazel Henderson, quoted in Joe Flower, "Discovering What Works: A Conversation with Hazel Henderson," *Healthcare Forum* 37, no. 5 (September/October 1994), available at http://www.well.com/user/bbear/henderson.html.

21. For a U.S. survey of the future challenges facing teaching hospitals, see Commonwealth Fund, Task Force on Academic Health Centers, *Envisioning the Future of*

Academic Health Centers (final report, New York, February 2003), available at http://www.cmwf.org/programs/taskforc/ahc_envisioningfuture 600.pdf.

22. Richard Normann, *Reframing Business* (London: Wiley, 2003), 63–64. See also the Shahal website (http://www.shahal.co.il/).

23. Andrew Moore, quoted in Julia Feinnman, "Too Much Information?" *Observer* (U.K.), November 11, 2001, available at http://www.guardian.co.uk/Archive/Article/0,4273,4296523,00.html.

24. For a useful collection of press stories on the subject of health-monitoring devices and services, see the Bodymedia website (http://www.bodymedia.com/press/overview.jsp).

25. "Ubiquitous Commerce: Online Medicine Cabinet," available on the Accenture Technology Labs website at http://www.accenture.com/xd/xd.asp?it=enweb&xd=services%5Ctechnology%5Ctech_medcab.xml.

26. David Batty, "Support Networks," *Guardian* (U.K.), January 10, 2003, available at http://www.guardian.co.uk/online/news/0,12597,872352,00.html. Cottam and Leadbeater have this to say about support networks: "The front line of health care is not where professionals dispense their knowledge to patients, but where people look after themselves to prevent ill-health or cope with it." They describe how techniques for the self-management of arthritis, developed at Stanford University in the 1980s, have informed the design of an Expert Patient Programme set up by Britain's Department of Health. The platform is based on the principle that people with a chronic disease are often best placed to manage it. "Know-how and advice has to be close at hand for people to draw on where and when it's most appropriate. Expert patients and carers could become peer-to-peer providers of support," they conclude. Hilary Cottam and Charles Leadbeater, *Health: Co-creating Services* (London: Design Council, 2004). In the United States, researchers at the University of Wisconsin are supporting a peer-to-peer network among women with breast cancer that enables patients to support each other with positive outcomes in terms of attitudes and well-being. See the Comprehensive Health Enhancement Service (CHESS) website (http://chess.chsra.wisc.edu/Chess/). A description of the system's service design is available at http://www.psychooncology.net/forum/CHESS.html.

27. According to the Mental Health Foundation, Google lists nearly twelve million mental health pages, including seven interactive forums on depression. The Open Directory project, the most comprehensive human-edited directory of websites, lists more than six thousand mental health sites. Ibid.

28. Cottam and Leadbeater, *Health: Co-creating Services*. Other data here are from taken from two reports from the United Kingdom's National Health Service Health Modernization Agency: "A New Platform For Social Innovation: Service Design For Health Care" and "Raising the Bar in Health and Social Care Locally and

Internationally," available on the National Health Service website at http:// www.nhssurveys.org/categories.asp?parent=117 and at http://www.modern.nhs.uk/ pursuingperfection.

29. James Pirkl, "Age Design" (lecture delivered at the Netherlands Design Institute, Amsterdam, 1995; transcript available at http://www.zuper.com/portfolio/real_ndi/ publications/3d/pirkl.html).

30. Ibid.

31. In 2004, the European Design for Ageing Network (DAN) evolved into the Include Network. An archive of DAN activities and publications is available at http:// www.hhrc.rca.ac.uk/programmes/designage/DAN.

32. A study of three thousand North American seniors by the Markle Foundation found that fully 30 percent of them felt "a strong need to keep up with the latest developments in technology" and that those aged eighty and over "care a lot about their ability to learn how to work new electronic products." In many respects older people are advanced consumers of technology: They were the first group for whom technology was a means, not an end in itself—a means, in particular, to better communications, which are more important than gadgets and high-tech physical aids to the welfare of older people.

33. "Digital Home Technologies for Aging in Place," available on the Intel website at http://www.intel.com/research/exploratory/digital_home.htm.

34. "CAST Work Programs," available on the CAST website at http://www.agingtech .org/workprograms.aspx.

35. Eric Britton's paper "Rethinking Work: New Concepts of Work in a Knowledge Society" was first published in 1993. Since then it has undergone continuous development on the "New Ways to Work in an Information Society" website (http:// www.ecoplan.org/new=work/nw_index.htm).

36. For an insightful review of the changing job market, see Jonathan Cave, "Old Bits in New Bytes: Implications of the 'New' Economy of Information, Knowledge and Belief for Working Life" (paper presented at "eWork," Helsinki, Finland, September 12, 2001, available at http://www.telework2001.fi/Cave.ppt).

37. The Conference Board, "U.S. Job Satisfaction Hits Record Low" (press release, September 18, 2003, available at http://www.conference-board.org/utilities/ pressDetail.cfm?press_ID=2227).

38. Fabiana Scapolo and Gustavo Fahrenkrog, *Employment and Welfare in 2010* (Seville, Spain: European Commission Directorate-General's Joint Research Centre, Institute for Prospective Technological Studies, 1999, available at http://futures.jrc .es/reports/introfutures-vs6.pdf).

39. Ann Oakley, *The Sociology of Housework* (London: Blackwell, 1974).

40. Sakiko Fukuda-Parr, ed., *United Nations Development Programme Human Development Report* (New York: Oxford University Press, 2003), 141.

41. Alan Atkisson, "Economics in the Solar Age" (interview with Hazel Henderson), *In Context*, no. 25 (1990), available at http://www.context.org/ICLIB/IC25/Hendrson.htm.

42. For a short explanation of how to design and set up a LETS, see Michael Linton and Angus Soutar, *The LETSystem Design Manual* (Courtenay, British Columbia: Landsman Community Services, 1994), available at http://www.gmlets.u-net.com/design/home.html.

43. Riel Miller, *The Future of Money: Making 21st Century Transitions Happen* (Paris: Organisation for Economic Cooperation and Development, 2003).

44. Edgar S. Cahn, "On LETS and Time Dollars," *International Journal of Community Currency Research* 5 (2001), available at http://www.le.ac.uk/ulmc/ijccr/vol4-6/5no2.htm.

45. "Four Core Principles," available on the Time Dollars website at http://www.timedollar.org/cp_four_core_principles.htm.

46. Margrit Kennedy, "Practical Cases Today: Embryos of a New Economy," chap. 7 in *Interest and Inflation Free Money: Creating an Exchange Medium That Works for Everybody and Protects the Earth and the Environment* (Okemos, Mich.: Seva International, 1995), available at http://userpage.fu-berlin.de/~roehrigw/kennedy/english/chap7.htm.

47. Ibid.

48. In a private communication in June 2004.

49. Robin Dunbar, *Grooming, Gossip, and the Evolution of Language* (Cambridge, Mass.: Harvard University Press, 1997).

50. Leading social-software pundits and practitioners Clay Shirky, Liz Lawley, Ross Mayfield, Sébastien Paquet, and David Weinberger run a blog called Many2Many (http://www.corante.com/many/).

51. Howard Rheingold, *Smart Mobs: The Next Social Revolution* (Cambridge, Mass.: Perseus, 2003). Rheingold's last chapter, "Always-On Panopticon—or Cooperation Amplifier?" is worth reading in its entirety for its critique of the idea that this is an either/or question.

52. James Maxmin and Shoshana Zuboff, *The Support Economy* (New York: Viking, 2002). The authors also run a website (http://www.thesupporteconomy.com) that presents complementary information. The trouble with the marketization of care is

that a business model based on discrete transactions does not mesh with the continuous, long-term, 24/7 demands of caring for people with chronic conditions.

53. Chrysanthos N. Dellarocas, "The Digitization of Word-of-Mouth: Promise and Challenges of Online Feedback Mechanisms" (MIT Sloan Working Paper No. 4296-03, March 2003, available through the Social Science Research Network Electronic Library at http://papers.ssrn.com/sol3/papers.cfm?abstract_id=393042).

54. Yochai Benkler, "Coase's Penguin, or, Linux and the Nature of the Firm," *Yale Law Journal* 112, no. 3 (December 2002), available at http://www.benkler.org/CoasesPenguin.html.

55. Investigations of possible open-source approaches to care have given rise to the concept of what Pekka Himanen and his colleagues have termed "civil communities of practice." "Some significant subset of social problems that communities confront are or can be structured as knowledge creation and/or problem solving domains similar to the 'problems' that the open source software community has found new ways to 'solve'. The tools and governance principles of the open source software community, in some modified form, could yield new approaches to community organization and problem solving." It's an enticing prospect that raises the question: What incentives and design principles will facilitate the development of civil communities of practice? Jerome A. Feldman, Pekka Himanen, Olli Leppänen, and Steven Weber, *Open Innovation Networks: New Approaches to Community Organization and Problem Solving* (Helsinki: The Finnish National Fund for Research and Development, 2004), 4, available online at http://www.sitra.fi/Report.

56. Eve Mitleton-Kelly, "Ten Principles of Complexity and Enabling Infrastructures," chap. 2 in *Complex Systems and Evolutionary Perspectives of Organisations: The Application of Complexity Theory to Organisations*, ed. Eve Mitleton-Kelly (London: Elsevier, 2003).

57. Valdis Krebs, "Social Networking in Academia" (2002), available at http://www.orgnet.com/Erdos.html.

58. For a report on scenarios for the use of complexity tools in a European policy context, see Peter Johnston, ed., *Complexity Tools in the Evaluation of Policy Options for a Networked Knowledge Society* (Brussels: European Commission, 2003).

59. Some useful resources are available at CPSquare (http://www.cpsquare.com/PGs/index.htm), an online "town square" for community-of-practice practitioners.

60. For more information about Büber and his ideas, see the Martin Büber website at http://www.buber.de/en/.

61. Mark K. Smith, "Association, La Vie Associative, and Lifelong Learning," *The Encyclopedia of Informal Education* (2000, last updated 2004), available at http://www.infed.org/association/b-assoc.htm.

62. Ibid.

7 Learning

1. Ivan Illich, *Deschooling Society* (Harmondsworth, England: Penguin, 1976).

2. Ken Ducatel and James P. Gavigan, *Employment and Employability in 2010 Europe* (Seville, Spain: Institute of Prospective Technological Studies, Joint Research Center, Commission of the European Community, 2000).

3. Caroline Nevejan, *Synchroon\Asynchroon: Onderwijsvernieuwing in de informatiesamenleving* (Synchronous\Asynchronous: Educational Renewal in the Information Society) (Amsterdam: Hogeschool van Amsterdam, 2003). See also Hogeschool van Amsterdam (Amsterdam University of Professional Education), ed., *Project Leren Leren en Kennismethodiek* (The Learning to Learn and Knowledge Methods Project) (Amsterdam: Hogeschool van Amsterdam, 1999).

4. The researcher I met, Sally Brown, had used the research to publish a book: Sally Brown and Angela Glasner, eds., *Assessment Matters in Higher Education: Choosing and Using Diverse Approaches* (London: Taylor and Francis, 1999).

5. David Hargreaves, *The Mosaic of Learning: Schools and Teachers for the Next Century* (London: Demos, 1994).

6. Howard Gardner and T. Hatch, "Multiple Intelligences Go to School: Educational Implications of the Theory of Multiple Intelligences," *Educational Researcher* 18, no. 8 (1989), 4–9. For an excellent summary of Gardner's wide-ranging work, see Mark K. Smith, "Howard Gardner and Multiple Intelligences," *The Encyclopedia of Informal Education* (2002, last updated 2004), available at http://www.infed.org/thinkers/gardner.htm.

7. Titus Alexander, *Family Learning* (London: Demos, 1997).

8. Ducatel and Gavigan, *Employment and Employability in 2010 Europe.*

9. Brian Ruttenbur and Ginger Spickler, *eLearning: The Engine of the Knowledge Economy* (Memphis, Tenn.: Morgan Keegan, 2000).

10. Ibid.

11. Jerry Wind and David Reibstein, "Just-in-Time Education: Learning in a Global Information Age," available at http://knowledge.wharton.upenn.edu/articles.cfm?catid=3&articleid=236.

12. The World Education Market, the world's first global trade fair for education, was established in 1999 and took place annually until 2003. As this book went to press, the website (http://www.wemex.com) was not online.

13. UNext attracted such investors as Michael Milken, the financier, and Larry Ellison, chief executive officer of Oracle Corporation. Among its higher-education partners supplying course content were Carnegie Mellon, Columbia, and Stanford Universities, the University of Chicago, and the London School of Economics and

Political Science. By the autumn of 2001, citing the need to operate in a "fiscally conservative manner," the Deerfield, Illinois–based company had cut its workforce by 42 percent, laying off 135 of its 325 employees. Katherine S. Mangan, "Expectations Evaporate for Online MBA Programs," *Chronicle of Higher Education*, October 5, 2001, available at http://chronicle.com/free/v48/i06/06a03101.htm.

14. The assets of Hungry Minds were acquired by the textbook publisher John Wiley. See the organization's former website at http://www.hungryminds.com/.

15. Fathom struggled to attract both students and outside investors, forcing the university to spend ten million dollars after its launch to keep the project afloat. Over sixty-five thousand of Fathom's visitors enrolled in courses and seminars, and the company went on to form alliances with such prestigious partners as the British Broadcasting Company. But visitors are no longer able to purchase courses through Fathom, which has become an archive website.

16. Carol A. Twigg, "Notes for the June 4–5, 1997 NLII-ITP Symposium on Creating and Delivering Collegiate Learning Materials in a Distributed (Networked) Learning Environment: A Business Model for University-Corporate Collaboration," available on the EDUCAUSE website at http://www.educause.edu/ir/library/html/nli0007.html.

17. Charles Vest, quoted in Carey Goldberg, "Auditing Classes at M.I.T., on the Web and Free," *New York Times*, April 4, 2001, available at http://education.mit.edu/tep/11125/opencourse/.

18. Seymour Papert, *The Children's Machine: Rethinking School in the Age of the Computer* (New York: Harper Collins/Basic Books, 1994).

19. David Forrest, "The High Price of Higher-Education Stocks," March 9, 2004, available on the Motley Fool website at http://www.fool.com/news/commentary/2004/commentary040309df.htm.

20. Most colleges with significant e-learning offerings employ private companies—e-learning call centers—that serve hundreds of colleges from the same technical support center. Nortel Networks and United Parcel Service, which are active in this market, charge institutions per-minute fees for each call or e-mail message that comes in. With prices in the range of sixty to ninety cents a minute, a typical phone call may cost an institution twenty dollars. This adds up.

21. The University of Phoenix Online does not quote lump-sum prices for its MBA programs, but its website states that "while the cost of attending a private college is over $20,000 a year at some schools, the cost of attending University of Phoenix Online is less than half that." "Cost," available on the University of Phoenix Online website at http://www.mba-programs-online.com/university-of-phoenix/cost.htm.

22. Larry Bouthillier, "Harvard Business School Website: A Case Study" (speech delivered at the conference "OroOro TeachersLab," Amsterdam, January 27, 2001, available at http://www.teacherslab.hva.nl/transcripties/html/bouthilliertrans.html).

23. Ibid.

24. Charles Hampden-Turner, "Perspectives on Management in the Americas," in *Regional Encyclopedia of Business and Management*, vol. 1: *Management in the Americas*, ed. M. Warner (London: Thomson Learning), 94–108.

25. John Seely Brown and Paul Duguid, *The Social Life of Information* (Cambridge, Mass.: Harvard Business School Press, 2000), 224.

26. Linda Anderson, "Corporate Learning—New Learning Models under Scrutiny," *Financial Times*, March 22, 2004, available at http://news.ft.com/servlet/Content Server?pagename=FT.com/StoryFT/SpecialFullStory&c=StoryFT&cid=1079419779518 &p=1079419779922.

27. For a startling account of the scale of the information overload that afflicts technical professionals, see William Horton, *Designing and Writing Online Documentation* (New York: Wiley, 1994).

28. For an excellent review of Illich's work on deschooling, learning webs, and the disabling effect of professions, see Mark K. Smith, "Ivan Illich: Deschooling, Conviviality and the Possibilities for Informal Education and Lifelong Learning," *The Encyclopedia of Informal Education* (2001, last updated 2004), available at http://www .infed.org/thinkers/et-illic.htm.

29. Hargreaves, *The Mosaic of Learning*, 43.

30. Tom Bentley, *Learning beyond the Classroom: Education for a Changing World* (London: Routledge/Demos, 1998).

31. Research cited in Nevejan, *Synchroon\Asynchroon*, 30.

32. e-Learning Centre, "Learning by e-mail," in *e-Learning Center's Guide to e-Learning*, available at http://www.e-learningcentre.co.uk/guide2elearning/2-8/2-8-6 .htm.

33. Time redesign, in the form of more flexible schedules, has started to emerge in some real-world schools. Thomas Telford, one of the highest-performing public schools in the United Kingdom, also has the longest school day in that country— between 31 and 35 hours a week, compared to a U.K. national average of 23.5. According to the Design Council, which has studied the case, these longer hours are less chopped up and predetermined than is usual in the British system. Each day is divided into two sessions, morning and afternoon. Staggered lunch and breakfast breaks limit congestion and disruption. A pupil will spend the whole morning on a subject, usually in the same classroom, but with a number of different teachers who work in a team. Hilary Cottam, ed., *Changing Behaviors* (London: Design Council, 2001).

34. John Seely Brown and Paul Duguid, *Universities in the Digital Age* (Palo Alto, Calif.: Xerox Palo Alto Research Center, 1995), 17.

35. Twigg, "Notes for the June 4–5, 1997, NLII-ITP Symposium on Creating and Delivering Collegiate Learning Materials in a Distributed (Networked) Learning Environment."

36. The percentage of corporate education programs delivered via the class-room decreased from 64 percent to 39 percent between 1999 and 2003. "eLearning Statistics," available on the Managers Forum website at http://www.managersforum .com/eLearning/Statistics.htm.

37. Seely Brown and Duguid, *The Social Life of Information.*

38. For a longer discussion of the concept of learning geographies, see John Thackara, *The New Geographies of Learning* (Amsterdam: Hogeschool van Amsterdam, 2001).

39. Giulio Ceppi, "Introduction," in *Children, Spaces, Relationships: Metaproject for an Environment for Young Children*, ed. Giulio Ceppi and Michele Zini (Milan: Domus Academy, 1998), 14. See also "Reggio Emilia Philosophy," available on the Document Young Children's Learning website at http://www.youngchildrenslearning .ecsd.net/reggio%20emilia%20philosophy.htm. In the United Kingdom, the National Endowment for Science Technology and the Arts has published a report describing how suppliers, teachers, and children might develop these close working practices to achieve the dual aims of "good pedagogy and profitable products." The report is available online at http://www.nestafuturelab.org/research/findings/handbooks/02 _01.htm.

40. Charles Hampden-Turner and Alfons Trompenaars, *The Seven Cultures of Capitalism* (New York: Bantam Doubleday Dell, 1993). The book is a classic comparative study of attiudes toward work and money in eight developed countries. For an in-depth look at the role played by projects in education, design educator Alain Findeli recommends Jean-Pierre Boutinet, *Anthropologie du Projet* (Anthropology of the Project) (Paris: PUF, 2003).

41. The number of computers obtained by U.S. schools and used by teachers and students increased throughout the 1990s, as it had during the previous decade. However, according to a paper published in March 2004 for the Office of Technology Assessment, the fact that computers are used primarily by one or two students at a time means that the density of computers in comparison to the number of potential student users remains small. Henry Jay Becker, *Analysis and Trends of School Use of New Information Technologies* (report prepared for the U.S. Congress, Office of Technology Assessment, Washington, D.C., March 2004, available at http://www.gse.uci.edu/ doehome/EdResource/Publications/EdTechUse/C-TBLCNT.htm).

42. Consortium for School Networking, ed., "Taking TCO (Total Cost of Ownership) to the Classroom: A School Administrator's Guide to Planning for the Total Cost of New Technology" (white paper, Consortium for School Networking, Washington, D.C., July 2001, available at http://classroomtco.cosn.org/tco2class.pdf).

43. Thomas A. Stewart, "What Information Costs," *Fortune*, July 10, 1995, 120. Stewart says the figure is based on data from Stephen Roach, chief economist of Morgan Stanley, Inc.

44. Stephen Heppell, *Schools in the Learning Age* (London: Campaign for Learning, 2000).

45. Howard Gardner, quoted in David Georgi and Judith Crowe, "Digital Portfolios: A Confluence of Portfolio Assessment and Technology," *Teacher Education Quarterly* 25, no. 1 (Winter 1998), 73–84, available at http://www.teqjournal.org/backvols/1998/25_1/1998v25n108.pdf.

46. J. C. Herz, "Gaming the System: What Higher Education Can Learn from Multiplayer Online Worlds" (2002), available on the EDUCAUSE website at http://www.educause.edu/ir/library/pdf/ffpiu019.pdf.

47. The number—3,600 pounds—was quoted in a BBC-1 news bulletin of September 6, 2004.

48. Theodor Zeldin, *Conversation: How Talk Can Change Our Lives* (New York: Hidden Spring, 2000).

49. Telephones had appeared in the principal's office by the end of the 1920s, and classroom intercoms permitted administrators to make schoolwide announcements; electric bells kept students and teachers to a daily schedule; and buses transported students to school from faraway locations. Larry Cuban, "Techno-Reformers and Classroom Teachers," *Education Week*, October 9, 1996, available at http://www.edweek.org/ew/vol-16/06cuban.h16.

50. Howard Rheingold, *Smart Mobs: The Next Social Revolution* (Cambridge, Mass.: Perseus, 2003).

51. See the Slashdot website (www.slashdot.org).

52. For an English-language summary of the event, see http://www.teacherslab.hva.nl/tekstdoorklikengelsvervolg.html.

53. William M. Snyder and Xavier de Souza Briggs, *Communities of Practice: A New Tool for Government Managers* (Arlington, Va.: IBM Center for the Business of Government, November 2003), available at http://www.businessofgovernment.org/pdfs/Snyder_report.pdf. See also Etienne Wenger, Richard McDermott, and William M. Snyder, *Cultivating Communities of Practice* (Cambridge, Mass.: Harvard Business School Press, 2002).

54. Esther Dyson, *Release 2.0: A Design for Living in the Digital Age* (New York: Broadway Books, 1997).

55. For an excellent collection of his writings, interviews, and essays, see Glen W. Norton's Jean-Luc Godard Web Page (http://www.geocities.com/Hollywood/Cinema/4355/).

56. Sonia Livingstone, "How Children Use Media Today" (speech delivered at the conference "OroOro Teachers Lab," Amsterdam, January 25, 2001, available at http://www.teacherslab.hva.nl/transcripties/html/livingstonetrans.html).

57. Douglas Rushkoff, quoted in Chris Mitchell, "Making Sense of the Future" (interview with Douglas Rushkoff), *Spike* (February 1997), available at http://www.spikemagazine.com/0297rush.htm.

58. J. C. Herz, "50,000,000 Star Warriors Can't Be Wrong," *Wired* 10, no. 6 (June 2002), available at http://www.wired.com/wired/archive/10.06/lucasarts.html.

59. Ibid.

60. Ibid.

61. Ibid.

62. Statistics from U.S. Bureau of Labor Statistics, cited in Marcia L. Conner, "Perpetual Innovation through Informal Learning," *Business Know-How* (September 2004), available at http://www.businessknowhow.com/growth/innovation.htm.

63. Pekka Himanen, *The Hacker Ethic, and the Spirit of the Information Age* (New York: Random House, 2001), 205.

8 Literacy

1. Malcolm Gladwell, *The Tipping Point* (New York: Little Brown, 2000).

2. William Horton, *Designing and Writing Online Documentation* (New York: Wiley, 1994).

3. Edward O. Wilson, *Consilience: The Unity of Knowledge* (London: Little Brown, 1998).

4. Horton, *Designing and Writing Online Documentation*.

5. Ibid.

6. Peter Lyman and Hal R. Varian, "How Much Information 2003?" (research report, School of Information Management and Systems, University of California at Berkeley, 2003, available at http://www.sims.berkeley.edu/research/projects/how-much-info-2003).

7. For a theoretical analysis of the information explosion, see Pierre Levy, *The Virtual Economy*, available at http://www.chairetmetal.com/levy-ang2.htm.

8. Danny Hillis, "High-Speed Information" (presentation at Doors of Perception 4: Speed, Amsterdam, November 7, 1996).

9. A recent development is that several dozen companies, government agencies, and universities have banded together in the Open Geospatial Consortium (OGC).

Homeland security rather than environmental awareness has prompted the move. In the words of its website (http://www.opengeospatial.org/), "Timely, accurate geospatial information and geoprocessing services—easily accessible and capable of being shared across federal, state, and local jurisdictions and multiple security levels—are fundamental to Critical Infrastructure Protection. Homeland Security will be seriously hampered without the real-time ability to quickly visualize patterns of activity and understand the multi-layered, location-based context of emergency situations."

10. David Rokeby, "Seen" (presentation at Doors of Perception 7: Flow, Amsterdam, November 14–16, 2002, available on the Doors of Perception website at http://flow .doorsofperception.com/content/rokeby_trans.html).

11. The global market for such sensors will reach fifty billion dollars in 2008. Intechno Consulting, in Switzerland, lists an extraordinary array of devices that are already on the market: binary sensors, position sensors, speed/RPM sensors, navigation sensors, acceleration sensors, force sensors, torque sensors, distance sensors, tilt sensors, pressure sensors, filling sensors, flow sensors, temperature sensors, photo detectors, image sensors, acoustic sensors, current sensors, magnetic sensors, humidity sensors, chemical sensors for gases, chemical sensors for liquids, and biosensors. See "Sensor Markets 2008," available on the Intechno Consulting website at http:// www.intechnoconsulting.com/Sensors%202008.htm.

12. Promotional materials for the GammaMaster, available at www.gammawatch .com.

13. Haz-Mat appears to have ceased selling its products online but its site, renamed Emergency Net News (http://www.emergency.com/hzmtpage.htm), includes articles about hazardous materials and research related to weapons of mass destruction.

14. DLESE is a grassroots community effort involving educators, students, and scientists working together to improve the quality, quantity, and efficiency of teaching and learning about the Earth system at all levels. The Black Rock Forest project is documented at http://www.ldeo.columbia.edu/edu/DLESE/BRF/.

15. The Data Harvester (http://ingrid.ldgo.columbia.edu/SOURCES/.BRF/.Weather/ .Station/.top.html) is a tool for accessing and thinking about environmental data.

16. Natalie Jeremijenko, "Against Virtualized Information: Tangible and Open-Ended Strategies for Information Technology," part of "STATEMENT" (April 7, 2003), available at http://cat.nyu.edu/natalie/projectdatabase/.

17. Bjorn Lomborg, *The Skeptical Environmentalist: Measuring the Real State of the World* (Cambridge: Cambridge University Press, 2001).

18. For a helpful reminder of the difference between prediction and scenario making, see Andrew Curry, "From Foresight to Scenarios—Landscaping, Methodology and Tools" (paper presented at European Commission Workshop Directorate General Research K-1, Brussels, July 5, 2002).

19. Gary Reiner, quoted in Ludwig Siegele, "The Real-Time Economy: How about Now?" *The Economist*, February 1, 2002, available at http://www.cfo.com/article.cfm/3003286/1/c_2984786.

20. Siegele, "The Real-Time Economy."

21. "Now that we can do anything, what will we do?" Massive Change (http://massive.change.com) is the title of an exhibition, book, and "international discursive project" organized by Bruce Mau Design and the Institute Without Boundaries.

22. Unisys 3D Visible Enterprise home page, available on the system's website (www.3DvisibleEnterprise.com).

23. Ivan Illich, *Vernacular Values* (1980), available at http://www.preservenet.com/theory/Illich/Vernacular.html.

24. Martin Jay, "The Speed of Light and Virtualized Reality," chap. 8 in *The Robot in the Garden: Telerobotics and Telepresence in the Age of the Internet*, ed. Ken Goldberg (Cambridge, Mass.: MIT Press, 2000).

25. Susan Sontag, *On Photography* (Harmondsworth, England: Penguin, 1977).

26. Matthew Chalmers, "Re-place-ing Space: The Roles of Place and Space in Collaborative Systems," in *Proceedings of the 1996 ACM Conference on Computer Supported Cooperative Work*, ed. Steve Harrison and Paul Dourish (Boston: ACM Press, 1996).

27. Maurice Merleau-Ponty, *The Phenomenology of Perception*, 2nd ed. (London: Routledge, 2002).

28. Dag Svanaes, *Understanding Interactivity: Steps to a Phenomenology of Human-Computer Interaction* (Trondheim, Norway: Computer Science Department, Norwegian University of Science and Technology, 2000), available at http://www.idi.ntnu.no/~dags/interactivity.pdf.

29. Merleau-Ponty, *The Phenomenology of Perception*.

30. Lucy Suchman, *Plans and Situated Actions: The Problem of Human-Machine Communication* (Cambridge: Cambridge University Press, 1987).

31. For examples of organizations that hold such a philosophy, see "Selected Ecological and Environmental Organizations," available at http://www.rmetzner-greenearth.org/ecoorg.html.

32. Luis Fernández-Galiano, *Fire and Memory: On Architecture and Energy* (Cambridge, Mass.: MIT Press, 2000), 178.

33. Ken Goldberg, "Introduction: The Unique Phenomenon of Distance," chap. 1 in *The Robot in the Garden: Telerobotics and Telepresence in the Age of the Internet*, ed. Ken Goldberg (Cambridge, Mass.: MIT Press, 2000), available at http://ieor.berkeley.edu/~goldberg/art/tele/intro.html.

34. Terry Winograd and Fernando Flores, *Understanding Computers and Cognition: A New Foundation for Design* (New York: Addison-Wesley, 1987), 48.

35. Ben Shneiderman, "The Limits of Speech Recognition," *Communications of the ACM* 43, no. 9 (September 2000), 63–65, available at http://portal.acm.org/citation.cfm?id=348941.348990.

36. Winograd and Flores, *Understanding Computers and Cognition*.

37. Ways to design the exploration of data aurally involve two approaches: sonification (data-controlled sound) and audification (audible playback of data samples). The most common application is the real-time monitoring of multivariate data. The website of the International Community for Auditory Display (ICAD) (http://www.icad.org/) includes a helpful glossary.

38. The Sounding Object (http://www.soundobject.org/intro.html) is part of the Disappearing Computer Initiative of the European Commission's Information Society Technologies (IST) program in the Future and Emerging Technologies (FET) department.

39. Ryan J. Cassidy, Jonathan Berger, Kyogu Lee, Mauro Maggioni, and Ronald R. Coifman, "Auditory Display of Hyperspectral Colon Tissue Images Using Vocal Synthesis Models," in *Proceedings of ICAD 04—Tenth Meeting of the International Conference on Auditory Display*, Sydney, Australia, July 6–9, 2004, ed. Stephen Barrass and Paul Vickers, available at http://www.icad.org/websiteV2.0/Conferences/ICAD2004/papers/cassidy_berger_lee.pdf.

40. David Jameson, quoted in Jennifer Sullivan, "Bringing Sound into the PC Foreground," *Wired News*, March 9, 1998, available at www.wired.com/news/news/technology/story/10792.html.

41. Sullivan, "Bringing Sound into the PC Foreground."

42. William W. Gaver, "Auditory Interfaces," in *Handbook of Human-Computer Interaction*, 2nd ed., ed. Allen Dix (Upper Saddle River, N.J.: Prentice-Hall), 1003–1041. Gaver's chapter is a key reference work concerning the use of nonspeech audio in computer interfaces, with discussion of perspectives on hearing and strategies for organizing and mapping sounds to interface events.

43. Marinetti continued: "One must imitate the movements of machines with gestures; pay assiduous court to steering wheels, ordinary wheels, pistons, thereby preparing the fusion of man with the machine, to achieve the metallicity of the Futurist dance." Filippo Tommasso Marinetti, *Manifesto of the Futurist Dance* (July 8, 1917), available on the Futurism and Futurists website at http://www.futurism.org.uk/manifestos/manifesto53.htm.

44. Ernst Gombrich, *The Sense of Order: A Study in the Psychology of Decorative Art*, 2nd ed. (London: Phaidon, 1994). Gombrich's book, originally published in 1979, includes fascinating insights into the psychology of decorative art.

45. David Toop, "Life in Transit," in *Sonic Process*, ed. Christine van Assche (Barcelona: Actar, 2002).

46. R. M. Schafer, *The Tuning of the World* (New York: Knopf, 1977), republished as *The Soundscape* (Rochester, Vt.: Destiny Books, 1994).

47. Benjamin U. Rubin, "Audible Information Design in the New York City Subway System: A Case Study" (paper presented at the International Conference on Acoustic Display, Glasgow, Scotland, 1998, available at http://www.earstudio.com/projects/ P_subpage/subway.pdf). A case study (with audio files) is also available at http:// www.earstudio.com/projects/P_subpage/subway_middle.html.

48. Elliman, a graphic designer, works with typefaces, test patterns, and the human voice. The quotations here are from his lecture at the conference "Design Recast" at the Jan van Eyck Academy, Maastricht, in June 2002. A version of the talk was later published in *Wired:* Paul Elliman, "Now Hear This. Voice Space: When Space Starts Speaking, We Listen," *Wired* 11, no. 6 (June 2003), available at http://www.wired .com/wired/archive/11.06/voice_spc.html.

49. Ibid.

50. Michel Chion, *Audio-Vision* (New York: Columbia University Press, 1994). See also Kendall Wrightson, "An Introduction to Acoustic Ecology," *Soundscape: The Journal of Acoustic Ecology* 1, no. 1 (Spring 2000): 10–13, available at http://homepage. mac.com/kendallwrightson/ae/aecology.html; and the website of the World Forum for Acoustic Ecology (http://interact.uoregon.edu/MediaLit/WFAE/home/index .html). For an excellent collection of resources on the artful uses of sound in environments, see Janek's Sound/Art/Installation & Music Resource (http://www.audioh .com/information/soundartresource.html). Also useful are the proceedings of the Symposium on Sound Design, available at http://www.design-sonore.org/. For design experiments in the use of sound in urban contexts, see also the website of the consulting firm Genesis Psychoacoustics, available at http://www.genesis.fr/english/ act3.htm, and the work of Yon Visell and Karmen Franinovic, available at http:// www.zero-th.org.

51. Ken Goldberg, ed., *The Robot in the Garden: Telerobotics and Telepresence in the Age of the Internet* (Cambridge, Mass.: MIT Press, 2000).

52. Robert Levine, *A Geography of Time: The Temporal Misadventures of a Social Psychologist* (New York: Basic Books, 1997).

53. Kate Fox, "Culture," in *The Smell Report* (Oxford, England: Social Issues Research Center), available at http://www.sirc.org/publik/smell_culture.html.

54. Kate Fox, "The Human Sense of Smell," in *The Smell Report* (Oxford, England: Social Issues Research Center), available at http://www.sirc.org/publik/smell_human .html.

55. Joseph Nathaniel Kaye. "Symbolic Olfactory Display" (master's thesis, Massachusetts Institute of Technology, Cambridge, Mass., 2001, available at http://xenia.media.mit.edu/~jofish/thesis/symbolic_olfactory_display.html).

56. Ibid.

57. Rob Strong and Bill Gaver, "Feather, Scent and Shaker: Supporting Simple Intimacy," in *Proceedings of the Conference on Computer Supported Cooperative Work (CSCW)* (Boston: ACM, 1996).

58. Armando Iannucci (column), *London Times*, April 24, 2004.

59. See the Büber website at http://www.buber.de/en/.

60. Ivan Illich, "Silence Is a Commons" (speech delivered at Asahi Shimbun Symposium "Science and Man—The Computer-Managed Society," Tokyo, March 21, 1982, available at http://www.preservenet.com/theory/Illich/Silence.html).

61. Theodor Zeldin, *Conversation: How Talk Can Change Our Lives* (New York: Hidden Spring, 2000).

62. John Shotter, "The End of Rational Planning and the Turn to Conversational Communities" (2000), available on The Gurteen Knowledge website at http://www.gurteen.com/gurteen/gurteen.nsf/0/FFF7259BA0FF856380256AD500472B37/.

63. "A Brief History of Temporal Art," available on the Franklin Furnace website at http://www.franklinfurnace.org/timebase.html.

64. Robert Irving, *Being and Circumstance: Notes towards a Conditional Art* (San Francisco: Lapis with the Pace Gallery, 1988). Simon Vinkenoog made a similar point about poetry: "In any flourishing, living civilization, above all in archaic cultures, poetry has a vital function that is both social and liturgical. All antique poetry is at one and the same time ritual, entertainment, artistry, riddle making, doctrine, persuasion, sorcery, soothsaying, prophecy, and competition." Simon Vinkenoog, "Play and Poetry" (presentation at Doors of Perception 5: Play, Amsterdam, November 26, 1998, available on the Doors of Perception website at http://museum.doorsofperception.com/doors5/content/vinkennog.html).

65. Sontag, *On Photography*, 9.

66. Natalie Jeremijenko, "Opinion," available on the Core 77 website at http://www.core77.com/reactor/opinion_natalie.asp.

67. Artist and cultural critic Eduardo Kac has investigated the philsophical and political dimensions of communications processes. He is also known as the creator of Alba, a fluorescent, genetically engineered rabbit. The quotation here is from his 1992 Siggraph paper, "Aspects of the Aesthetics of Telecommunications," available at http://www.ekac.org/Telecom.Paper.Siggrap.html.

9 Smartness

1. The subject matter of biomimetics is known by several names: bionics, biogenesis, biomimicry, and others. This chapter draws on Ed van Hinte's reports of the "Smart Materials and Systems" seminars organized in 1997 and 1998 at the Netherlands Design Institute, with the help of Julian Vincent. Vincent, who leads the Centre for Biomimetic and Natural Technologies at Bath University in the United Kingdom, says the concept describes "taking ideas from nature and implementing them in another technology such as engineering, design, computing, etc. The concept is very old (the Chinese wanted to make artificial silk 3,000 years ago; Democritus (460–370 BCE) also said it was absurd for men to vaunt their superiority over the animals when, in matters of great importance, it was they who were our teachers: the spider for weaving and mending; the swallow for architecture; the swan and the nightingale for singing. (The last animal is recounted in Bruce Chatwin's book *The Songlines*.) But the implementation is gathering momentum only recently because the science base can cope with the advanced techniques and our civilization is in ever increasing need of sympathetic technology." Centre for Biomimetics, "What Is Biomimetics?" available on the Centre's website at http://www.bath.ac.uk/mech-eng// biomimetics/about.htm.

2. Janine Benyus, *Biomimicry: Innovation Inspired by Nature* (New York: Morrow, 1997), chap. 1.

3. Ibid.

4. Paola Antonelli, *Mutant Materials in Contemporary Design* (New York: Museum of Modern Art, 1995).

5. Ezio Manzini, *The Material of Invention* (Cambridge, Mass.: MIT Press, 1996). This key text on "the relationship between technical evolution and design culture" was the product of an inquiry among Italian designers into the possibilities, limits, and design implications of new materials.

6. Julian Vincent, "Biomimetics," in *Smart Materials: Human-Machine Interaction*, ed. Gert Staal and Anne Voshol (Amsterdam: Netherlands Design Institute, 1997), 7–23.

7. Ibid.

8. "Achieving these goals," says a PARC statement, "will require a novel synthesis of technologies from the fields of active structural control, MEMS [micro-electro-mechanical systems], smart materials, and distributed computation to create intelligent surfaces and materials that not only sense, reason about, and interact with their environment, but that can fundamentally alter both their own behavior and the behavior of other objects in their vicinity." "MEMS/Smart Matter Research at PARC," available on the PARC website at http://www2.parc.com/spl/projects/smart-matter/.

9. Ed van Hinte, Marc Neelan, Jacques Vink, and Piet Vollaard, *Smart Architecture* (Rotterdam: 010 Publishers, 2003). The outcome of a research project by the Smart

Architecture Foundation (www.smartarch.nl), this book contains examples involving climate control, supplemented with new ideas on planning, building and construction, and the application of intelligent systems, all contributing to sustainability.

10. "MEMS/Smart Matter Research at PARC."

11. The key book on the subject is by Luis Fernández-Galiano, *Fire and Memory: On Architecture and Energy* (Cambridge, Mass.: MIT Press, 2000). Setting out to compensate for the "scandalous absence of energy considerations in architectural analysis and criticism," Galiano distinguishes between the energy of construction and the energy of maintenance. In North America, where buildings account for 65 percent of electricity consumption, 26 percent of total energy use, and 30 percent of greenhouse-gas emissions, the economic arguments do now seem to be generating change. Rebecca Flora of the Green Building Alliance, a group that promotes sustainable architecture, says, "Going green saves money by reducing long-term energy costs. On average green buildings in the US use 30 percent less energy than conventional buildings. The 2 percent increase in construction costs typically pays for itself in lower running costs within two years." "The Rise of the Green Building" (Report), *The Economist Technology Quarterly*, December 4, 2004, 12–17.

12. For a useful review of intelligent buildings, design, and building management systems, see Gary Mills, "Intelligent Buildings Design and Building Management Systems: Overview of 'Intelligent Buildings' and 'Intelligent Homes' Technologies," available on the BusinessBalls website at http://www.businessballs .com/intelligentbuildingsdesign.htm. An online magazine called *Automated Buildings* also provides links to extensive resources on the subject (http://www .automatedbuildings.com/resources/linksys.htm). The use of daylight in shopping complexes also appears to increase sales. The Heschong Mahone group, a California-based consultancy that specializes in energy-efficient building technologies, found that sales were as much as 40 percent higher in stores lit with skylights. Quoted in *The Economist Technology Quarterly*, December 4, 2004.

13. For more information about these projects, see the NOX Architects website (http://www.noxarch.com/flash_content/flash_content.html). See also Julien Devereux and Martin C. Pedersen, "How Buildings Breathe," *Metropolis* (March 2004), available at http://www.metropolismag.com/html/content_0304/bre/.

14. For a lighter look at some other lessons to be learned from penguins and polar bears, see "P~Animals," available on the Pathys Place website at http://groups.msn .com/PathysPlace/panimals.msnw. See also Julian F. V. Vincent and Darrell L. Mann, "Systematic Technology Transfer from Biology to Engineering," *Philosophical Transactions of the Royal Society of London A* 360, 159–174 (published online January 11, 2002), available at http://www.bath.ac.uk/mech-eng/biomimetics/TRIZ.pdf.

15. An example I know well was the Netherlands Design Institute in Amsterdam, where I worked as director from 1993 to 1999. This beautiful canal-side building

was rebuilt completely for our use—a conversion that included the removal of several floors to create spectacular translucent spaces. The result, although gorgeous, was a serious decrease in the building's energy performance—according, at least, to several environmentally conscious designers and architects who came to the building, often to hear people like Julian Vincent, who is quoted extensively in this chapter!

16. Julie Wosk, "Mutant Materials in Contemporary Design: Exhibition Review," *Design Issues* 12, no. 1 (Spring 1966), 63–69.

17. For examples of the ways that nature "can serve as a model not just for passive materials and structures, but also for systems that can respond," see "New Materials for the New Age," available on the website of the Centre for Biomimetic and Natural Technologies at http://www.bath.ac.uk/mech-eng//biomimetics/newmats.htm.

18. Vincent's work on the properties of collagen is reported in Adriaan Beukers and Ed van Hinte, *Lightness: The Inevitable Renaissance of Minimum Energy Structures* (Rotterdam: 010 Publishers, 1998).

19. This particular research prompts one to contemplate a number of highly profitable technology transfer opportunities in the domain of medical prosthetics. For a summary of current and recent research projects at the Centre for Biomimetic and Natural Technologies, see "Current and Recent Projects," available on the Centre's website at http://www.bath.ac.uk/mech-eng//biomimetics/Projects.htm.

20. Straight transfer of a material or structure from the natural world to engineering technology is not usually useful; what is more promising is the transfer of design principles. Several communities of practice in the field of biomimetics are listed by the Resource Discovery Network at http://www.rdn.ac.uk/resourcefinder/?query=biomimetic.

21. Martin Kemp, "Building a Model Dragonfly," in *Smart Materials: Human-Machine Interaction*, ed. Gert Staal and Anne Voshol (Amsterdam: Netherlands Design Institute, 1997), 47–55.

22. Ibid. Kemp also participated in an expert meeting at the Netherlands Design Institute in March 1998 whose results are available in Ed van Hinte, *Smart Design* (Amsterdam: Netherlands Design Institute, 1998).

23. Although the electric-toothbrush story appears in dozens of documents on the Internet, I have not been able to locate an authoritative technical source for the statistic "three thousand lines of code." This particular urban legend probably originated in James Gleick, "Inescapably Connected: Life in the Wireless Age," *New York Times*, June 2001, available at http://www.jr.co.il/articles/connect.txt.

24. Vincent and Mann, "Systematic Technology Transfer from Biology to Engineering." The consultants charged with finding a way to modernize Britain's crumbling

west coast railway line thought they'd hit on a magic bullet: a white-hot software so-lution—"blocking"—that would allow the huge task to be completed cheaply. There was just one problem: Blocking had never worked in the real world. A *Guardian* writer, James Meek, spent a whole year investigating the saga of "incompetence, greed and delusion" behind Britain's biggest public works project. It's a terrific piece of journalism about a complex subject—and a salutary reminder that the integration of cyberspace and real space will always be fraught with more problems than tech-nology marketers acknowledge. James Meek, "The 10 Billion Pound Train Crash," *Guardian* (U.K.), April 1, 2004, p. 2, available at http://www.guardian.co.uk/transport/Story/0,2763,1183210,00.html.

25. Overall's research is described by Vincent in "Biomimetics."

26. Julian Vincent, "Stealing Ideas from Nature," in *Deployable Structures*, ed. S. Pellegrino (Vienna: Springer, 2001), 51–58.

27. Ibid.

28. PRé Consultants, "Ecodesign Tools," available on the PRé website at http://www.pre.nl/ecodesign/ecodesign.htm.

29. Philip Ball, "Life's Lessons in Design," *Nature* 409 (January 18, 2001), 413–416.

30. Jack Ganssle, on the website of the Ganssle Group (http://www.ganssle.com/).

31. Slogan of the website for Embedded.com (http://www.embedded.com/).

32. The number 150 is a guesstimate. Kevin Kelly stated in *Out of Control* that the number of microprocessors in the world had reached six billion—one chip for every human on Earth—as of 1997. Kevin Kelly, *Out of Control: The New Biology of Machines, Social Systems, and the Economic World* (New York: Perseus, 1998), 11. There are no audited figures for unit volumes of embedded systems, in part because embedded systems are deployed by a wide range of unconnected industries, from consumer electronics, process control systems, and aircraft to in-car systems and many other applications. And they often don't belong to an individual: Microsoft calls them "non-personal computer devices." The embedded-systems industry tends to be measured by value: In 2003, according to the *Mirus Online Newsletter*, the global embedded systems market was approximately $71 billion. M. Fung, "A Spotlight on the Embedded Software Industry," *Mirus Online Newsletter* 1, no. 4 (July 2001), available at http://www.imakenews.com/rcwmirus/e_article000029606.cfm.

33. Ted Lewis, "Digitopolis Meets Calm Tech," *Computer* (September 1997), available at http://www.nps.navy.mil/cs/lewis/articletxt/sept97/digitopolis.htm.

34. The phrase "Internet of things" was coined at the EPCglobal Network (where EPC stands for "electronic product code"), a global consortium of retailers and aca-demics based at the Massachusetts Institute of Technology (MIT). Founded in 1999

by Gillette, Procter and Gamble, and Unilever, the consortium now boasts one hundred global companies and five of the world's leading research centers, including the University of Cambridge and MIT. According to one network member, Verisign, the network "has the potential to be much larger and more complex than the network of websites on the Internet. The Domain Name System (DNS), which converts domain names to IP addresses, processes over 10 billion queries per day. The Object Name Service (ONS), which will provide similar services for the EPCglobal Network, is expected to process more than 100 billion queries a day." "FYI: The EPCglobal Network: 'The Internet of Things,'" available on the Verisign website at http://www.verisign.com/products-services/naming-and-directory-services/directory-services/epc -network-services/page_001196.html.

35. For a well-informed review of the field, see Neil Gershenfeld, *When Things Start to Think* (New York: Henry Holt, 1999).

36. For a large archive of Sterling's writings, see http://www.viridiandesign.org/.

37. For a fascinating account of how industrial design adapted to the coming of the electrical age, see Tilmann Buddensieg, *Industriekultur: Peter Behrens and the AEG, 1907–1914* (Cambridge, Mass.: MIT Press, 1984).

38. See the account of the project on the Microsoft Research website at http://research.microsoft.com/easyliving.

39. Bahar Barami, "Market Trends in Homeland Security Technologies" (paper presented at the IEEE Conference on Technologies for Homeland Security, Cambridge, Mass., April 21–22, 2004), available at http://www.volpe.dot.gov/ourwork/dimensions/050604/trends.doc.

40. In the words of its website (http://conference.digitalidworld.com/2004/), Digital ID World "provides an environment in which enterprises, service providers, financial institutions, government officials and vendors have meaningful interactions about the issues and future of the digital identity industry. Attendees consist of CEO's, CTO's, CIO's, senior architects, privacy and security officers, product development and marketing managers, senior IT managers, industry analysts, pundits, visionaries and personalities shaping the identity space."

41. Louisa Liu and Robin Simpson, "China Starts Rollout of National ID Smart Card" (February 19, 2002), available on the Gartner Group website at http://www4.gartner.com/DisplayDocument?doc_cd=104570.

42. Mike Davis, *Beyond Bladerunner: Urban Control and the Ecology of Fear* (New York: New Press, 1993), 21.

43. Donna Haraway, "A Cyborg Manifesto: Science, Technology, and Socialist-Feminism in the Late Twentieth Century," in *Simians, Cyborgs and Women: The Reinvention of Nature* (New York: Routledge, 1991), 149–181, available at http://www.stanford.edu/dept/HPS/Haraway/CyborgManifesto.html.

44. A case study about Oticon is included in John Thackara, *Winners! How Today's Successful Companies Innovate by Design* (London: Ashgate, 1997).

45. According to an article on About.com, "The Extracorporeal Liver Assist Device (ELAD) is the first artificial liver to use cells from humans rather than from pigs. The device is used to sustain patients awaiting a liver transplant or whose own liver is not functioning and needs to recover." "Artificial Liver" (April 8, 1999), available on the About.com website at http://biology.about.com/library/weekly/aa040899.htm.

46. A BBC story on artificial skins explains: "A self-repairing plastic 'skin' has been developed and tested by U.S. scientists. The smart type of plastic, which automatically knits together when cracked or broken, could one day be used to make artificial organs. The material contains microcapsules filled with a special healing agent. Like human skin, it bleeds and heals itself, offering a potential breakthrough in vital materials used in surgical implants. It could also prove useful for making rocket and spacecraft components, which cannot be repaired once they are in use." "Scientists Develop Artificial Skin" (February 15, 2001), available on the *BBC News* website at http://news.bbc.co.uk/1/hi/sci/tech/1170304.stm. A more comprehensive review of skin substitutes may be found on the website of the Burn Survivor Resource Centre at http://www.burnsurvivor.com/skin_substitutes.html.

47. Thomas K. Grose, "Smart Parts," *Prism* 11, no. 9 (May–June 2002), available at http://www.prism-magazine.org/mayjune02/prosthesis.cfm.

48. Ibid.

49. PubMed, for example, a service of the National Library of Medicine, includes over fifteen million citations for biomedical articles dating back to the 1950s. (The search engine for the site's database is available at http://www.ncbi.nlm.nih.gov/entrez/query.fcgi.) The website of a related service called Medline receives more than fifty million visits a year.

50. The subject of electronic patient records is complex, and ethically sensitive—but is also big business. A private-enterprise entity, The Medical Records Institute, has been established to promote the implementation of mobile health care (m-health) and electronic order entry (EOE) technologies. According to the institute's website (http://www.medrecinst.com/), its National Conference on m-health and EOE "is the only one of its kind analyzing leading edge mobile healthcare and EOE technologies."

51. Although Web technology enables access to the full text of online versions of scientific journals, many publishers have opted for paid-subscription models—and thereby restrict access to their journals' contents. However, both the *British Medical Journal* and *Science* have said they support a new site, Free Medical Journals (http://www.freemedicaljournals.com/), that aspires to provide free access to 1,380 medical publications.

52. Drug information is such a valuable information business in its own right that privately owned online and wireless-enabled services are proliferating. They have names like Lexi-Drugs Platinum, Tarascon Pocket Pharmacopoeia, ePocrates Rx Pro, and Clinical Pharmacology OnHand.

53. Patient-monitoring systems are already a six-billion-dollar business in the United States alone. The main products today are blood glucose test strips and optical sensors, followed by multiparameter telemetry stations and home apnea, cholesterol, coagulation, EEG/EMG, and blood pressure monitors. In the pipeline are multiparameter products for blood pressure and pulse, cardiac, anesthesia and respiratory, neurological, blood glucose, fetal, and pediatric conditions. A four-thousand-dollar report on the market, published by Freedonia, is available on the Chiltern Magazine Services' Business Research website at http://www.biz-lib.com/ZFRPT.html.

As much effort goes into the remote monitoring of equipment as of patients. A company called Tadlys builds asset location networks that help staff members locate expensive equipment, prevent its disappearance, and enable full utilization of portable medical apparatuses. See "Hospital Solutions," available on the Tadlys website at http://tadlys.com/pages/solution_content.asp?iGlobalId=2.

54. Using a small prototype transmitter (roughly the size of a deck of cards) embedded with a microchip, and a slightly larger receiving device, the researchers can transmit a preprogrammed electronic business card between two people via a simple handshake. What's more, the prototype allows data to be transmitted from sender to receiver through up to four touching bodies. For basic information about personal area networks, see "PAN Fact Sheet," available on the website of IBM's User Systems Ergonomics Research (USER) group at http://www.almaden.ibm.com/cs/user/pan/pan.html.

55. Arthur Kroker and Michael A. Weinstein, "The Hyper-Texted Body, Or Nietzsche Gets a Modem," in *Data Trash: The Theory of the Virtual Class* (New York: St. Martin's, 1994), available at http://www.ctheory.net/text_file.asp?pick=144http://ctheory.net/book_default.asp.

56. Magnetoencephalography enables noninvasive studies of brain function to be carried out to within a few millimeters and on a millisecond scale of temporal resolution. Neuromag's software is able to sample up to 450 channels simultaneously. Further information is available on Neuromag's website (http://www.neuromag.com/main.html).

57. Yonmoy Sharma, quoted in "Remote Control Brain Sensor," *BBC World News*, November 17, 2002, available at http://news.bbc.co.uk/2/hi/health/2361987.stm.

58. The AmI vision is enshrined in an evolving series of policy documents. The latest of these is Information Society Technologies Advisory Group (ISTAG), ed., *Ambient Intelligence: From Vision to Reality* (Brussels: European Commission, 2003), available at http://www.cordis.lu/ist/istag-reports.htm.

59. George Metakides and Thomas Skordas, "Major Challenges in Ambient Intelligence" (presentation at "Tales of the Disappearing Computer," Santorini, Greece, June 2003, available at http://ilios.cti.gr/DCTales/presentations/Santorini_TALES _GM_TSk_light.pdf).

60. Greger Linden, "Proactive Computing and Proact" (presentation at "Tales of the Disappearing Computer," Santorini, Greece, June 2003). The archive for Proact (The Research Programme on Proactive Computing), the consortium Linden leads, is available at http://www.aka.fi/index.asp?id=c36cc39f901d43279aa3c90cd5934a4c.

61. Scott Makeig, "New Insights into Human Brain Dynamics" (presentation at Society for Psychophysiological Research Symposium, San Diego, Calif., October 22, 2000), available at http://www.sccn.ucsd.edu/~scott/spr00.html. According to Makeig, "rapid advances in available technology for recording high-density EEG, MEG and MRI signals from the human brain afford an unprecedented opportunity to observe and model human brain dynamics during a very wide range of human experience and task performance. Interpreting the mass of derived data requires new computational tools."

62. In their search to determine cognitive and emotional states of mind remotely, researchers are developing techniques to measure a person's pupil dilation, where a person is looking, and how much cognitive effort is required. See William S. Riippi, "Identification Systems: Policy, Process, and Technology—Choices for an Integrated Solution" (presentation at GTC West, 2003), available as part of "Public Safety & Homeland Security Speeches" on the MTG Management Consultants website at http://www.mtgmc.com/expertise/speeches ps.shtml.

63. Intel explains that "the emergence of a new genre of machine learning tools firmly grounded in statistical methods is particularly exciting. Systems use uncertainty to support robotic hypothesis generation, a key stepping stone to anticipation." Intel's vision on proactive computing and its possible applications is described in "Exploratory Research: A Future of Proactive Computing," available on the Intel website at http://www.intel.com/research/exploratory/. For its part, IBM plans to create "systems that configure and manage themselves under human supervision—an approach often called autonomic computing." IBM concedes, in an aside, that the introduction of autonomic computing "will change the relationships between systems and people" and that "not a lot is known about this kind of transformation in the human-computer relationship." From the online summary of the Conference on the Human Impact and Application of Autonomic Computing Systems, IBM T. J. Watson Research Center, Yorktown, N.Y., April 21, 2004, available at http://www.almaden.ibm.com/asr/chiacs.

64. M. Satyanarayanan, "A Catalyst for Mobile and Ubiquitous Computing," *Pervasive Computing: Mobile and Ubiquitous Systems* 1, no. 1 (January–March 2002), 5. Satyanarayanan is the journal's editor.

65. Policy on, and evaluation of, AmI research is a continuous process that is recorded in documents that are continually updated. The quotations used here are from Information Society Technologies Advisory Group, *ISTAG in FP6: Working Group 1. IST Research Content. Interim Report June 9, 2003* (Brussels: European Commission, 2003).

66. "You're Hired," *The Economist*, September 18, 2004, 20, 21. When an IVR/speech system does not meet customers' expectations, they become frustrated and hang up or "zero out" to a live agent. According to Forrester Research, customer satisfaction levels with IVR systems fall in the 10 percent range, compared with a satisfaction rate of approximately 80 percent for face-to-face interactions. What a surprise. According to industry expert Tal Cohen, companies continue to foist automated services onto us because if you or I talk to a human being, it costs the company $10 per call handled. Tal Cohen, "Optimizing IVR/Speech Using Customer Behavior Intelligence" (June 21, 2004), available on the Technology Marketing Corporation website (TMCnet) at http://www.tmcnet.com/tmcnet/articles/2004/062104tc.htm.

67. Elizabeth Herrell, "Speech-Enabled Interactive Voice Response Systems Help Hold Down Costs," Forrester Research, December 4, 2001, available on the Forrester website at http://www.forrester.com/Research/LegacyIT/Excerpt/0,7208,26227,00.html.

68. Cohen, "Optimizing IVR/Speech Using Customer Behavior Intelligence."

69. James Woudhuysen, "What Next in IT?," Spiked Online, January 15, 2001, available at http://www.spiked-online.com/Printable/000000005437.htm.

70. Information Society Technologies Advisory Group, *ISTAG in FP6*.

71. Skill shortage numbers are somewhat unreliable, but the numbers quoted here were based on a significant research project in seventeen European countries (the EU member states, plus Norway and Switzerland) undertaken by the International Data Corporation (IDC) for European Information Technology Observatory (EITO). See the data tables available on the EITO website at http://www.eito.com/tables.html. In Europe alone, there is a shortage of 1.5 million information technology workers. A question arises: Does this mean that every day of the year, 1.5 million days of IT maintenance and development is not getting done? I have not been able to locate any study of the effects on our IT systems—and us—if 548 million days of maintenance are indeed missed each year. Information is available on the Doors of Perception website at http://doors8delhi.doorsofperception.com/.

10 Flow

1. In addition to the interview quoted from here, the Simeon ten Holt archive (http://www.simeontenholt.com/) contains downloadable extracts from performances of ten Holt's work.

2. Manuel Castells, *The Rise of Network Society* (London: Blackwell, 1996), 412.

3. The quotations from John Carroll in this chapter come from his book *Making Use*, a study of "the dynamic tension between specification and imagination" in the design of complex systems. This book is comparable in importance to Donald Schön's *The Reflective Practitioner—How Professionals Think* (New York: Basic Books, 1983). John M. Carroll, *Making Use: Scenario-Based Design of Human-Computer Interactions* (Cambridge, Mass.: MIT Press, 2000).

4. Theodor Zeldin, *Conversation* (New York: Hidden Spring, 2000). A variety of case studies in which conversation is a medium of change and transformation are available on the Oxford Muse website (http://www.oxfordmuse.com/).

5. Brian Arthur, quoted in an interview "Conversation with W. Brian Arthur," by Joseph Jaworski, Gary Jusela, and C. Otto Schanmer at Xerox Parc, Palo Alto, Calif., April 16, 1999, available at http://www.dialogonleadership.org/Arthur-1999.html.

6. Alain Findeli, "Rethinking Design Education for the 21st Century: Theoretical, Methodological, and Ethical Discussion," *Design Issues* 17, no. 1 (Winter 2001).

7. Peter Bøgh Andersen, "Interacting with Dynamic Environments—Maritime Instrumentation as an Example" (paper presented at the Nordic Interactive Conference, Copenhagen, November 1, 2001, available at http://www.nordic-interactive .org/nic2001/conference/parallel3/andersen.shtml).

8. Carroll, *Making Use*, 329.

9. As Carroll observes, many important consequences for people reveal themselves only through the course of extended use. Ibid., 45. The FileMaker Pro database in the Doors of Perception office is a case in point: It was first set up for us in 1993— and has been changing more or less continuously ever since. The more we fiddle with it, the more we want to fiddle. Fiddling begets more fiddling. We could probably keep our FileMaker wizard, Jan Jaap Spreij, busy one hundred hours a week— and we are only a small group of people.

10. Hippocrates, *Ancient Medicine: Airs, Waters, Places* (Cambridge, Mass.: Harvard University Press, 1923).

11. Peter Drucker, *Post-capitalist Society* (Oxford: Butterworth-Heinemann, 1993).

12. Ezio Manzini, "Space and Pace of Flows" (presentation at Doors of Perception 7: Flow, Amsterdam, November 14–16, 2002, available on the Doors of Perception website at http://flow.doorsofperception.com/content/manzini_trans.html).

13. Malcolm Gladwell, *The Tipping Point* (New York: Little Brown, 2000).

14. Tom Bentley, *Learning beyond the Classroom: Education for a Changing World* (London: Routledge/Demos, 1998).

15. Edward O. Wilson, *Consilience: The Unity of Knowledge* (London: Little Brown, 1998).

16. Susantha Goonatilake, "The Shift to Asia: Cultural Implications for Science and Technology" (presentation at Doors East, Bangalore, India, December 2003, available on the Doors East website at http://www.doorseast.com/transcriptions/goonatilake _txt.html).

17. Susantha Goonatilake, *Toward a Global Science: Mining Civilizational Knowledge* (Bloomington: Indiana University Press, 1998).

18. Goonatilake, "The Shift to Asia."

19. Based on his experience setting up First Direct, Gavaghan has developed a process that he calls the Unique Assembly of Tried and Tested Components (UATTC). I am a member, with Gavaghan, of a consortium, Spirit of Creation (http://www .spiritofcreation.com), that is applying UATTC and other recombinatory techniques to the development of new educational and research institutions.

20. Yves Doz, *From Global to Metanational: How Companies Win in the Knowledge Economy* (Boston, Mass.: Harvard Business School Press, 2002).

21. Harry Kunzru, "One Year On: How Bright Does the Futurecasters' Future Look?," *Mute*, no. 19 (May 2001), 23.

22. Ibid.

23. Manzini, "Space and Pace of Flows."

24. For an example of the genre, see "Do It Yourself: Self-Service Technologies, Such as Websites and Kiosks, Bring Both Risks and Rewards," *The Economist*, September 16, 2004, available at http://economist.com/opinion/displayStory.cfm?story_id= 3196309.

25. Løvlie and his colleagues made a presentation on the time-banking scenario, using the evidencing technique, at the Doors East conference in Bangalore, India, in December 2003; slides from the presentation are available on the Doors East website at http://www.doorseast.com/transcriptions/lovlie/index.html. A related scenario, having to do with car sharing and mobility, is available on the Doors of Perception website at http://static.doorsofperception.com/2004roundtable.

26. These engineers and planners were from Rijkswaterstaat (Directorate General for Public Works and Water Management).

27. A. den Doolaard, *De Waterweg Herovered* (Conquest of the Waterways: Reshaping Wet Nature and Society) (Rotterdam: Comité Nationale Herdenking, 1947). A. den Doolaard was the pseudonym of Cornelis Johannes George Spoelstra (1901–1994).

28. Michiel Schwarz, "Expo 2000 Netherlands Story Line" (request for proposal, Netherlands Pavilion at Expo 2000 Hannover, Foundation Holland World Fairs,

1998); Michiel Schwarz, *Holland schept ruimte: Het Nederlands paviljoen op de wereldten-toonstelling EXPO 2000 te Hannover* (Holland Makes Space: The Dutch Pavilion of Expo 2000 in Hannover) (Blaricum/Den Haag: V+K Publishing/Inmerc, SNW, 1999).

29. Hilary Cottam and Charles Leadbeater, *Open Welfare: Designs on the Public Good* (London: Design Council, 2004). A related online discussion forum is available at http://www.designcouncil.org/blog/red.

30. Sourceforge, "Software Map," available at http://sourceforge.net/softwaremap/trove_list.php (statistics accurate as of September 16, 2004).

31. Felix Stalder and Jesse Hirsh, "Open Source Intelligence," *First Monday* 7, no. 6 (June 2002), available at http://firstmonday.org/issues/issue7_6/stalder/index.html.

32. Thomas Goetz, "Open Source Everywhere," *Wired* 11, no. 11 (November 2003), available at http://www.wired.com/wired/archive/11.11/opensource.html?pg=1& topic=&topic_set=.

33. Stalder and Hirsh, "Open Source Intelligence."

34. Lawrence Lessig, *The Future of Ideas: The Fate of the Commons in a Connected World* (New York: Random House, 2001).

35. Website of the Agile Alliance (http://www.agilealliance.com/home).

36. "Manifesto for Agile Software Development," available on the manifesto's website (http://www.agilemanifesto.org).

37. A useful portal to companies and organizations rethinking themselves as providers of product-service systems is the website of SusProNet (http://www.suspronet.org/fs_aboutsuspronet.htm). Software development companies are moving toward a model of selling services rather than products. "Tools used to test software are often open source, but by paying 'rent' clients get the benefit of the company's expertise," according to a recent article. "Managing Complexity," *The Economist* (Special Report), November 27, 2004, 75–77.

38. Alan Cooper, *The Inmates Are Running the Asylum* (Indianapolis, Ind.: SAMS [MacMillan Computer Publishing, 1999]).

39. Carroll, *Making Use*, 8.

40. Eugenio Barba, address to the Institute Superior de Artes on the occasion of its awarding him an honorary doctorate, Havana, Cuba, February 6, 2002, available at http://www.odinteatret.dk/general_information/pdf_filer/havanaenglish.pdf. See also Eugenio Barba, *The Paper Canoe: A Guide to Theatre Anthropology* (London: Routledge, 1995).

What to Read Next

Ten Books to Read Next

Bentley, Tom. *Learning beyond the Classroom: Education for a Changing World*. London: Routledge/Demos, 1998.

Benyus, Janine. *Biomimicry: Innovation Inspired by Nature*. New York: Morrow, 1997.

Calvino, Italo. *Six Memos for the Next Millennium*. London: Cape, 1992.

Carroll, John M. *Making Use: Scenario-Based Design of Human-Computer Interactions*. Cambridge, Mass.: MIT Press, 2003.

Elbek, Uffe, ed. *KaosPilot A–Z*. Aarhus, Denmark: KaosPilots, 2004.

Fernandez-Galiano, Luis. *Fire and Memory: On Architecture and Energy*. Cambridge, Mass.: MIT Press, 2000.

Hawken, Paul, Amory B. Lovins, and L. Hunter Lovins. *Natural Capitalism: The Next Industrial Revolution*. London: Earthscan, 1999.

Levine, Robert. *A Geography of Time: The Temporal Misadventures of a Social Psychologist*. New York: Basic Books, 1997.

Rheingold, Howard. *Smart Mobs: The Next Social Revolution*. Cambridge, Mass.: Perseus, 2003.

Seely Brown, John, and Paul Duguid. *The Social Life of Information*. Cambridge, Mass.: Harvard Business School Press, 2000.

A Book a Week for a Year

Agamben, Giorgio. *The Man without Content*. Palo Alto, Calif.: Stanford University Press, 1999.

Bentley, Tom. *Learning beyond the Classroom: Education for a Changing World*. London: Routledge/Demos, 1998.

Benyus, Janine. *Biomimicry: Innovation Inspired by Nature*. New York: Morrow, 1997.

Beukers, Adriaan, and Ed van Hinte. *Lightness: The Inevitable Renaissance of Minimum Energy Structures*. Rotterdam: 010 Publishers, 1998.

Brand, Stewart. *How Buildings Learn—What Happens after They Are Built*. New York: Penguin, 1994.

Calvino, Italo. *Six Memos for the Next Millennium*. London: Vintage, 1996.

Carroll, John M. *Making Use: Scenario-Based Design of Human-Computer Interactions*. Cambridge, Mass.: MIT Press, 2003.

Ceppi, Giulio, Analia Cervini, and Juan Keyser. *Mobile Embodiments: New Convergences in Mobile Telephony*. Ivrea, Italy: Interaction Design Institute Ivrea, 2004.

Dinkler, Soke, and Christoph Brockhaus, eds. *Connected Cities: Processes of Art in the Urban Network*. Ostfildern-Ruit, Germany: Hatje Cantz, 1999.

Duffy, Francis. *Architectural Knowledge*. London: Spon, 1998.

Dupuy, Jean-Pierre. *Medicine and Power: A Tribute to Ivan Illich* (Paris: Centre National de Recherche Scientifique [CNRS], 2003.

Dyson, Esther. *Release 2.0: A Design for Living in the Digital Age*. New York: Bantam Dell, 1997.

Elbek, Uffe, ed. *KaosPilot A–Z*. Aarhus, Denmark: KaosPilots, 2004.

Fernández-Galiano, Luis. *Fire and Memory: On Architecture and Energy*. Cambridge, Mass.: MIT Press, 2000.

Gladwell, Malcolm. *The Tipping Point*. New York: Little Brown, 2000.

Goldberg, Ken, ed. *The Robot in the Garden: Telerobotics and Telepistemology in the Age of the Internet*. Cambridge, Mass.: MIT Press, 2000.

Gombrich, E. H. *The Sense of Order*. London: Phaidon, 1979.

Goonatilake, Susantha. *Toward a Global Science: Mining Civilizational Knowledge*. Bloomington: Indiana University Press, 1998.

Gray, John. *Straw Dogs: Thoughts on Humans and Animals*. London: Granta, 2002.

Hajer, Maarten, and Arnold Reijndorp. *In Search of New Public Domain: Analysis and Strategy*. Rotterdam: Netherlands Architecture Institute, 2001.

Hawken, Paul, Amory B. Lovins, and L. Hunter Lovins. *Natural Capitalism: The Next Industrial Revolution*. London: Earthscan, 1999.

Himanen, Pekka. *The Hacker Ethic, and the Spirit of the Information Age*. New York: Random House, 2001.

Holloway, Richard. *Looking in the Distance: The Human Search for Meaning.* Edinburgh: Canongate, 2004.

Hunt, Tristram. *Building Jerusalem: The Rise and Fall of the Victorian City.* London: Weidenfeld and Nicolson, 2004.

Illich, Ivan. *Deschooling Society.* Harmondsworth, England: Penguin, 1976.

Illich, Ivan. *Energy and Equity.* London: Calder and Boyars, 1974.

Jégou, François, and Ezio Manzini. *Sustainable Everyday: A Catalogue of Promising Solutions.* Milan: Edizione Ambiente, 2004.

László Barabási, Albert. *Linked: The New Science of Networks.* New York: Perseus, 2002.

Laurel, Brenda. *Utopian Entrepreneur.* Cambridge, Mass.: MIT Press, 2001.

Lessig, Lawrence. *The Future of Ideas: The Fate of the Commons in a Connected World.* New York: Random House, 2001.

Levine, Robert. *A Geography of Time: The Temporal Misadventures of a Social Psychologist.* New York: Basic Books, 1997.

Lietar, Bernard. *The Future of Money.* London: Century, 2001.

Manguel, Alberto. *A History of Reading.* London: Harper Collins, 1996.

Mast, Gregory, ed. *Film Theory and Criticism.* 5th ed. Oxford: Oxford University Press, 1998.

McCullough, Malcolm. *Abstracting Craft.* Cambridge, Mass.: MIT Press, 1996.

Mulgan, Geoff. *Connexity: How to Live in a Connected World.* London: Chatto and Windus, 1997.

Orr, David. *Ecological Literacy: Education and the Transition to a Postmodern World.* Albany: State University of New York Press, 1992.

P.M. (pseudonym). *Bolo Bolo.* New York: Autonomedia, 1995.

Rheingold, Howard. *Smart Mobs: The Next Social Revolution.* Cambridge, Mass.: Perseus, 2003.

Rifkin, Jeremy. *Time Wars: The Primary Conflict in Human History.* New York: Simon and Schuster, 1989.

Ross, Andrew. *Strange Weather: Culture, Science and Technology in the Age of Limits.* London: Verso, 1991.

Roszak, Theodore, Mary E. Gomes, and Allen D. Kanner, eds. *Ecopsychology.* San Francisco: Sierra Club Books, 1995.

Schechner, Richard. *Performance Studies: An Introduction.* London: Routledge, 2002.

Schlosser, Eric. *Fast Food Nation*. New York: Perennial, 2002.

Seely Brown, John, and Paul Duguid. *The Social Life of Information*. Cambridge, Mass.: Harvard Business School Press, 2000.

Sonnabend, Regina. *Serve City: Interactive Urbanism*. Berlin: Jovis Verlag, 2003.

van Hinte, Ed, Marc Neelan, Jacques Vink, and Piet Vollaard. *Smart Architecture*. Rotterdam: 010 Publishers, 2003.

Vincent, Julian V. F. *Structural Biomaterials*. Princeton, N.J.: Princeton University Press, 1998.

von Weizsäcker, Ernst, Amory Lovins, and L. Hunter Lovins. *Factor Four: Doubling Wealth, Halving Resource Use*. London: Earthscan, 1997.

Wilson, Edward O. *Consilience: The Unity of Knowledge*. London: Little Brown, 1998.

Worpole, Ken, and Liz Greenhalgh. *The Richness of Cities: Urban Policy in a New Landscape*. London: Comedia/Demos, 1999.

Zimmerman, Brenda, Curt Lindberg, and Paul Plsek. *Edgeware: Complexity Resources for Health Care Leaders*. Irving, Texas: VHA Inc. (Plexus Institute), 2001.

Bibliography

Alakeson, Vidhaya, ed. *Making the Net Work: Sustainable Development in a Digital Society*. London: Forum for the Future/Xeris, 2003.

Alexander, Christopher, Sara Ishikawa, and Murray Silverstein. *A Pattern Language: Towns, Buildings, Construction*. New York: Oxford University Press, 1977.

Alexander, Titus. *Family Learning*. London: Demos, 1997.

Antonelli, Paola. *Mutant Materials*. New York: Museum of Modern Art, 1996.

Antonelli, Paola. *Workspheres: Design and Contemporary Work Styles*. New York: Museum of Modern Art, 2001.

Bakker, Conny, ed. *Smart Materials*. Amsterdam: Netherlands Design Institute, 1997.

Barba, Eugenio. *The Paper Canoe: A Guide to Theatre Anthropology*. London: Routledge, 1999.

Barley, Nick, ed. *Breathing Cities: The Architecture of Movement*. Basel, Boston, and Berlin: Birkhauser, 2000.

Bauman, Zygmunt. *Liquid Modernity*. Cambridge, England: Polity, 2000.

Beolchi, Luciano, ed. *Telemedicine Glossary*. Brussels: European Commission, 2003.

Bergson, Henri. *Duration and Simultaneity*. Indianapolis: Bobbs-Merrill, 1965.

Berners-Lee, Tim. *Weaving the Web: The Original Design and Ultimate Destiny of the World Wide Web*. New York: Harper Collins, 1999.

Birkenshaw, Julian, and Peter Hagstrom, eds. *The Flexible Firm: Capability Management in Network Organizations*. Oxford: Oxford University Press, 2000.

Boekraad, Hughes, ed. *The New Academy: Papers for the Barcelona Symposium*. Breda, The Netherlands: Academy St. Joost, 1997.

Bonsiepe, Gui. *Interface: An Approach to Design*. Maastricht: Jan van Eyck Academy, 1998.

Boutinet, Jean-Pierre. *Anthropologie du Projet*. Paris: PUF, 2003.

Bradburne, James. Collecting Interaction: Digital Craft and the Museum of the Twenty-First Century. Unpublished paper, Museum of Applied Arts Frankfurt, 2000.

Bradburne, James. Digital Craft. Unpublished paper, Museum of Applied Arts Frankfurt, 2000.

Braddock, S. E., and Marie O'Mahony. *Techno-Textiles: Revolutionary Fabrics for Fashion and Design*. London: Thames and Hudson, 1998.

Brand, Jan, Ritsaert ten Cate, Akki Colenbrander, and Catelijne de Muijnk. *The Art Academy of the 21st Century*. Bedum, The Netherlands: Profiel, 1999.

Brand, Stewart. *How Buildings Learn—What Happens after They Are Built*. New York: Penguin, 1994.

Brand, Stewart. *The Clock of the Long Now: Time and Responsibility*. London: Phoenix, 2000.

Brezet, Han, Philip Vergragt, and Tom van der Horst, eds. *Vision on Sustainable Product Innovation*. Amsterdam: BIS Publishers, 2001.

Brickwood, Cathy, ed. *New Media Culture in Europe*. Amsterdam: De Balie, 1999.

Capra, Fritjof. *The Web of Life*. New York: Random House, 1996.

Castells, Manuel. *The Information Age: Economy, Society and Culture*. 2nd ed. Malden, Mass.: Blackwell, 2000.

Ceppi, Giulio, and Michele Zini, eds. *Children, Spaces, Relationships: Metaproject for an Environment for Young Children*. Milan: Domus Academy, 1998.

Changeux, Jean-Pierre, and Paul Ricoeur. *Ce qui nous fait penser: Le nature et le regle* (What Makes Us Think: Nature and Law). Paris: Odile Jacob, 2000.

Chion, Michel. *Audio-Vision*. New York: Columbia University Press, 1994.

Cohen, Daniel. *Our Modern Times: The New Nature of Capitalism in the Information Age*. Cambridge, Mass.: MIT Press, 2003.

Cooper, Alan. *The Inmates Are Running the Asylum*. Indianapolis: SAMS (Macmillan Computer Publishing), 1999.

Corbin, Alain. *Time, Desire and Horror: Towards a History of the Senses*. Cambridge, England: Polity, 1995.

Cottam, Hilary, and Charles Leadbeater. *Health: Co-creating Services*. London: Design Council, 2004.

Croall, Jonathan. *LETS Act Locally: The Growth of Local Exchange Trading Systems*. London: Gulbenkian, 1997.

Csikszentmihalyi, Mihaly. *Flow and the Psychology of Discovery and Invention.* New York: Harper, 1996.

Culshaw, B. *Smart Structures and Materials.* London: Artech House, 1965.

Cusveller, Sjoerd, Oene Dijk, and Kirsten Schipper. *Remaking NL: Cityscape, Landscape, Infrastructure.* Amsterdam: S@M, 2001.

Davidson, Robyn, ed. *The Picador Book of Journeys.* London: Pan Macmillan, 2000.

Davis, Mike. *Beyond Bladerunner: Urban Control and the Ecology of Fear.* New York: New Press, 1993.

de Kerckhove, Derrick. *The Skin of Culture: Investigating the New Electronic Reality.* Toronto: Somerville House, 1995.

de Landa, Manuel. *A Thousand Years of Nonlinear History.* Cambridge, Mass.: MIT Press, 1997.

DiBona, Chris, Sam Ockman, and Mark Stone, eds. *Open Sources: Voices from the Open Source Revolution.* Sebastopol, Calif.: O'Reilly, 1999.

Dinkler, Soke, and Christoph Brockhaus, eds. *Connected Cities: Processes of Art in the Urban Network.* Ostfildern-Ruit, Germany: Hatje Cantz Verlag, 1999.

Dourish, Paul. *Where the Action Is: The Foundations of Embodied Interaction.* Cambridge, Mass.: MIT Press, 2001.

Downs, Anthony. *Still Stuck in Traffic: Coping with Peak-Hour Traffic Congestion.* Washington, D.C.: Brookings Institution Press, 2004.

Ducatel, Ken, and James P. Gavigan. *Employment and Employability in 2010 Europe.* Seville: Institute of Prospective Technological Studies, Joint Research Centre, Commission of the European Community, 2000.

Dudek, Mark. *Kindergarten Architecture: Space for the Imagination.* London: Chapman and Hall, 1996.

Dunbar, Robin. *Grooming, Gossip, and the Evolution of Language.* Cambridge, Mass.: Harvard University Press, 1997.

Dunne, Anthony, and Fiona Raby. *Design Noir: The Secret Life of Electronic Objects.* London: August/Birkhäuser, 2001.

Dupuy, Jean-Pierre. *Medicine and Power: A Tribute to Ivan Illich.* Paris: Ecole Polytechnique, Centre National de Recherche Scientifique (CNRS), 2003.

Ehrlich, Paul. *New World, New Mind.* London: Paladin, 1991.

Ferry, Luc. *The New Ecological Order.* Chicago: University of Chicago Press, 1995.

Florida, Richard. *The Rise of the Creative Class: And How It's Transforming Work, Leisure, Community, and Everyday Life.* New York: Perseus Books, 2002.

Flusser, Vilem. *The Shape of Things: A Philosophy of Design.* London: Reaktion, 1999.

Forsebäck, Lennart. *Case Studies of the Information Society and Sustainable Development.* Brussels: European Commission Information Society Directorate General, 2000.

Forsyth, Richard. *Machine Learning.* London: Chapman and Hall, 1989.

Gandhi, Mukesh V., and Brian S. Thompson. *Smart Materials and Structures.* London: Chapman and Hall, 1990.

Gardner, Howard. *The Unschooled Mind: How Children Think and How Schools Should Teach.* New York: Basic Books, 1993.

Graham, Stephen, and Simon Marvin. *Splintering Urbanism: Networked Infrastructures, Technological Mobilities, and the Urban Condition.* London: Routledge, 2001.

Gray, Alasdair. *Lanark: A Life in Four Books.* Glasgow: Canongate, 1985.

Gray, Charles Hable, ed. *The Cyborg Handbook.* London: Routledge, 1995.

Griffiths, Jay. *Pip-Pip: A Sideways Look at Time.* London: Flamingo, 2000.

Hall, Edward T. *The Silent Language.* New York: Doubleday, 1959.

Hamilton, Clive. *Growth Fetish.* London: Pluto, 2004.

Hampden-Turner, Charles, and Fons Trompenaars. *Mastering the Infinite Game: How East Asian Values Are Transforming Business Practices.* London: Capstone, 1997.

Hargreaves, David. *The Mosaic of Learning: Schools and Teachers for the Next Century.* London: Demos, 1994.

Heppell, Stephen. *Schools in the Learning Age.* London: Campaign for Learning, 2000.

Herz, J. C. *Joystick Nation: How Videogames Gobbled Our Money, Won Our Hearts, and Rewired Our Minds.* London: Abacus, 1997.

Hillis, W. Daniel. *The Pattern on the Stone.* New York: Basic Books, 1999.

Hillman, Mayer, and Stephen Plowden. *Speed Control and Transport Policy.* London: Policy Studies Institute, 1996.

Hilty, Lorenz M., and T. F. Ruddy. Resource Productivity in the Information Age. Chapter 3 in *Indicators of Sustainable Development,* edited by Olli Hietanen. Helsinki: Finnish Society for Future Studies, 2002.

Hofmeester, Kay, ed. *Presence: New Media for Older People.* Amsterdam: Netherlands Design Institute, 1999.

Holland, John H. *Adaptation in Natural and Artificial Systems*. Ann Arbor: University of Michigan Press, 1975.

Horton, William. *Designing and Writing Online Documentation*. New York: Wiley, 1994.

Huizinga, Johan. *Homo Ludens: A Study of the Play-Element in Culture*. Boston: Beacon Press, 1955.

Hussey, Andrew. *The Game of War: The Life and Death of Guy Debord*. London: Cape, 2001.

Hutton, Will, and Anthony Giddens, eds. *On the Edge: Living with Global Capitalism*. London: Vintage, 1999.

Illich, Ivan. *Tools for Conviviality*. London: Calder and Boyars, 1973.

Information Society Technology Advisory Group (ISTAG). *Scenarios for Ambient Intelligence in 2010*. Seville, Spain: Institute for Prospective Technological Studies, 2001.

Irving, Robert. *Being and Circumstance: Notes towards a Conditional Art*. San Francisco: Lapis with the Pace Gallery, 1988.

Johnson, Robert R. *User-Centered Technology: A Rhetorical Theory*. Albany: State University of New York Press, 1998.

Johnston, Peter, ed. *Information Societies Technologies Conference*. Helsinki: European Commission, 2000.

Jones, John Chris. Softecnica. In *Design after Modernism: Beyond the Object in Design*, edited by John Thackara, 216–226. London: Thames and Hudson, 1987.

Kafai, Yasmin B., and Mitch Resnick. *Construction in Practice: Designing, Thinking, Learning in a Digital World*. Hillsdale, N.J.: Erlbaum, 1996.

Kelly, Kevin. *Out of Control: The New Biology of Machines, Social Systems, and the Economic World*. New York: Perseus, 1995.

Kennedy, Margrit. *Interest and Inflation Free Money*. Sydney: Social Entrepreneurial Ventures Asia, 1995.

Krausse, Joachim, and Claude Lichtenstein, eds. *Your Private Sky: R. Buckminster Fuller and The Art of Design Science*. London: Müller/Birkhäuser Verlag, 1999.

Lakoff, George, and Mark Johnson. *Metaphors We Live By*. Chicago: University of Chicago Press, 1980.

Landauer, Thomas K. *The Trouble with Computers: Usefulness, Usability, and Productivity*. Cambridge, Mass.: MIT Press, 1996.

Latour, Bruno, and Catherine Porter. *Aramis: Or the Love of Technology*. Cambridge, Mass.: Harvard University Press, 1996.

Laurel, Brenda. *Computers as Theatre*. New York: Addison-Wesley, 1991.

Laurel, Brenda, ed. *Design Research: Methods and Perspectives*. Cambridge, Mass.: MIT Press, 2003.

Lave, Jean, and Etienne Wenger. *Situated Learning: Legitimate Peripheral Participation*. Cambridge: Cambridge University Press, 1991.

Lawrence, Eleanor, ed. *Henderson's Dictionary of Biological Terms*. 11th ed. London: Longman, 1995.

Maas, Winy. *Five Minute City: Architecture and (Im)mobility*. Rotterdam: Episode, 2003.

Maas, Winy, and Jacob van Rijs. *FARMAX: Excursions on Density*. Rotterdam: 010 Publishers, 1998.

Mamet, David. *Three Uses of the Knife: On the Nature and Purpose of Drama*. New York: Vintage, 1998.

Manovich, Lev. *The Language of New Media*. Cambridge, Mass.: MIT Press, 2001.

Manzini, Ezio. *Artefatti: Verso una nuova ecologia dell'ambiente artificiale* (Artifacts: Toward a New Ecology of the Artificial Environment). Milan: Edizioni Domus Academy, 1990 (published in French and Spanish).

Manzini, Ezio. *HK Lab*. Hong Kong: Portefaix Map, 2002.

Manzini, Ezio. *The Material of Invention*. Cambridge, Mass.: MIT Press, 1996.

Manzini, Ezio. *Product-Service Systems and Sustainability*. Paris: United Nations Environment Programme, 2002.

Manzini, Ezio. *Solution Oriented Partnership: How to Design Industrialised Sustainable Solutions*. Cranfield, England: Cranfield University Press, 2004.

Manzini, Ezio, and Marco Susani. *The Solid Side*. Naarden, The Netherlands: V + K, 1995.

Manzini, Ezio, and Carlo Vezzoli. *Product-Service Systems and Sustainability: Opportunities for Sustainable Solutions*. Paris: United Nations Education Programme, 2003.

Maxmin, James, and Shoshana Zuboff. *The Support Economy*. New York: Viking, 2002.

McCullough, Malcolm. *Abstracting Craft*. Cambridge, Mass.: MIT Press, 1996.

McCullough, Malcolm. *Digital Ground*. Cambridge, Mass.: MIT Press, 2004.

McNeill, J. R., and William H. McNeill. *The Human Web: A Bird's Eye View of World History*. New York: Norton, 2003.

Millar, Jeremy, and Michiel Schwarz, eds. *Speed: Visions of an Accelerated Age*. London: Photographers' Gallery, 1998.

Mitchell, William J. *The Reconfigured Eye: Visual Truth in the Post-photographic Era.* Cambridge, Mass.: MIT Press, 1992.

Miyake, Riiche, and John Thackara, eds. *T-Zone.* Brussels: Europalia, 1990.

Mok, Clement. *Designing Business.* San Jose, Calif.: Adobe, 1996.

Mulder, Arjen. *Levende systemen: reis naar het einde van het informatietidperk* (Living Systems: Travels to the End of the Information Age). Amsterdam: Van Gennep, 2002.

Mulder, Arjen, and Jacqueline Tellinga. *L'Europe à Grande Vitesse* (High-Speed Europe). Rotterdam: Netherlands Architecture Institute, 1996.

Nevejan, Caroline. *Synchroon-asynchroon: Onderwijsvernieuwing in de informatiesamenleving* (Synchronous-Asynchronous: Educational Renewal in the Information Society). Amsterdam: Hogeschool van Amsterdam, 2003.

Norman, Donald A. *Things That Make Us Smart: Defending Human Attributes in the Age of the Machine.* New York: Addison-Wesley, 1993.

Normann, Richard. *Reframing Business.* London: Wiley, 2003.

Norretranders, Tor. *The User Illusion: Cutting Consciousness Down to Size.* New York: Viking, 1998.

Papanek, Victor. *Design for the Real World: Human Ecology and Social Change.* New York: Random House, 1972.

Phillips, Adam. *The Beast in the Nursery.* London: Pantheon, 1998.

Polanyi, Michael. *Personal Knowledge.* Chicago: University of Chicago Press, 1958.

Rifkin, Jeremy. *The Age of Access.* London: Penguin, 2000.

Rifkin, Jeremy. *The End of Work: The Decline of the Global Labor Force and the Dawn of the Post-market Era.* New York: Putnam, 1995.

Roberts, Paul. *Images: The Piano Music of Claude Debussy.* New York: Amadeus, 1996.

Sachs, Wolfgang. *The Development Dictionary: A Guide to Knowledge as Power.* London: Zed, 1992.

Sachs, Wolfgang. *Global Ecology: A New Arena of Political Conflict.* London: Zed, 1993.

Sahlins, Marshall. *Stone Age Economics.* New York: Aldine de Gruyter, 1972.

Schivelbusch, Wolfgang. *The Railway Journey: The Industrialization of Time and Space in the Nineteenth Century.* Berkeley and Los Angeles: University of California Press, 1987.

Schön, Donald. *The Reflective Practitioner—How Professionals Think.* New York: Basic Books, 1983.

Schor, Juliet B. *The Overspent American: Upscaling, Downshifting, and the New Consumer.* New York: Basic Books, 1998.

Schwarz, Michiel. *Holland schept ruimte: Het Nederlands paviljoen op de wereldtentoonstelling EXPO 2000 te Hannover* (Holland Makes Space: The Dutch Pavilion at Expo 2000 in Hannover). Blaricum/Den Haag: V + K, 1999.

Seelig, Thomas, Urs Stahel, and Margin Joeggi, eds. *Trade: Commodities, Communication and Consciousness.* Zurich: Scalo, 2001.

Simon, Herbert. *The Sciences of the Artificial.* Cambridge, Mass.: MIT Press, 1996.

Smith, Mark K. *Online Encyclopedia of Informal Education.* Available at http://www.infed.org/association/b-assoc.htm. 2002.

Soja, Edward W. *Postmodern Geographies: The Reassertion of Space in Critical Social Theory.* London: Verso, 1989.

Sontag, Susan. *Regarding the Pain of Others.* London: Hamish Hamilton, 2003.

Sorkin, Michael, and Sharon Zukin, eds. *After the World Trade Center: Rethinking New York City.* New York: Routledge, 2002.

Sudjic, Deyan. *The 100 Mile City.* London: Harper Collins, 1993.

Svanaes, Dag. *Understanding Interactivity: Steps to a Phenomenology of Human-Computer Interaction.* Trondheim, Norway: Computer Science Department, Norwegian University of Science and Technology, 2000.

Thackara, John. *Lost in Space: A Traveller's Tale.* Haarlem, The Netherlands: De Grafische Haarlem, 1994.

Thackara, John. *Winners! How Today's Successful Companies Innovate by Design.* London: Gower, 1999.

Thackara, John, ed. *Design after Modernism: Beyond the Object in Design.* London: Thames and Hudson, 1987.

Tukker, Arnold, Peter Eder, and Erick Haag. *Ecodesign: The European State of the Art.* Seville, Spain: Institute for Prospective Technological Studies, 2000.

Uricchio, William. *Media, Simultaneity, Convergence: Culture and Technology in an Age of Intermediality.* Utrecht, The Netherlands: Universiteit Utrecht, 1997.

van Assche, Christine, ed. *Sonic Process.* Barcelona: Actar, 2002.

van Hinte, Ed. *Eternally Yours: Visions on Product Endurance.* Rotterdam: 010 Publishers, 1997.

van Hinte, Ed. *Smart Design.* Amsterdam: Netherlands Design Institute, 1999.

van Hinte, Ed, and Conny Bakker. *Trespassers: Inspirations for Eco-efficient Design*. Rotterdam: 010 Publishers, 1998.

Vincent, Julian V. F. Borrowing the Best from Nature. In *Encyclopaedia Britannica*, 168–187. Chicago: Encyclopaedia Britannica, 1995.

Virilio, Paul, and Mark Polizzotti. *Speed and Politics: An Essay on Dromology*. New York: Semiotext(e), 1986.

Vogel, Steven. *Life's Devices: The Physical World of Animals and Plants*. Princeton, N.J.: Princeton University Press, 1989.

Wackernagel, Mathis, and William Rees. *Our Ecological Footprint: Reducing Human Impact on the Earth*. Canada: New Society, 1996.

Weber, Steven. *The Success of Open Source*. Cambridge, Mass.: Harvard University Press, 2004.

Wenger, Etienne, Richard McDermott, and William M. Snyder. *Cultivating Communities of Practice*. Cambridge, Mass.: Harvard Business School Press.

Williams, David, ed. *Collaborative Theatre: The Théâtre du Soleil Sourcebook*. London: Routledge, 1999.

Whitelegg, John. *Critical Mass: Transport Environment and Society in the Twenty-First Century*. London: Pluto, 1997.

Whitelegg, John, and Gary Haq, eds. *The Earthscan Reader in World Transport Policy and Practice*. London: Earthscan, 2003.

Winograd, Terry, and Fernando Flores. *Understanding Computers and Cognition: A New Foundation for Design*. New York: Addison-Wesley, 1987.

Yeang, Ken. *Bioclimatic Skyscrapers*. London: Artemis, 1994.

Index